THE DEATH OF ASYLUM

THE DEATH OF
ASYLUM

*Hidden Geographies of the
Enforcement Archipelago*

ALISON MOUNTZ

 UNIVERSITY OF MINNESOTA PRESS
Minneapolis • London

Portions of chapters 3 and 4 were originally published as "Mapping Remote Detention: Dis/location through Isolation," in *Beyond Walls and Cages: Prisons, Borders, and Global Crisis,* edited by Jenna Loyd, Matthew Mitchelson, and Andrew Burridge, 27–41 (Athens: University of Georgia Press, 2012), and as "The Enforcement Archipelago: Detention, Haunting, and Asylum on Islands," *Political Geography* 30, no. 3 (2011): 118–28.

Published by the University of Minnesota Press
111 Third Avenue South, Suite 290
Minneapolis, MN 55401-2520
http://www.upress.umn.edu

Printed in the United States of America on acid-free paper

The University of Minnesota is an equal-opportunity educator and employer.

Library of Congress Cataloging-in-Publication Data
Names: Mountz, Alison, author.
Title: The death of asylum : hidden geographies of the enforcement archipelago / Alison Mountz.
Description: Minneapolis : University of Minnesota Press, 2020. | Includes bibliographical references and index. | Summary: "Alison Mountz traces the global chain of remote detention centers used by states of the Global North to confine migrants fleeing violence and poverty, using cruel measures that, if unchecked, will lead to the death of asylum as an ethical ideal" —Provided by publisher.
Identifiers: LCCN 2019054492 (print) | ISBN 978-0-8166-9710-6 (hc) | ISBN 978-0-8166-9711-3 (pb)
Subjects: LCSH: Refugees—Government policy—Western countries. | Detention of persons—Moral and ethical aspects. | Asylum, Right of.
Classification: LCC JV6346 .M697 2020 (print) | DDC 362.87/56091821—dc23
LC record available at https://lccn.loc.gov/2019054492

To my parents and my sister, who taught me to remember the past and enjoy the present while working for a better future; and to my children, beautiful daily reminders that the future is a brighter place already

No man is an island entire of itself; every man is a piece of the continent, a part of the main. If a clod be washed away by the sea, Europe is the less, as well as if a promontory were, as well as a manor of thy friends or of thine own were. Any man's death diminishes me, because I am involved in mankind. And therefore never send to know for whom the bell tolls; it tolls for thee.

—JOHN DONNE, *Devotions upon Emergent Occasions*

Although we might argue that it would be impractical to write obituaries . . . for all people, I think we have to ask, again and again, how the obituary functions as the instrument by which grievability is publicly distributed. It is the means by which a life becomes, or fails to become, a publicly grievable life, an icon for national self-recognition, the means by which a life becomes noteworthy. . . . The matter is not a simple one, for, if a life is not grievable, it is not quite a life; it does not qualify as a life and is not worth a note. It is already the unburied, if not the unburiable.

—JUDITH BUTLER, *Precarious Life*

Contents

Asylum:
An Obituary

Border deaths at sea are increasing at alarming rates. While many mourn this loss of life, another death goes unnoticed: the death of asylum itself. This death is visible where money is invested in walls, fences, interception, and detention rather than in processing claims and legal avenues to entry. People who are starving or displaced by violence must travel somewhere to survive. If one country locks its doors, they must knock elsewhere. Recent border deaths are, therefore, not only a European or North American crisis but part of a relational, global geography. As Canada, Australia, the United States, and other countries close their doors to people fleeing strife and persecution, these countries become complicit in their deaths elsewhere. Amid these moves, the right to asylum is being buried, disappearing in public discourse and in the closure of geographical and legal routes to safe haven.

The loss of asylum is a loss to be grieved like any other.

Asylum was born in Geneva, a child of state-sanctioned atrocity and subsequent displacement during World War II. This lineage assured its place among human rights conventions developed after 1945 to protect victims of oppression. The 1951 Convention Relating to the Status of Refugees was designed to prevent further abandonment of those displaced.

Asylum offered the right to seek protection from a well-founded fear of persecution. In its seventy years, asylum helped millions flee persecution, enjoying its greatest support from Canada, Australia, and the United States. Each now shuts down paths to protection in its own way, as countries of the Global North attempt to contain displacement and countries in the Global South invest more heavily to provide shelter.

Asylum's deterioration began at sea in the Caribbean in the early 1980s, when the United States intercepted, detained, and returned Haitian and Cuban nationals. Other countries followed suit, contravening international obligations to protect by prohibiting people from landing on sovereign territory where they accrue the right to make a claim. Potential asylum seekers are, thereby, prevented from seeking asylum.

The United States responded to a 2014 surge in asylum seeking by Central Americans by building its largest detention facility in Dilley, Texas. Authorities detained women and children there while also moving processing offshore. When a surge happened again a few years later, Donald Trump's administration separated families and children, reduced access to asylum to particular social groups, and moved processing offshore through bilateral agreements with Mexico and Guatemala. Although the violence that drove the exodus from Central America continues, the effect was a steep drop-off in asylum claims from Honduras, El Salvador, and Guatemala and a steep climb in violence targeting those displaced and in limbo in Mexico. By 2018, U.S. authorities had separated families, detaining children in facilities along the border, and forced asylum seekers into limbo in Mexico.

Asylum became diseased in public discourse, declining rapidly in its final years. Children crossing into the southwestern United States were called illegal, treated as security threats, admonished, detained, and told to go home by hysterical protestors who trod on familiar territory: "not in my backyard." These protestors would like their country to abdicate obligations under international law.

Many people seeking asylum travel by boat. Marine arrivals inspire fears of invasion and cost, and politicians stoke these fears. Australia banishes asylum seekers to island countries that are not bound by the Convention and therefore offer few chances for asylum. It funds detention in Nauru (a small independent state), on Papua New Guinea's Manus Island, and across Indonesia, places where rights violations of those detained—including sexual violence and deprivation—have been well documented. People detained on these islands respond with hunger strikes, self-immolation, and other attempts at suicide and expressions of protest. Australian authorities respond, in turn, by paying for their imagined resettlement in Cambodia and beyond.

Asylum died a sudden death in Canada, until recently a leading advocate among Western countries offering protection. After enjoying global repute as a leader in refugee resettlement and refugee claimant programs, thanks largely to mass resettlement in the early 1980s of more than sixty thousand Indochinese displaced during the Vietnam War, at the same time that it opted to resettle displaced Syrians from camps, Canada recently continued to close doors to and open space in detention facilities for asylum seekers, expanding the Safe Third Country Agreement to limit access to asylum in 2019.

When the United Nations High Commissioner for Refugees (UNHCR) reported a 54 percent rise in claims worldwide in 2014, Canada boasted a 49 percent drop in claims and recently reached its lowest rate of resettled refugees in decades. In 2013, when the number of people making asylum claims globally grew by 24 percent, the number making claims in Canada fell by 49 percent (Government of Canada 2019, 47; United Nations High Commissioner for Refugees [UNHCR] 2014b).

In 2019, the UNHCR reported 70.8 million displaced people around the globe. In the same year, the United States resettled the lowest number of people since it had begun refugee resettlement.

Meanwhile, asylum *seeking* is reaching new heights globally. By the end of 2018, 3.5 million people awaited adjudication of their asylum claims, according to the UNHCR (2019).

As the number of asylum seekers rose globally, some European Union (EU) states refortified national borders, Australia once again relegated asylum seekers to reopened detention facilities offshore, and the United States banned asylum seeking and all travel from several countries by executive order.

In Canada, cancerous language criminalized asylum seekers as security threats, labeled terrorists before they ever landed. This language metastasized with importation of U.S. and Australian politics and practices of intercepting and detaining people deemed illegal and bogus refugees rather than asylum seekers. Though small in number, boat arrivals catalyzed dramatic changes, including mandatory and indefinite detention. These mirrored efforts to deny landing to Indians who were British subjects on the *Komagata Maru* in 1914 and German Jews on the *St. Louis* in 1939.

To block asylum seeking, governments invest in policing and detention to contain displacement elsewhere. Divesting from protection involves looking away from humanitarian crises from Central America to the Mediterranean and Syria.

Governments are complicit in migrant deaths due to their heavy investments in border enforcement and detention, when research shows consistently over time that deterrence fails. Deterrence is perhaps the most expensive and lasting public policy failure of our time. Between 2006 and 2015, EU states invested €299 million in enforcement operations at sea through Frontex alone (Frontex 2016). Italy, Malta, and Greece expanded detention and deportation. In 2014, the U.S. border enforcement budget was $19 billion. During the Barack Obama administration, approximately four hundred thousand were detained and deported.

And still, people came. They endured perilous journeys and spent years languishing in detention and limbo en route. In 2015, the *Economist* estimated that 1 million people were waiting on the north coast of Africa as thousands more embarked across the Indian Ocean.

In its heyday during the Cold War, asylum enjoyed nearly universal respect. Asylum was unique in protecting those who used grit and determination to land in a country that adjudicated claims. Authorities retained the right to determine which claims were accepted. Although never guaranteed, asylum will be remembered for the right at least to be heard.

Asylum is survived by the United Nations High Commission for Refugees and by the principle of protection in countries of origin—the idea that people be protected at home. Asylum is also survived by its cousin, the refugee camp. Its prognosis is more robust: some 16 million people now live in protracted refugee situations, displaced for five years or more. While those displaced and held in camps do not enjoy the same recognition in law, they proved more palatable politically for providing the displaced with basic shelter closer to home. Recent years have seen the proliferation of temporary-seeming sites where displaced people seek shelter, from France's Calais to Rohingya in Bangladesh and Syrians in Turkey, and the increased use of remote islands to confine and isolate.

Judith Butler (2004) writes that obituaries facilitate the public distribution of grief. Asylum will be remembered by those it saved and for those whom it could not. It leaves behind a dark world, drowning in its own cynicism.

Preface

The Search for Safe Haven

Too many people are dying in their search for political asylum. As a result, and for additional reasons detailed in this book, *asylum itself is in crisis.* Asylum was institutionalized as a tool of global governance to resettle the displaced of World War II. Its legal basis is in the 1951 Convention Related to the Status of Refugees and the 1967 Protocol. These allow people to make a claim for protection based on a well-founded fear of persecution in the country from which they seek asylum. As of 2015, 148 states were parties to the Convention, to the Protocol, or to both—roughly three-quarters of all countries (UNHCR 2015c).

I spent several years researching the detention of asylum seekers on remote islands. In this research, I found the creation of endless islands on, through, within, and beyond these research sites. Consider the irony of the detention facility built on a remote island at sea. The notion that a newcomer to a small, isolated island community might easily escape is absurd. People can, however, be placed at a geographical and social distance from the mainstream, hidden from view on islands. The global growth in detention and the strategic use of islands to detain people in search of protection from persecution—to thwart human mobility through confinement—is part of the death of asylum. Can access to protection be provided behind bars? Can asylum be accessed remotely? And if so, what is the quality of that access?

When I began doing research for this book about offshore enforcement, I wrote and thought often about the *erosion* of access to asylum. As time went on, my research on border enforcement on islands and at sea emboldened me to argue that we are witnessing the *death* of asylum in the interstitial spaces of crossing between states.

What does it mean that asylum is in crisis and dying today, nearly seven decades after its formal inception in international law? This is not, of course, a literal argument but one informed by political analysis and theories of social death, grievability, and meanings of haunting. In fact, the relationship between actual physical deaths and the social death of asylum proves illuminating, as I will show. On one hand, the *search for asylum*—asylum seeking itself—has not died but intensified, with more people displaced from their homes since World War II (UNHCR 2014b). The UNHCR reported a 24 percent rise in claims globally in 2013 over 2012 (UNHCR 2014b) and a 54 percent rise in claims globally in 2014 over 2013 (UNHCR 2016d), with the percentage expected to be higher again in each subsequent year. In the face of increases in asylum seeking and associated deaths, states of the Global North have grown more creative and aggressive in keeping asylum seekers away from sovereign territory rather than redoubling their efforts to resettle so many people on the move. In 2012, for example, Australia extended use of reopened island detention facilities on foreign soil. EU member states continued to fortify boundaries across the Mediterranean and around the Spanish exclaves of Melilla and Ceuta in Morocco, as deaths of people trying to enter the EU without authorization rose precipitously (International Organization for Migration [IOM] 2015). Like migrants, the death of asylum is itself mobile, not bound by national boundaries but instead moving across regions as "fast policy transfer" (Peck and Theodore 2015) of best practices of exclusion.

The rise in detention and asylum claims has corresponded with an ongoing discursive and political crisis, so that at the same time the number of displaced people and asylum claims increases, the idea of asylum dies. Over the last twenty years, since a spike in claims in the late 1980s and early 1990s, people seeking asylum have been criminalized, vilified in public discourse as "bogus refugees," "queue jumpers," "illegal" when traveling by boat (Hall 2013), and threats to national security. As the very ideas of asylum and the "legitimate" asylum seeker disappear (Macklin 2005) with the social death of the asylum seeker, these discursive crises lead to legislative and enforcement changes that make it more difficult to make a claim. Among these changes is the intensification of offshore border enforcement—the practice of stopping people on their journeys long before they reach sovereign territory to make a refugee claim. Paths to safe haven are blocked through offshore interception and detention, enforcement measures put into place during crises. These measures make crossing more precarious, contributing to the well-documented rise in border deaths (Weber and Pickering 2011; De Bruycker et al. 2013; IOM 2015; Spijkerboer et al. 2015; Williams and Mountz 2016).

The rise in asylum claims has corresponded with profound forms of exceptionalism surrounding the search for protection. Seeking asylum is increasingly discussed as something abnormal, unusual, threatening, or even criminal: it is rendered exceptional, despite increasing numbers of claims. This exceptionalism manifests materially in the shrinking of paths to refuge as the industries and spaces of detention and border enforcement expand globally (Sampson 2013). The discursive crisis contributes to the advancement of practices, policies, and laws that prevent people from arriving and making asylum claims.

The global growth in detention is also contributing to the asylum crisis. More countries are detaining, and those that do detain are expanding their infrastructure and criteria to detain (Sampson 2013, 9–10). Much of this expansion happens along transit routes, areas that people cross on their way elsewhere, where they aim to seek livelihood or protection. There is a clear relationship between the global expansion of detention and border enforcement industries; the precarity (Fassin 2013), politicization (Squire 2011), and discursive disappearance of asylum; and the shrinking of spaces of refuge. Instead of finding more robust forms of protection, people on the move are growing ever more precarious, and this trend toward precarity has been well documented among all people on the move—refugees, asylum seekers, temporary foreign workers, permanent residents, and even citizens who increasingly find themselves at risk of losing their citizenship status (Macklin 2015).

Crisis politics surround discourses of migration and asylum seeking, attaching criminality and illegality to people in search of protection. These politics are killing the principle of protection embedded in asylum. The politics of asylum and the social death of the asylum seeker have so distorted the principles of protection that policy makers and scholars alike have lost the moral compass of what is at stake. In recent years, Australia and the United States have "traded" asylees who were accepted as refugees but not allowed to land. People attending rallies for U.S. presidential candidate and then president Donald Trump chanted against refugees. As the EU intensified enforcement, people displaced from Africa and the Middle East ended up stuck in north Africa or displaced to South and Central America. The EU struck a deal with

Turkey to keep asylum seekers there (van Liempt et al. 2017). More than
one million displaced Syrians in Turkey were denied access to health
care, education, or work, establishing conditions for their exploitation
(Baban et al. 2017). Similarly, the United States funded Mexico, and the
country went from transit zone to destination for Central Americans
(Seelke and Finlea 2016).

In 2017, when asylum seekers from the African continent, the Caribbean, and Central America crossed into Canada from the United
States to make asylum claims, I was interviewed on Canada's national
news by Canadian Broadcasting Corporation news anchor Ian Hano-
mansing. His last question was, "What will stop them from coming?"
This question signaled clearly the death of asylum: the inability for an
asylum seeker to be thought of as someone authentically in need of
and exercising her right to protection. Instead, the primary framing
of contemporary asylum seekers has become precisely the question of
how to make them stop. This situation began in the 1970s with modern
practices of interception at sea but has grown more acute in the decades
since, with the criminalization of asylum seekers and securitization of
migration. State efforts to exclude asylum seekers unfold violently on
the bodies of asylum seekers, and this form of state violence needs to
be rendered visible, its implications discussed and debated rather than
hidden from view. This book it not mere provocation but instead offers
empirical evidence of death. It is not comfortable, but it is happening,
more intensely with each passing day and with each new pushback
policy designed to restrict access to safe haven.

ON CRISIS

People have a tendency to overuse the word *crisis* in relation to migration, even reconceptualizing much human movement writ large as
"crisis migration" (e.g., Martin et al. 2014). While there is no doubt that
humanitarian crises are unfolding, this book contributes to the necessary and collective reframing (e.g., Mainwaring 2019) of what, where,
when, and just whose crises these are.

The case for crisis is often overstated and misplaced. The exodus of
approximately 4.8 million Syrian nationals from conflict in that country
offers one example (UNHCR 2016d). This mass migration was often

spoken of in global news as the EU's crisis, with the arrival of more than a million asylum seekers in 2015. Empirically speaking, if there was a crisis, it was first and foremost a crisis for displaced Syrians, and possibly the neighboring states that host them in the region, including Jordan, Lebanon, Turkey, and Iraq. Jordan's Zaatari camp, for example, operated close to full capacity by 2016, with approximately 79,326 refugees (UNHCR 2016b). Lebanon, a country of 4.5 million people, had 1.8 million Syrians living there at the end of 2015 (UNHCR 2016c).

Migration crises persist because crisis does political work. During times of so-called migration crises, states expand their powers and enhance and reconfigure enforcement regimes. Eruptions due to crisis are important moments to pay attention to when sovereign efforts to control migration and mobility expand outward, when more restrictive measures are placed on movement (Mountz 2010). Boat arrivals tend to provoke crises, which become openings when enforcement agendas are advanced. Crisis is thus a productive time to advance national (and supranational) security agendas. These advances prove even more acute in border areas where scholars shift the location of crisis from migration to sovereignty itself. Much early literature on globalization stated that nation-states were "losing control" because of intensified globalization and were reasserting their power through control of the border (Sassen 1996), with the construction of walls and fences attributed to failures in sovereignty (Brown 2010).

Borderlands—where I have spent much of my time conducting research in recent years—are an important geographical location from which to examine these questions (Anzaldúa 1987). Although they may be geographically remote, they are far from marginal. They are at the heart of this book and its analysis. The year 2015 saw an escalation of attention to Mediterranean crossings from Turkey to Greece, after years of North African crossings to Italy and Malta. The crossing of more than one million migrants to Europe in 2015 was that year's crisis. By 2017, and continuing into 2019, international attention and daily headlines shifted to the Rohingya. Scholars in the fields of border, island, and migration studies have long shown that we need to shift these seemingly peripheral zones from margin to center to understand sovereignty and the geopolitics of displacement. Small or remote places are not inconsequential. Instead, they are key to understanding power relations that shape entry and exclusion.

Struggles to enter expose the creative uses of geography and legality to restrict access to rights that people accrue once they land on sovereign territory, including the right to seek asylum. Of late, most efforts to seek asylum have been framed as crises, with authorities stating a preference to choose whom to resettle, rather than responding to the unruly and unexpected "spontaneous arrival."

It is important to query and contextualize the word *crisis* and also to show just how productive the word can be for sovereign power and its geographical incursions through border enforcement offshore. Rather than a failure in sovereignty, crises become productive moments for extensions of sovereign power and its regulation of territory and human mobility.

ON WALLS AND WALLING, ISLANDS AND ISOLATION

Globally, the main response to so-called migration crises is to contain and isolate—to build walls, fences, and detention facilities. So prolific is this walling that transnational journeys no longer resemble a border crossing as a singular event but rather a proliferating series of spaces of confinement and limbo that migrants move through for years: the camp, the ship, the detention center, the island. These are the spaces that I explore in this book.

Unfortunately, people are not talking about these threats to asylum or the containment of displacement to the Global South, in large part because potential asylum seekers are hidden from view, either offshore or in plain sight in the criminalizing discourse that turns them into security threats and illegal or "impossible subjects" (Ngai 2008). The social death of detained or excluded people seeking asylum construes them as racialized nonpersons without rights (Cacho 2012). Border enforcement proves central to the production of these hidden geographies and deadly subjectivities. Through enforcement, the border is now produced as a series of proliferating forms of isolation. These islands—which I refer to as the enforcement archipelago—mask the violence of confinement and exclusion.

Although there is much evidence of the deaths of *people* in this book, I argue that we are witnessing the slow death of asylum itself in the enforcement archipelago. By death of asylum, I do not mean that asylum has ceased to exist but rather that it is in crisis and under threat of disappearance. This crisis is evident in law, public discourse, politics, and practice. The death of asylum involves a social death, the contours of which I explore in the introduction.

As you read this book, a definitive geographical shift in border enforcement will become evident: the border has moved ever farther offshore. In the process, the walls or fortified barriers that once delineated the geographical boundaries of sovereign territory have themselves moved offshore and taken new spatial form. The border is no longer a line, a wall, or a crossing. These border sites persist in their symbolic power at the same time that they are left to decay. Borders now operate as more dynamic, mobile, and persistent geographical forms of enclosure and confinement. Although I began by studying these forms of isolation on islands, I find them to be reproduced everywhere as the border takes on the form of the island and, in this spatial form, moves both offshore and into the interior of mainland territories.

ENGAGING DEATH

As such, the death of asylum is not happening in any one place, although its history will be traced to particular times and places through a genealogy of externalization in chapter 1. Instead, the death of asylum is transpiring through a global constellation of sites where people and places are exploited to carry out exclusion.[1] It is a place where the death of asylum can be witnessed and a place that mirrors trends in migration and foretells the death of asylum elsewhere. Spectacular enforcement operations carried out within the archipelago mask more mundane forms of violence churning quietly, daily, beneath its surface: physical harms and losses that people endure as they move through proliferating spaces of confinement at sea and on land, separated from family, community, and livelihood. The enforcement archipelago is a material location but also a metaphor for the death of asylum.

To develop this argument, I begin with Judith Butler's (2004, 2009) writing about death and the politics of memorialization. I extend her work on precarious life to the realm of migration and asylum seeking. For Butler, people's precarity owes to their devaluation and dehumanization. Building on her work, I demonstrate the physical, ontological, and political death of asylum throughout this book. Physical deaths relate directly to state mobilities: as enforcement intensifies and extends well beyond boundaries of sovereign territory, more physical deaths of migrants occur. The field of offshore policing expands, resulting in fewer geographical or legal routes to becoming an asylum seeker. Asylum thus dies an ontological death due to the impossibility of becoming an asylum seeker. Physical deaths are forgotten, and violence is hidden. The subjectivity of asylum seekers disappears, replaced by other kinds of subjectivities: the victim rescued or not rescued, the "good" refugee resettled, the security threat precluded offshore. Border deaths disappear benignly into everyday life. Citizens of the so-called Global North complacently accept the fact of faraway others' immobility, detention, and death as their governments invest staggering resources into policing the boundaries between states. This is the political death of asylum.

In each subsequent chapter, I trace the architecture of the archipelago in different kinds of sites (such as islands and detention facilities) and different regions. Butler's (2004, 2009) assessment of the precarity of life lends insight into the collective failure to grieve and respond to migrant losses. She argues that loss is politicized and holds the potential to mobilize political communities through individual and collective processes associated with mourning and grieving. She shows, however, that some lives and some deaths count more than others to the international community: "Certain lives will be highly protected, and the abrogation of their claims to sanctity will be sufficient to mobilize the forces of war. Other lives will not find such fast and furious support and will not even qualify as 'grievable'" (Butler 2004, 32). The relative values assigned to life are often revealed during periods of conflict and displacement—and the periods of memorialization that follow. In the introduction, I extend and apply Butler's analysis to the death of asylum in the enforcement archipelago.

Three kinds of death emerge in Butler's (2004, 31–35) reflection on precarious life: physical death of the body, ontological death through dehumanization and devaluation, and subsequent political death with the deceased forgotten rather than mourned. These three forms of death operate along a continuum that helps to explain the relationship between the physical harm to and deaths of migrants to the ontological disappearance and political death of asylum. With violence and migrant deaths on the rise, asylum is shrinking (physical), disappearing (ontological), and dying (political). These are three different but related phenomena—shrinking, disappearing, and dying—related to Butler's exploration of the devaluation of lives. Close examination of the continuities between them as they are lived by migrants offers insight into the embodiment of forms of exclusion that scholars often theorize but too often leave as disembodied categories in their texts.

Butler (2004, 32–33) explores death as both physical and ontological when she asks, "What is real? Whose lives are real? How might reality be remade?" She connects physical violence and unreality, what she calls the "derealization" of what it is to be human, with politics: "What, then is the relation between violence and those lives considered as 'unreal'? Does violence effect that unreality? Does violence take place on the condition of that unreality?" (Butler 2004, 33). These are important questions to ask about the international response to the many forms of violence harming migrants in the name of enforcement. What is it that prompts a response to some losses but not to others? And just what kinds of responses are these?

More scholars are exploring the fine line between humanitarian rescue and border enforcement (Ticktin 2011; Campesi 2014; Williams 2014, 2015). Sometimes the response to losses of life at sea involves greater enforcement, often narrated in the name of humanitarian rescue. Other times, more sobering processes of memorialization are staged. Both are explored in this book.

In the United States, when presidential hopefuls Donald Trump and Scott Walker proposed to wall off the country on all sides, the border enforcement budget was already approximately $19 billion in 2014 (*Capitol Times* 2014). The American Immigration Council (2019) estimates that the federal government has spent $330 billion on immigration enforcement since the creation of the Department of Homeland Security in 2003. In the EU, Frontex (the coordinating agency of the external border) estimated that 219,476 people—the majority fleeing conflict in Syria, Gaza, and Libya—crossed the Mediterranean in 2014 (Frontex 2015a). In response, EU member states invested more than €299 million into operations coordinated by Frontex on the Mediterranean between 2006 and 2015 (Frontex 2016; Williams and Mountz 2016).[2] In 2015, the EU offered Turkey €3 billion to close its borders, an offer it turned down. In 2016, Turkey accepted a deal to "take back" migrants attempting to enter Europe via the Aegean Sea (Faiola and

White 2016). In 2014, Australia announced a payment of AU$35 million to Cambodia over a four-year period to resettle asylum seekers it detained in Nauru and on Papua New Guinea's Manus Island. In 2016, when Papua New Guinea courts ruled detention of asylum seekers on behalf of Australia unlawful, Australia reiterated its refusal to resettle anyone detained, including those who had been determined Convention refugees. And between 2014 and 2015, the United States funded greater enforcement of the southern borders of Mexico and Central American countries through its Plan Frontera Sur, estimated to cost in the tens of millions, to reduce the flow of asylum seekers to its own sovereign territory, resulting in growth in detention, violence, and the militarization of borders south of the United States (Nazario 2015; Hiemstra 2019b). These figures show coordinated and significant investments in policing the borderlands.

Mass migrations by sea are not new but historical phenomena with numerical ebb and flow. The decontextualization and detachment of marine travel from the past through presentist crisis narratives prompt repeated political crises onshore. To return to the Mediterranean example, the EU appeared to falter for a time in the wake of heightened Mediterranean crossings. In response to the 2015 influx of displaced Syrians, member states responded with disparate policies, alternatively opening their doors to welcome Syrians in the cases of Sweden and Germany and closing them in the case of the Balkan states. Yet the response of EU states offshore was remarkably well coordinated by Frontex, through interception and detention.

Within this morass, islands emerge as sites in the borderlands where struggles over entry and exclusion transpire. States create two tiers of access through the manipulation of offshore searches for asylum and territorial jurisdiction. Islands proliferate as the border crossing recedes from view. Stitched together, sites of enforcement operate as an enforcement archipelago. Throughout this text, I visit these sites within the enforcement archipelago. The mundane forms of violence enacted and endured there on a daily basis are hidden beneath spectacular forms of enforcement. This violence—the spectacular and the hidden—portends the death of asylum.

As asylum dies a death with spatial, social, discursive, political, material, and legal dimensions, I illustrate that islands and archipelagoes imagined as peripheral prove central to its demise. Islands are used as material sites of exclusion but also function as a spatial form mobilized everywhere to create legal exceptionalism and isolation. As evidence, I trace the creation of endless islands, spaces of confinement in the enforcement archipelago designed through creative interplay between geography and legality offshore—and, ultimately, onshore too.

GEOGRAPHICAL AND TEXTUAL TRAJECTORIES

This book is organized to trace trajectories of authorities and migrants and their encounters throughout the archipelago. Part I traces state mobilities and physical deaths: the movement of the state offshore as borders are dislodged, displaced, and relocated to create the dynamic infrastructure of the enforcement archipelago. Part II shows ontological death: *how* spaces of asylum are shrinking geographically, legally, numerically, and discursively. This shrinking is expressed through the proliferation of spaces of containment and isolation, including the detention center and the island. Sites of refuge have been supplanted by discourses and practices of exceptionalism that increasingly engulf asylum claimants and their applications, overshadowing the spirit of protection with which the Convention Relating to the Status of Refugees and its 1967 Protocol were designed. I ask what kinds of refuge proliferating spaces of containment offer. Part III explores consequences of the political death of asylum: the hidden nature of offshore geographies and the social movements that struggle to locate, map, and in other ways make visible all that has been concealed from view.

The book's geographically driven organization maps the growth of enforcement archipelagoes across regional borderlands involving maritime and island landscapes where asymmetries between Global North and South erupt. Mapping the enforcement archipelago illuminates proliferating forms of spatial isolation and how they are used by states of the Global North to shrink spaces of asylum and offload the management of displacement by confining people in interstitial locations. The book investigates the archipelago in specific sites, beginning with the border and following its enforcement in ever more remote locations offshore where authorities and migrants first encounter each other on transnational migrant routes, closer to or even within regions of origin.

Each chapter traces the geography of one general kind of site and a specific location within an enforcement archipelago, offering both empirical evidence and genealogies showing how this expansive movement offshore has transpired globally across sites. Chapter 1, "Externalizing Asylum: A Genealogy," heeds Walters's (2008) call to pay more attention to the sites where land meets sea. In it, I develop a genealogy of the term *externalization* that spans several decades and does not yet exist in the literature on migration enforcement. The genealogy traces offshore exclusionary practices that today would be labeled externalization but that existed before the term came into existence. I begin with U.S. interception of Cuban and Haitian nationals at sea in the 1970s and 1980s. Although the practice was seen as an obvious effort to undermine international law, it moved slowly into the realm of normalcy in the ensuing decades across a number of regions. The late 1980s and early 1990s saw the development and subsequent thickening of immigration control networks offshore. The 2000s showed the diffusion of externalization as an effective and widely accepted practice to shut down routes to asylum. The most recent period can be characterized by freneticism around these impulses to move ever farther offshore and deeper into zones of origin and transit routes. The chapter moves beyond a more traditional historical narrative to posit a series of critical securitizing moments when externalization was advanced in different regions, ending with contemporary offshore moves by Canada and the United States. Each critical juncture involves a recurring mix of mandatory detention policies, border enforcement crises related to boat arrivals, criminalization of asylum seekers, expansion of detention capacity, and securitization through antiterrorism legislation post-9/11 that *expanded* on seeds planted earlier. With its global narrative, this chapter provides a crucial backdrop for chapters to come by weaving together the history of externalization across sites.

To understand the "securitization of migration" (e.g., Huysmans 2006) and trace the development of the enforcement archipelago, it is essential to begin with the border. Chapter 2, "The Border Becomes the Island," explains spatial shifts in the operation of the topological border: one that grows ever more transnational, productive, dynamic, vertiginous, and haunting, remaking remote sites of enforcement like small islands along the way. There, states increasingly invest in the intimacies of daily life, exercising biopolitical power through remote detention and outsourcing, resulting in the simultaneous expansion and fragmentation of border enforcement. The border and sovereign power are reconfigured through this blurring of onshore and offshore sites. Amid security "crises," states undermine access to legal representation, human rights, and avenues to asylum (Mountz and Hiemstra 2014). These sovereignties reach offshore, moving the border to the bodies of asylum seekers, carrying out detention in ambiguous places between states through "third parties." As a result, it becomes more difficult to trace accountability back to the sovereign power contracting out enforcement. This chapter examines the role of in/visibility and violence as the performative state traffics in all that is hidden, groundwork for exploration of the violence and continuum of death that lie beneath the topography of the archipelago. It explores Italy's enforcement archipelago, including Lampedusa and the Mediterranean Sea.

Chapter 3, "The Island within the Archipelago," details the strategic uses of islands that emerged as a pronounced pattern in my research on new tactics of enforcement. Islands become "hot spots" where physical geography does some of the work of isolation, a platform for material infrastructure of migration control built on histories of occupation and colonization. Islands thus prove a key component of the enforcement archipelago: as material staging ground to confine, figurative infrastructure mobilized to confine elsewhere, and metaphor for the death of asylum. States are using islands to build the archipelago based on their place in the geographical imagination and the idea that information, people, and resources can somehow be contained, controlled, and hidden on islands. Authorities attempt to use islands to control migration by capturing "populations of concern" and detaining them at sites where they are isolated from communities of advocacy and where they enter into spatial, temporal, and legal zones of limbo. I look at the place of the island within the archipelago and find that the spatial form proliferates as the topological border remakes islands into carceral spaces. I develop the argument that the island as spatial form moves recursively onshore and offshore, connecting mainland and island detention and processing regimes and legal schemata. The chapter connects distant and distinct locations that prompt reexamination of geographies of sovereign power from the outside in. What is a detention center, if not an island?

Chapter 4, "Remote Detention: Proliferating Patterns of Isolation and Confinement," locates and details emergent spatial patterns and practices in the detention of migrants, drawing primarily on discussion of the U.S. detention system. Whereas Giorgio Agamben (1998) theorizes the historical trajectory of the modern camp as one that is perpetually reconstituted everywhere and excludes no one, this chapter posits the island as a kind of camp and contemporary detention practices as strategically located in particular times and places to position particular populations in marginalized, exploitable locations. As the genealogy of externalization shows, the United States plays a leading role in developing and implementing exclusionary enforcement practices designed to externalize asylum and detention. The United States today holds the largest population of detainees and the most expansive landscape of detention onshore with the greatest reach offshore. Numbers of detainees and deportees reached historic highs during the first Obama administration. In 2009, 383,000 foreign nationals were detained in the United States (Office of Immigration Statistics 2010). In 2011, some 430,000 foreign nationals were detained (Office of Immigration Statistics 2011) in facilities ranging from 200 to 300.[3] In 2015, a total of 209 facilities were in use (ICE 2015). As of December 8, 2015, 30,374 people were detained, with a capacity of at least 39,609 beds for detainees (ICE 2015).

Within the U.S. system, detainees are hidden in a variety of ways. Sometimes detention facilities are themselves remote: distanced from powerful urban centers and legal representation, dispersed, detached, hidden. Through dispersal, a degree of geographical and legal *ambiguity* accompanies the many disparate locations of detention. In other cases, detainees may be held in urban centers and mainstream facilities, essentially hidden in plain sight. In addition to drawing on original empirical research, chapter 4 introduces efforts to map detention being undertaken at national and transnational scales.

The mapping of exclusion brings into relief the subsequent shrinking of spaces of asylum that preclude refuge, brought to life in the book by the narratives of authorities and asylum seekers navigating these spaces. Their locations and journeys demonstrate the potential disappearance of the asylum seeker as the border is dynamically and perpetually reconstituted. Chapter 5, "Mobilizing Islands to Restrict Asylum Onshore in Canada (or the Death of Asylum, Even in Canada)," shows how these changes are happening in Canada. Since establishing its refugee system, Canada has garnered a global reputation for resettlement of asylum seekers from situations where they were caught between states. Canada is now shifting from a space of refuge to a place where asylum is treated as exceptional rather than the norm, where access has been curtailed through a series of creative legal maneuvers. Recent legislative changes to asylum seeking in Canada serve as a case to illustrate how the discourse of exceptionalism that surrounds and criminalizes asylum seeking actually works its way into legislation and shrinks paths to asylum. Canada is an important example because of the place it occupied until recently as a global leader in refugee resettlement practices. More recently, recent legislation targets asylum seekers, who face increased deterrence, criminalization, and punitive measures. These include mandatory detention, lists of safe countries whose nationals face expedited access to asylum with fewer chances for appeal, lists of dangerous countries whose nationals face lengthier security checks upon making claims for asylum, and greater concentration of discretionary power with the minister to intervene and adjudicate cases. By detailing how routes to and spaces of asylum disappeared offshore and onshore in Canada, I show that islands have been mobilized even in a country that does not detain on islands.

I end with the countertopographies of activists fighting to counter these exclusions, exploring feminist countertopographies (Katz 2001) enacted by detainees, activists, and advocates who use tools like mapping and communications via social media to transcend the isolating and alienating islands of the enforcement archipelago. Chapter 6, "The Struggle," examines the intimate entanglements between border enforcement, detention, the erosion of asylum, and activism—key among the forces countering the death of asylum. Countless creative, productive encounters happen daily in these seemingly forgotten zones. States, migrants, and activists work dialectically as they move between administrative, urban centers of power and more marginal spaces of sovereignty. As states expand outward and pursue ever more creative geographies of detention through isolation and the use of distance, people located within and beyond detention facilities respond with creative and pronounced strategies designed to overcome tactics of distance and isolation. These material countertopographies are designed to counter the isolating impulses of the topological border with a politics of location. In this chapter, I detail various campaigns, such as visiting detainees, posting bail, legal advocacy, mapping projects, and other strategic political interventions. I also explore the broad range of people involved in social movements designed to free people from detention. By looking especially at advocacy aimed to challenge extraterritorial enforcement practices, this chapter argues that activists engage the same transnational landscape as states with distinct political projects to create radical spaces of hope: spare rooms for refugees, letter-writing campaigns, bus tours to detention centers, artistic renditions of spaces of detention, and investigative reports that expose human rights abuses. I also examine detainee involvement in these efforts. By accessing technology and social media, they work toward freedom collaboratively with people on the outside. By discussing campaigns carried out by activists in Australia, Europe, and the United States, I examine the politics and resources they have mobilized in attempts to form countertopographies to state tactics of exclusion. These countertopographies build on a politics of location: locating, mapping, documenting, and memorializing to confront contemporary forms of exclusion.

The conclusions explore the implications of this research for the continuation of contemporary exclusionary policies, including trends in privatization of detention and the contracting out of asylum processing. Drawing together the material presented and current rounds of exclusion ongoing, I argue that hidden geographies of enforcement require ontologies of exclusion, a restless questioning of what is known about offshore enforcement and how more can be known about what is happening in the borderlands of nation-states. This concluding essay asks from what vantage points the death of asylum can be witnessed or not witnessed and what kinds of witnesses we might become. Given that most violent episodes only rarely reach the international community, more intense scrutiny of the marginal zones between states is needed. Given the continuum of violence and death readily apparent in this study of the enforcement archipelago, this essay suggests that we make good on Butler's call for political community in the shared, relational experiences of grief and mourning.

Acronyms

CARL	Canadian Association of Refugee Lawyers
CBP	U.S. Customs and Border Patrol
CBSA	Canadian Border Services Agency
CIC	Citizenship and Immigration Canada
DCO	Canada's Designated Countries of Origin List
DHS	U.S. Department of Homeland Security
EU	European Union
ICE	U.S. Immigration and Customs Enforcement
IOM	International Organization for Migration
IRCC	Immigration, Refugees, and Citizenship Canada
IRPA	Canada's Immigration and Refugee Protection Act
MSF	Médecins Sans Frontières
STCA	Safe Third Country Agreement
UNHCR	United Nations High Commissioner for Refugees

Introduction

Mapping Death in the Enforcement Archipelago

From Afghanistan I went to Pakistan; from Pakistan, to Iran; from Iran, to Turkey, Greece and then Italy. Part by car, part on foot, part on a rubber dinghy, at sea.... Then, inside a truck ... I was arrested [in Greece] because I was illegal.... I had just called my mother reassuring her that I was in Greece. I thought that was part of Europe, too, so I ... I didn't expect what they did to me. If Greek police catch you ... they'll give you a good thrashing. I called my mom, I said I am arrived, so don't worry now we'll see what we can do from here. As soon as I hang up—it was a telephone booth— I get out, and two steps ahead I'm caught by the police.... They took us to prison. I did a month inside. More than a month inside. There was no hope, I didn't even have the guts to call my mother.... I had called her some time before, telling her that I was in Greece, didn't I?
—Khalil, an eighteen-year-old Afghan man, interviewed in
Sicily in July 2011, recounting two attempts to enter the EU

This young Afghan man whom we interviewed in Sicily had made two attempts to enter the EU. Even a brief recollection of his journey shows the futility of deterrence measures and the incredibly circuitous and costly lengths migrants will travel to enter. Khalil reached Italy as an unaccompanied minor after two attempts. During the first attempt, he was arrested in Greece, imprisoned in Turkey for a month (perhaps longer), and returned to Afghanistan. His journey—mapped in Figure 1— was undertaken on foot, by rubber dingy at sea, and by truck.

Such journeys among Afghans continued while those undertaken by Syrians increased in number. In these journeys, migrants cross multiple borders, travel via different vehicles, and encounter authorities and periods of stasis and limbo along the way. In January 2014, the UNHCR (2014a) reported the deaths of twelve people who were intercepted and in the process of being towed back toward Turkey by a Greek Coast Guard vessel when the migrant ship capsized. The

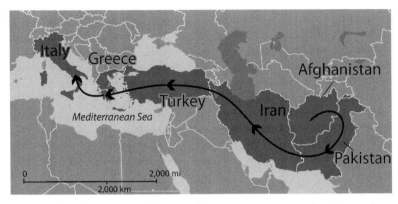

FIGURE 1. Map of one young Afghan man's migration journey undertaken on foot, via a rubber dinghy, and by truck. This journey involved two attempts to travel from Afghanistan to Italy. Based on an interview in Sicily.

sixteen surviving Afghan and Syrian passengers were then held on the Greek island of Leros. Greek authorities denied that they had been towing the boat to Turkey, suggesting instead that it was being towed to Farmakonisi Islet when it capsized. Their claims contradicted those of the sixteen survivors. Both the Human Rights Commissioner of the Council of Europe and the UNHCR condemned the pushbacks. UNHCR's southern Europe regional representative lobbied the Greek government to bring the survivors to mainland territory, stating, "Survivors need to be quickly moved to the mainland so that their needs can be better looked after" (UNHCR 2014b). This response reveals a premise that remoteness is used to deny access to social and legal support, whereas proximity to mainland territory is assumed to provide more access or publicity. Similar events transpired in August 2014 and again in January 2015: migrant boats capsized while being towed (Keep Talking Greece 2015). Later that year, Greek islands became a major conduit for Syrians traveling to Europe, and local communities and visiting authorities grew increasingly overwhelmed at the scale of arrivals. Lesvos Island, like other islands and other routes to the EU, was transformed slowly from a space of transit to one of confinement, with the local population overwhelmed (Afouxenidis et al. 2017). The EU responded with its "hot spot" strategy, mobilizing sites of enforcement (Vradis et al. 2019).

Whether physical abuse or directional reversals, encounters with authorities increasingly entail the prevention of people from seeking protection rather than the facilitation of protection. These tragic episodes involving boat travel illustrate the death of asylum in three parts. The first part involves the physical death of migrants as a direct result of mobile state enforcement infrastructure. Would those twelve people have died had they not been "rescued" by state authorities? Second, also witnessed in this scenario is the ontological death of asylum: towing a boat in reverse is a more literal form of what is often referred to as *pushback*—deterrence at sea—by authorities. Such action shows a refusal, preventing people from landing and becoming asylum seekers recognized as such by law. What does it mean when authorities literally reverse the path of those en route to claim asylum and, in so doing, land them at greater risk of physical harm? Once interception transpired and tragedy ensued, members of the group were held on an island, still not allowed onto mainland territory; geography was put to use to mediate their access. Asylum's political death, the third and final part, lies with the mundane nature and general acceptability of this news: a small group of people lost in a broader international field of shame. While the international community formally spoke in the case of the deaths on the towed boats, the vast majority of migrant stories are more akin to Khalil's experience: in the struggle to land, people quietly enter limbo for months or years at a time, lost and unheard at the margins of sovereign territory.

These incidents and conditions also expose the relationship between enforcement and humanitarianism narrated as rescue (Ticktin 2011; Williams 2014). While directly causal relations between state mobilities (the resources that states invest in moving infrastructure offshore to block access to asylum) and the physical deaths of migrants are not always discernable, greater enforcement at sea has been proven consistently to cause greater risk taking as smugglers and migrants attempt to evade authorities (Koser 2000; Nadig 2002; Barnes 2004; Fan 2008; Carling and Hernandez-Carretero 2011; Williams and Mountz 2016). The failure of boats to land, annual growth in losses of life at sea, and inhumane conditions in detention are all indicators of the death of asylum and the victory of enforcement over protection.

The EU-based organization PRO ASYL (2012) and Médecins Sans Frontières (2011b) documented terrible conditions in detention in the Evros borderland between Greece and Turkey. There migrants were held by Greek authorities for months at a time in spaces where they could not all sit or lie down simultaneously but instead had to take turns. The asylum acceptance rate in Greece between 2010 and 2015 was under 9 percent (Eurostat 2016).[1] In addition to the punitive, jurisdictional limbo of detention, many experienced beatings, torture, and sexual violence at the hands of authorities (Médecins Sans Frontières 2011a, 2011b). Cuban, Haitian, and Central American nationals endured similar conditions when detained along the border between Guatemala and Mexico, prompting their mass escape in 2019 (Stevenson 2019). Whose lives are saved or lost when interception and detention are narrated as humanitarian rescue? Alternatively narrated, these state responses endanger the very lives they were purportedly designed to preserve. Who is responsible for life and death, and what constitutes protection and violence in these contexts?

Judith Butler (2004, 2009) explores these questions in *Precarious Life* and *Frames of War,* asking whose deaths count and whose are silenced. I aim to extend Butler's (2004) analysis of "infinite detention," loss, and grief to include time spent in detention as a kind of living death or deathly living. Many kinds of death result from heavy investments by states of the Global North in erasing asylum from their purview in quiet efforts to contain displacement to the Global South, rather than processing claims on their sovereign territories. Spectacular forms of violence, such as boat losses and associated enforcement operations, mask the more mundane daily forms of violence experienced on a daily basis at sea and in detention. When caught up in enforcement operations, migrants and people seeking asylum experience another form of state violence: prolonged limbo in crossing and detention. People making precarious journeys at sea experience deathly forms of living and living deaths while time is suspended in remote sites of detention.

In what follows, I elaborate on the continuum of the three expressions of asylum's death, an argument developed across the three parts of this book. In part I, I show how evolving and expanding state mobilities contribute directly to physical deaths through the global growth of offshore policing and detention. In part II, the shrinking of space of asylum is tied intimately to its ontological disappearance. With nowhere to be, no path to becoming an asylum seeker, the very existence of asylum becomes threatened with extinction. This shrinking through ontological death also signals the disappearance of asylum as a possibility worth fighting for: its political death. The physical, ontological, and political deaths work together to seal the fate of asylum and asylum seekers.

STATE MOBILITIES AND PHYSICAL DEATHS IN THE ENFORCEMENT ARCHIPELAGO

Landscapes of asylum and refuge are changing globally, and dramatically so, along the edges of the Global North. On one hand, by 2016, more than sixty-five million people were displaced globally (UNHCR 2017), more than in any year since the end of World War II. At the same time, states were finding creative ways to shut down asylum seeking. As a result, young men like Khalil spent years trying to enter, only to find themselves confined, waiting, and in limbo, either in small spaces or in wide open expanses at sea.

Khalil's migration history (which extends well beyond the short narrative that opens this chapter) shows how perilous migrant journeys across borders can become. People facing intensified border enforcement take greater risks, crossing multiple borders and spending months and sometimes years in detention. As in Khalil's case, the journey may involve deaths of friends and family, brushes with death or brushes with one's own death; long periods of uncertainty when hope is lost; and several periods of confinement at sea and on land. Confinement happens in disparate kinds of places, such as unmarked warehouses, prisons, and boats, in different countries. At the hands of smugglers to whom they have paid significant resources, many people interviewed after these harrowing journeys are not even sure where they were detained. In no small part, this is due to the cat-and-mouse games, or what Peter Andreas (2009) calls "border games," played between human smugglers and state authorities who enforce borders. These games have intensified as investments in offshore enforcement have grown.

Over the last twenty years, nation-states have invested heavily to push border enforcement progressively farther offshore to stop unauthorized entry of migrants to work or make claims for asylum far away from sovereign territory. Authorities are mobilizing resources to prevent people from accessing rights, specifically the right to seek asylum—accrued, generally, when one lands on sovereign territory. Viewed collectively in the genealogy developed in chapter 1, enforcement practices show the progressive movement of the border farther offshore over time. As a result, enforcement archipelagoes of exclusionary infrastructure engulf people in the borderlands. There people struggle to enter as authorities work to keep them out of countries considered desirable places to seek asylum and livelihood (Nevins and Aizeki 2008). Recently, however, these peripheral edges of enforcement are sharpening in the borderlands between the regions that people leave and the regions that they take desperate measures to reach. By sharpening, I refer not to precision but to intensified state violence with the broad expansion of enforcement infrastructure: the remarkable financial investment and ubiquitous material proliferation of carceral spaces that people on the move encounter at every turn, the greater risks that they take to avoid them, and the subsequent growth in border-related injuries and deaths (Weber and Pickering 2011; UNHCR 2012; Spijkerboer et al. 2015; Last et al. 2017). Border deaths have increased significantly in the last fifteen years and reached historical highs in places such as the Mediterranean (European Migration Network 2015; IOM 2015). Numbers of asylum claims have also increased steadily over the last several years, reaching new highs in 2015 and 2019 (UNHCR 2016c, 2019).

Offshore enforcement in these border areas is important to map for a number of reasons, not least of which is the loss of life transpiring there. People are dying, and other people are mapping these deaths as families, activists, scholars, human rights monitors, and journalists attempt to account for offshore trends, trajectories, and human impacts in their own ways. Kira Williams and I joined in these efforts, working to collect, analyze, and map data on migrant deaths and boat losses at sea, alongside marine enforcement operations. We analyzed media databases and online reports and found a total of 175 boats lost and approximately 19,173 migrant deaths associated with these boat losses between 1990 and 2015. Most of the incidents were concentrated in time and space, occurring around the EU, Australia, and the United States between 2007 and 2015. The losses increased over time, with an especially high frequency between 2011 and 2015 (Williams and Mountz 2018). The greatest numbers were lost en route to the EU. The most commonly reported countries of origin for passengers involved with lost ships were Afghanistan (twenty-seven cases), Somalia (seventeen), Iraq (sixteen), Syria (sixteen), Palestine (fourteen), Iran (twelve),

Pakistan (eleven), and Haiti (ten) (Williams and Mountz 2016). The map of those lost reflects conflict-induced displacement as well as economic disparities across world regions.

In a simple exclusionary equation, states use geography strategically to undermine access to the rights accrued when a person lands on sovereign territory, including the right to seek asylum.[2] Stitched together, sites on the edges of sovereign space where struggles over access to rights transpire—islands, detention centers, ports of entry—constitute enforcement archipelagoes through which states of the Global North are shrinking spaces of asylum. These exclusions are sustained by processes of racialization, homogenization, criminalization, securitization, and dehumanization. Public narratives suggest that these offshore moves are necessary, designed to protect the vulnerability of the national public from the imagined threat of the other. These are bolstered by the association of asylum seeking with criminality and security threats. Such rationales are used to justify the continued territorial expansion outward to stop potential migrants and asylum seekers from reaching sovereign territory. As the enforcement archipelago expands, states shrink routes to livelihoods and protection, and violence against migrants intensifies.

The exclusionary infrastructure of the enforcement archipelago is an "architecture of enmity" (see Hyndman and Mountz 2007) designed with little regard for the protection of human life, whether lost quietly or in dramatic events that capture international attention. Human rights organizations have collected an overwhelming and condemning body of evidence showing that intensified enforcement has increased migrant deaths (e.g., Human Rights Watch 2009; Médecins Sans Frontières 2011b; Amnesty International 2012). Over a ten-year period from 2006 to 2016, Williams estimates that most migrants died crossing the central Mediterranean in 2014 and 2015, with 1,813 and 2,557 lost (Williams 2018), the highest counts since the UNHCR, Frontex, and the IOM started collecting data in 2006. From 2006, when 302 people were estimated to be lost in this crossing, to 2015, the number increased by 88 percent. In 2015, IOM estimated that migrant deaths peaked, exceeding thirty-seven hundred (IOM 2016), a tenfold increase in deaths over ten years.[3] Arrivals shifted to Greek islands, and in one month, October 2015, 135,000 people landed on the island of Lesvos alone (UNHCR 2015b); they subsequently shifted to Turkey, where Syrians entered into prolonged limbo with precarious legal status (Baban et al. 2017).

These numbers prove especially notable in the Mediterranean, where Italy estimates the "rescue" of some 169,264 people with its operations in 2014, including Mare Nostrum (Frontex 2015b, 2015c). In the wake of the 2013 sinking near Lampedusa, Italy launched Mare Nostrum, a marine operation narrated as humanitarian rescue in the Mediterranean, and a reference to the Roman Empire's use of the term to refer to the Mediterranean Sea in the context of expansionism (*Helsinki Times* 2014). When the Italian defense minister announced the end of Mare Nostrum at the end of October 2014, a spokesperson for Frontex stated, "Of course, we will also do search and rescue actions, but if you don't have enough capacity will you be there in time? I would expect many more sea deaths the moment that Mare Nostrum is withdrawn" (Davies and Nelson 2014). In 2015, Italy intercepted 149,390 passengers (Frontex 2015b, 2015c), with at least 2,557 deaths crossing the central Mediterranean (Williams and Mountz 2016).

Although numerically staggering, more than life has been lost. The physical disappearance of people is not the only kind of death transpiring in the hidden folds of the enforcement archipelago. While moved by and engaged in the work of documenting deaths offshore, I am also concerned with the slower death of asylum itself.

SHRINKING SPACES: THE ONTOLOGICAL DEATH OF ASYLUM

People displaced from home can broadly be placed into two categories grouped by location. The first category consists of people who leave home and relocate within the region, often seeking protection in an adjacent country and sometimes housed in camps run by the UNHCR (Hyndman 2000). Some prima facie refugees in camps hope for resettlement as Convention refugees by a third country with a refugee resettlement program (such as the United States, Canada, Australia, Sweden, or New Zealand). For this group, the quest for refuge translates into waiting in camps that can continue for years, or decades (Hyndman and Giles 2016). The second category of people also flee home but usually travel farther in an attempt to seek asylum and find work in another country using their own resources, without assistance or sanction from a state. They may attempt unauthorized entry to work in the underground economy or to make a claim for protection. This book is concerned primarily with the latter category: those attempting to reach sovereign territory, most often in the Global North, to work or make an asylum claim. They are excluded not only because their arrival is unexpected but because they are deemed unruly—not the displaced *chosen* for resettlement and deemed as safe (not a threat to security) by states.

As enforcement archipelagoes expand, those people seeking entry or protection find fewer avenues and instead encounter shrinking spaces of asylum, fewer legal paths, and proliferating spaces of confinement. Although the numbers of asylum seekers have climbed, with the highest numbers of asylum claims in the last twenty years, there are simultaneously fewer spaces of refuge, fewer paths to becoming an asylum seeker. While there exists no limit on the number of people who can seek or be granted asylum, increasing numbers of people are precluded from making claims. This absence of legal paths to protection fuels growth in statelessness, in unauthorized entry, and in people awaiting the opportunity to make claims in borderlands between home and aspirational destinations.

Policy makers and enforcement authorities label the second group who succeed in landing "spontaneous arrivals," or "irregular arrivals," in the case of Canada's 2012 legislation around designated foreign nationals (discussed in chapter 5). Many others do not succeed in landing: would-be asylum seekers who are struggling to land. Not all people on the move are seeking asylum, and not all people who seek asylum will fit into the definition of a refugee as defined by the 1951 Convention. But by precluding the chance for a landing and a fair hearing, the exclusions in the enforcement archipelago stage war on all people on the move. Mechanisms of securitization, such as increased visa requirements and fortified borders, ensnare everyone.

Routes to the Global North grow more perilous as the securitization of migration and asylum seeking intensifies (Huysmans 2000, 2006; Loyd and Mountz 2018). Securitization involves a shift in discourse *about* migrants and migration, making mobile people the objects of security. This discursive shift is accompanied by shifts in material geographies of exclusion that thwart human mobility and inhibit entry into sovereign territory. Would-be seekers of asylum and migrants increasingly find themselves caught in webs of security, including more aggressive offshore border policing practices, remote detention, antiterrorist legislation, and legally ambiguous zones of interception and detention between states. While some asylum seekers are resettled within the territory of signatory states to the 1951 Convention Relating to the Status of Refugees or its 1967 Protocol, many migrants and would-be asylum seekers en route remain in limbo in liminal zones, detained and hidden from view in places where an asylum claim cannot be made.

Aggressive offshore enforcement shuts down routes, demonstrating the ontological death of asylum: the impossibility of actually making a claim. As the archipelago extends farther offshore, the spaces where people can seek safe haven and better livelihoods shrink, resulting in the sorts of migrant journeys with which this chapter opened. Contemporary asylum journeys tend to involve many years, countries, vehicles, and spaces of confinement.

Spatially remote forms of detention and policing on islands and in foreign airports inhibit asylum seekers from making claims but also from accessing advocacy and claimant systems due to geographical distance (Basaran 2011). They also serve the purpose of hiding detainees from view of the public through various means of dispersal and isolation. Dispersal takes different forms in distinct national contexts throughout this book. The United States, for example, detains people in county jails where they are difficult to locate beyond dedicated federal detention facilities (discussed in chapter 4). Australian dispersal exploits the physical geography of islands (chapter 3).

Sometimes national authorities police their own borders to draw lines of exclusion, as in the case of the Italian Navy implementing a policy called *respingimento,* pushing ships away from territorial waters to prevent them from landing (discussed in chapter 1). In other cases, authorities essentially contract out externalization to private companies and other governments, and those "third parties"—from corporations to NGOs—are increasingly a subject of analysis (e.g., Flynn and Cannon 2009; Andrijasevic and Walters 2010). In 2011, for example, MSF researchers interviewed a migrant who experienced torture while imprisoned in Libya. The man was subjected to electric shock to his genitals while a Libyan prison guard shouted, "You want to go to Italy? This is Italy!" (Médecins Sans Frontières 2011b, 12). In addition to national governments, such as Libya and Indonesia, the IOM is a frequent beneficiary of funds to manage access to asylum outsourced through contracts. These third parties, whether government authorities, private contractors, or international organizations, crop up wherever migration crises occur. When we arrived to begin fieldwork on Christmas Island in 2010, for example, the IOM was just opening an office there. States of the Global North have been expanding fields of enforcement offshore since the 1990s (a chronology detailed in chapter 1). Through proliferating networks and nodes, they share information and enforcement practices. They are achieving the containment of asylum seeking by forming alliances to share interests, tactics, and data. For example, the Five Country Conference, known more informally as the Five Eyes—Australia, Canada, the United States, the United Kingdom, and New Zealand—share intelligence, including a database of fingerprints taken from people seeking asylum, and learn from one another's enforcement practices (MacCharles 2015).[4] Australia, Canada, the United States, and the United Kingdom have developed extensive "front-end security," from visa requirements that require biometrics from refugee-producing countries to interdiction abroad when airline liaison officers and immigration control officers operate informally to share information with counterparts (Canadian Council for Refugees 2003; Mountz 2010). Their authorities view "spontaneous arrivals," formerly asylum seekers, as security threats to target with enforcement. As numbers of people on the move without authorization increased throughout the 1990s, states intensified efforts to reduce spontaneous arrivals (Mountz 2010). Spectacular media events, such boat arrivals, stoked fear and anxiety about the usual tropes associated with migration, such as "flooding" (Bradimore and Bauder 2011). Terrorist attacks in the United States in 2001, Indonesia in 2002 (which killed Australian citizens), Spain in 2004, England in 2005, and, more recently, France in 2015 and Brussels in 2016 each led to the implementation of new security regimes and antiterrorism legislation that facilitated stricter border enforcement. Security agencies received an infusion of resources, and immigration departments saw radical overhauls. Without doubt, the death of asylum is bound up with the securitization of migration.

Migration's securitization and its intersection with neoliberal imperatives manifest in the reconfiguration of borders (Walters 2004; Sparke 2006). The EU, for example, harmonizes border enforcement and "externalizes" asylum by processing asylum seekers in transit countries along the edges of the new European perimeter (Betts 2004; Schuster 2005) (the subject of chapters 1 and 2). Each year, since EU expansions in 2004 and 2007, a new island along the southern margins of the EU becomes hotly contested terrain as asylum seekers, smugglers, and authorities shift routes from the Canary Islands to Lampedusa, Malta, Cyprus, and Greece. Canada, meanwhile, shrank routes to protection through recent rounds of legislation in the 2000s that targeted small numbers of refugee claimants and leveraged this securitized stance to strip access and rights from all categories of refugees, claimants, and permanent residents (Canadian Council for Refugees 2012)—discussed in chapter 5.

Authorities in the Global North advance enforcement strategies that increasingly contain displacement in the Global South (Hathaway 1998; Castles 2008). Wealthy countries that until recently had some of the highest rates of refugee resettlement per capita (Canada, Australia, and the United States) also boast the most sophisticated border management policies. Access to protection originally enshrined in international law in the 1951 Convention Relating to the Status of Refugees and its 1967 Protocol was celebrated only recently with the sixtieth anniversary of the Convention. The next anniversary threatens to signal not a celebration but a memorialization, an international community mourning the loss of access to protection for asylum seekers. As a result of years aggressively offshoring containment, the highest numbers of displaced groups are now located in the countries neighboring conflict zones, such as 4.8 million displaced Syrians in Jordan, Lebanon, and Turkey (UNHCR 2016b)—one measure of the containment of displacement in regions closer to home.

Of course, the distancing of the border is not only physical but social—carried out through a racialized process of othering. In this process, distant and unruly racialized bodies threaten the global order. As detention and enforcement grow more remote, so too do chances for political advocacy; therefore the ontological death is tied closely to the political death of asylum and the physical and social deaths of asylum seekers.

DISAPPEARANCE: THE POLITICAL DEATH OF ASYLUM

The state moves offshore to enforce exclusion, resulting in physical deaths; ontological death involves the resulting impossibility of becoming an asylum seeker due to this prevention of arrivals; and political death means essentially that no critical mass of people knows, cares, or responds to this situation. Aggressive offshore enforcement therefore also fuels and finds basis in the political death of asylum: with little political will to preserve access to asylum, governments invest fewer resources in processing claims robustly and fairly and more in ballooning border enforcement budgets designed to turn people away.

The enforcement archipelago traffics in the interplay between what can be seen and what can be hidden. The securitization of migration is premised on the racialized politics of fear of unknown others offshore. The dehumanizing discourse of racialized others masks the violence of enacting offshore enforcement in the name of national security. Hidden from view are the bodies of securitized migrants and the livelihoods, families, and communities in which they are embedded (Hiemstra 2019a). Throughout this book, I explore the interplay between hypervisible, spectacular infrastructures of enforcement and that which is hidden from view, the more insidious forms of violence at work beneath the surface.

This hiding is made possible by the political death of asylum, with subjectivities of asylum seekers foreclosed upon, the violence enacted on the body made possible through continual processes of forgetting and erasure. Much contemporary activism endeavors to counter this disappearance, building on the premise of humanizing, valuing life, and grieving loss through documentation, mapping, and memorialization—discussed in chapter 6.

The enforcement archipelago tends to come to the attention of national and transnational publics when physical deaths occur—sometimes within detention facilities but more so when they happen en masse at sea. The drowning of more than three hundred migrants in a sinking boat within sight of the small Italian island of Lampedusa in October 2013 is one example. The suspected killing of nearly five hundred migrants who were allegedly maneuvered by smugglers who then threatened them into submission in September 2014 is another. And yet death is a regular occurrence in the borderlands between disparate regions with asymmetrical economic fortunes. As one writer for the *New Yorker* noted after the boat capsized near Lampedusa, "dig further, and you'd have noticed that, with tick-tock regularity, migrants have been dying along its coast for quite some time" (Stillman 2013).

The political death of asylum is similarly a nonevent, a lesson in the dehumanizing dimensions of contradiction—a failure to know or remember those lost or the shame of remembering them in the wrong ways. In morbid acknowledgment of dehumanization and its failure to rescue the ship that sank in 2013, for example, Italy announced a state funeral and granted postmortem Italian citizenship to the dead, while detaining the survivors (Mainwaring 2014). These responses and associated bickering and posturing between Italy and Malta during search-and-rescue operations demonstrate the many ways in which loss is politicized. "With tick-tock regularity," geopolitical priorities prevail over human life.

The erasure of people and denial of the violence they experience have been more common responses to the loss of life than the granting of postmortem citizenship. Within the archipelago, enforcement leads to a loss of life obscured from view of national and transnational publics. Throughout this book, I explore both the spectacular (de Genova 2013) signs of enforcement and the hidden forces of exclusion at work beneath the surface. Building on the work of Butler (2004, 2009), Agamben (1998, 2005), and Gregory (2006, 2007), I link offshore exercises in sovereignty and biopower to violence. The existence of enforcement archipelagoes and deaths in the places where people are most desperate to enter wealthier, more stable states suggests that the community of nation-states about which Hannah Arendt (1958, 269) so famously and presciently wrote is growing less willing to protect the rights of those displaced and on the move. Arendt's writing remains as relevant today as it was in the aftermath of World War II.

Calling attention to spectacular performances of violence—such as muscular shows of border enforcement, interception, and detention—distracts from the more mundane violence that happens routinely, if more quietly, at sea and in detention. As a result, much activism operates with the impulse to document, show, locate, map, and remember. Activists and scholars alike have researched these movements between onshore and offshore practices and populations, sovereign and biopower, and the visibility and invisibility through which they operate. They have done so often with the simple impulse to locate the hidden. Paglen and Thompson (2006), for example, studied commercial airlines hidden in plain sight and the flight trackers who devoted themselves to finding their use for rendition in the global war on terror. Derek Gregory (2007), using Abu Ghraib and Guantánamo Bay as examples, and building on work by Michel Foucault and Giorgio Agamben, characterizes these sites as "vanishing points" produced creatively through the law: places where sovereign and biopower operate to invisibilize human suffering and failures to protect human rights and human life.

While Abu Ghraib prison in Iraq and the U.S. naval base at Cuba's Guantánamo Bay became iconic sites notorious for human rights abuses and U.S. detention of "foreign enemy combatants" during the war on terror (Butler 2004; Kaplan 2005; Gregory 2007), these are not the only sites where people and the state violence carried out against them are vanquished, intentionally hidden, and removed discursively from the frame (Butler 2009). Other, more mundane sites function as island vanishing points that require collective endeavors to unearth and understand the hidden geographical reconfigurations of sovereignty and subjectivity.

The enforcement archipelago surrounding the small Italian island of Lampedusa serves as a case in point, introduced here and discussed in more detail in chapter 1. Lampedusa has been a significant destination of migrants traveling from North Africa since the mid-1990s. Until about 2004, asylum seekers landing on the island would be relocated to Sicily and eventually make their way to other parts of Italy or other EU countries to work and seek asylum (Andrijasevic 2010). Since 2004, however, Italy has pursued exclusionary enforcement practices that follow a spatial logic of outward expansion. Following EU expansion in 2004, Lampedusa went from being an island of entry and transit to a site where migrants were detained and often deported. Rutvica Andrijasevic (2010) has traced this exclusion through the lens of the island detention facility and the reconfiguration of border politics. Her work reveals Lampedusa as a key location where the reconfiguration of sovereign territory produces new subjectivities. Rather than externalize asylum, she suggests, Italy is producing illegality on the island.

Within a few years, the Italian navy had intensified interception practices at sea and entered into bilateral agreements with Libya to return migrants intercepted and returned or detained and deported (most of whom were not Libyan). In 2007, Italy began to enforce its policy of *respingimento* with the 2007 Protocol of Joint Patrol of the Mediterranean with Libya. Often referred to as *pushback* in English, this involved more extensive collusion with Libyan authorities to intercept and return boats to northern Africa (Tazzioli 2011). In 2011, bilateral arrangements fell apart as Muammar Gaddafi was ousted and social unrest prevailed during the Arab Spring. Whereas 2010 had seen very few migrants detained on Lampedusa, more than fifty-seven thousand landed in Lampedusa in 2011 (Ministero dell'Interno 2011). Once the immediate crisis of the uprising subsided, bilateral agreements were reconstituted, and thousands of migrants continued to move through what has been characterized as a revolving door, attempting to migrate to the EU, being returned, trying again, spending time in detention, and making their way slowly through the enforcement archipelago, with far too many dying in the Mediterranean (IOM 2014). Human rights reports and research on this archipelago show its sinister spread from the southern frontier of the EU into northern Africa and back again as the mass displacement of Syrians has a similar effect on the Greek islands of Kos and Lesvos (Carling 2007b; Collyer 2007; Lutterbeck 2009).

Whereas Lampedusa once signified a path to protection where it was possible to land and make a claim for asylum, the island was slowly transformed over the space of a decade into a space of exclusion through detention and deportation, another node in the shrinking of access to asylum. Many struggles over migration on the island relate to visibility and memorialization—discussed in chapters 1 and 6.

Yet migrants do not vanish, in life or in death; instead, the violence they endure festers and erupts, making itself known time and again. As Butler (2004, 34) suggests, "violence renews itself in the face of the apparent inexhaustibility of its object." People do not disappear but continually reappear in spectral form. Authorities, local residents, and transnational migrant families and communities are drawn into and haunted by episodes of loss. They witness death, sometimes attempting rescue, sometimes pushing back against pushback. In December 2010, when a boat carrying ninety asylum seekers from Iraq and Iran sank off the ragged shores of Australia's Christmas Island (in Australian Overseas Territory), local residents watched in horror, unable to enter the rough waters risked routinely by those attempting to land on Australian overseas territory. In another symbolic gesture to render migrants strategically visible in one moment, only to invisibilize them again, the Australian government flew survivors from Christmas Island to memorial services for the dead held in Sydney in February 2011, only to return them to detention on Christmas Island afterward (Australian Broadcasting Corporation 2011). In another boomerang move, asylum seekers detained on Nauru in early 2016 were flown to Australian cities for medical treatment. When they challenged their return in court, they were found to be returnable (Doherty 2016). This decision prompted revitalization of the new sanctuary movement and the "Let Them Stay" campaign across Australia (Hodge 2019).

The archipelago produces life and death in myriad forms. Fierce struggles over body counts and memorialization are under way on islands and along borders. Embedded within these struggles are the mourning of continuous loss and fights to value life and count those who have been dehumanized. Efforts to trace biographies where no body has been found are themselves becoming an important, burgeoning field of research (Delano and Nienass 2014; Last et al. 2017). The role of the spectral incited activism, with EU-wide planning of a large commemorative memorial on Lampedusa in October 2014, accompanied by a declaration about the rights of migrants (Carta di Lampedusa 2014). As discussed in chapter 6, activists' efforts to document and memorialize loss can be understood as a direct response to the political death of asylum, the desire to fight for life to be preserved and for death and humanity to be recognized in the face of the ever-widening push to move the displaced farther offshore.

ARCHIPELAGOES

By mapping enforcement archipelagoes where migrant deaths transpire, I refer to exclusionary assemblages of ever-more dispersed practices, policies, people, sites, and tactics designed to restrict migrants' access to sovereign territory of states of the Global North against those aiming to work or seek protection. These material archipelagoes are expressions of state mobility; they involve the movement of state enforcement well beyond the borders of destination countries and deep into the transnational routes that people navigate at sea and on islands.

The archipelago is at once a natural form identified by physical geographers and a human geography built onto the landscape. The enforcement archipelagoes I map in this book are built into geopoliticized regional landscapes and overlain upon physical archipelagoes. They are constructed on foundations of geostrategic military history, colonization, asymmetrical economies, and imperial reach and crafted on island military infrastructures designed originally to form the basis— and bases—of American empire (Vine 2009). This infrastructure is now being repurposed to regulate human mobility and punish uninvited migration. The assemblage of the archipelago brings together sea and land, onshore and offshore, and hybrid forms and permutations of sovereign and nonsovereign territorial status. Jurisdictional issues therein raise important questions about the operation and reach of sovereign power and varied forms of citizenship and belonging. Agamben's (1998, 2005) topological thinking about the productive threshold between inside and outside proves central to recent geographical scholarship on sovereignty. He identifies the destabilization of internal and external territory and conceptualizes exceptional zones working through these binaries. Like Butler and Mbembe (2003), Agamben also conceptualizes the devaluation of life, specifically in relation to a figure of Roman law, *homo sacer* or "sacred man," a person without rights who is included in the juridical order only through exclusion.

Sites where this threshold is navigated and negotiated have sustained the attention of geographers: border, prison, body, sea, island (Mountz 2013). Other scholars have studied islands as nodes of sovereign power (e.g., Benton 2010; Khalil 2013). These thresholds are sites of crossing and flux between interiority and exteriority. They become places where sovereign power operates at the intersection of law, geography, and legal status. These places have thus captured the attention of legal geographers and legal scholars (Gregory 2007; Dastyari 2015).

Reconfigurations of sovereignty and subjectivity can be seen in migration studies where people grow ever more precarious as they approach borders, and in border studies where scholars have written about borders proliferating, present everywhere (Balibar 2002), onshore and offshore (Bigo 2000, 2002). More dispersed and transnational, changing geographies of the border aptly reflect shifting spaces of sovereignty (Sparke 2006). The spatial patterns emerging prompt examination of traditional political geographies of sovereign territory by moving analysis to the margins where remote processing happens along the edges of sovereign territory, where mobile state authorities and practices meet and immobilize migrants, and where the precariousness of ambiguous legal status intersects with the partiality of political status. Legality, securitization, and enforcement are pronounced and etched with contradictions on islands. There "offshoring" capitalizes on subnational island jurisdictions to shrink spaces of asylum legally (Durieux and McAdam 2004), numerically (Newland 2005; UNHCR 2007, 2008), and spatially (Mountz 2010).

Hidden prisons have long been identified through the metaphor of the archipelago, building on Solzehnitsyn's (1974) understanding of Russian prisons as gulag, dispersed, and unseen, in the Siberian hinterland (Applebaum 2003).[5] Foucault suggested in an interview that the archipelago was "the only truly geographical concept" (Gordon 1980, 68). Foucault's "carceral archipelago" captured "the way in which a form of punitive system is physically dispersed yet at the same time covers the entirety of a society" (cited in Gordon 1980, 68). The archipelago is often mobilized as a spatial metaphor to understand the distribution of power. Just as Foucault understood institutions to be reproduced as a form of social control within the social body (and beyond the spaces of institutions themselves), I see islands and archipelagoes as reproduced throughout society.

Gregory (2007) employs Foucault's "carceral archipelago" to explain contemporary war prisons and the topological connections between black sites developed during conflicts in Iraq and Afghanistan, particularly the legal treatment and isolation of noncitizens. His carceral archipelago advances through legal moves that solidify American exceptionalism and justify the evasion of international law in what Gregory (2004) calls the colonial present. Ann Stoler (2011, 2013) also extends and challenges Foucault's notion of the carceral archipelago. She locates "the carceral archipelago of empire" as a perpetually shifting geography that connects colonial spaces of confinement through "managed mobilities, mobilizing and immobilizing populations, dislocating and relocating peoples according to a set of changing rules and hierarchies that orders social kinds" (Stoler 2011). For Stoler (2011, 2013), the carceral archipelago becomes the grounds on which to map ruination, the debris of imperialism and colonialism.

Similarly, the enforcement archipelago functions as an emergent process premised on the dispersal of enforcement infrastructure and people seeking asylum. Productive, creative topological processes of border enforcement lead to material topographies of exclusion: fixed sites of exclusion that immobilize people (detailed in chapter 2). Tracing the genealogies of these exclusions—externalization, excision, interception, interdiction—requires understanding present and past. These topological relations and processes produce material effects: distinctive offshore spaces such as the U.S. unincorporated territory of Guam, the Australian overseas territory of Christmas Island, and Australian-funded detention facilities on many different Indonesian islands. On islands, the detachment of migrants from sovereign territory and the rights they would accrue upon landing proves an important part of the violence that engulfs people in offshore detention facilities. Offshoring intensifies precarity.

The archipelago has also become an important metaphor for understanding sovereign power and the particular forms of imperialism, empire, and colonialism in which states are engaged in the present (Gregory 2004, 2007; Stoler 2011, 2013). As Stoler and Gregory observe, the archipelago is not a static form but perpetually in motion through the ruination of imperialism (Stoler 2013). Much current scholarship on imperialism and empire locates islands not as marginal but rather as central to understanding how power operates (e.g., Burnett 2005; Lipman 2012).

The archipelago thus functions as an apt spatial metaphor through which to understand geographical shifts in migration enforcement and the broader geopolitical relations of power where these are formed. The term references a constellation of sites of securitization where migrants encounter authorities and become ensnared in nets of border security and detention. The archipelago mobilizes and advances the death of asylum by capitalizing on and mobilizing the spatial form of the island within uneven fields of power and mobility.

ISLANDS

Within but distinct from archipelagoes, islands also function as spatial metaphors of confinement through which to understand configurations of power. As Foucault observed about prisons and other state spaces, the *dispositif,* the island is reproduced throughout society, and the archipelago is a form often mobilized in contemporary analyses of power. What is a prison if not an island?

States have long used islands as sites of experimentation (Taussig 2004; Baldacchino and Milne 2006; Sheller 2009) or for attempts to control or exert influence (Vine 2009) and to extract resources or attract profit in other ways (Baldacchino 2007). Islands function as both material locations and spatial forms that shift in the operation of power. The form of the island can also be found in recent conceptual thought about sovereignty, imperialism, post/colonialism, and the "debris of empire" (Moore 2000). In the resurgence of the study of political geography post-9/11 (Mountz 2013), the role of islands has once again come to the fore, utilized to understand new forms of warfare, such as what Gregory (2011) calls the "everywhere war," the proliferating network of small U.S. bases globally (Davis 2011), or the rendition flights and black sites of the war on terror (Paglen and Thompson 2006). Nodes in a network recur in various iterations: Gregory's (2007, 206) vanishing points where states use geography to evade international laws and conventions in militarized locations such as Guantánamo Bay (Butler 2004; Kaplan 2005; Gregory 2007) and Diego Garcia (Vine 2009; Sidaway 2010) and Vine's (2012) "lily pad" strategy. The lily pad involves the strategic location of proliferating, small forward-operating U.S. bases as a form of imperialism constructed to exert regional control. Whether discussed explicitly or operating as underlying logic, island and archipelago are reproduced across spatial concepts of these nodes, networks, and constellations.

The island appears and is reproduced in other forms: bases, bodies, prisons, all islands of a kind. As the global war on terror reestablishes geopolitical uses of territory that enable states to circumvent international conventions and international law, political geographers and theorists study that which is silenced or removed from the frame: civilian deaths (Butler 2004; Gregory 2004), black sites (Gregory 2007), rendition (Paglen and Thompson 2006), and proliferating small bases as new forms of warfare (Vine 2012). Much of this silencing and disappearing involves the production of exceptional states and spaces through the law (Gregory 2007; Delaney 2010). The production of exclusion through the law becomes a basis for the creation of islands in the form of confinement.

In Agambenian terms, islands parallel the spatial form of the camp, with the potential to be mobilized and reproduced anywhere, also representing movement of the concept of the island beyond the geographic location of the island. Indeed, Minca (2007, 78, 90) finds in Agamben's and Gregory's (2004) writing a new spatial ontology of power, with camp and permanent state of exception "a new nomos on global politics." Is the camp the island of the twenty-first century? And if so, how might the mobilization of the island as a territorial expression of power overcome important critiques of Agamben's writing (e.g., Pratt 2005; Mitchell 2006; Ramadan 2012), such as the absence of human agency?

In the enforcement archipelago, the spatial forms of borderlines and borderlands have been supplanted by islands: proliferating spaces of confinement and a primary spatial form of exclusion. We see not only the proliferation of crossings but the proliferation of spaces of confinement. Crossing itself is no longer an apt metaphor in border studies; instead, it has been replaced by the "revolving door" and legal limbo. The death of asylum progresses as people move in and out of a zone where they find themselves in continual motion, yet rarely achieving entry.

The island proliferates as a spatial form of confinement as the colonial past haunts and erupts into the colonial present. High-security facilities on islands function as islands. Cells for solitary confinement grow in use as detainees are separated from one another. Within these facilities, the use of these islands of confinement and suicide attempts accelerate hand in hand. People detained there become profoundly isolated: islands (bodies) within islands (detention facilities) within islands.

As Savitri Taylor (2005) argues, legal forms of exceptionalism, such as excision of borders for the purposes of migration, are attached to migrants' bodies. Those intercepted and detained in Australia's excised zones carry that excision on the body, with limited access to protection even once they pass the threshold between island and mainland territories. This isolation constitutes the proliferation of islands within islands. Through creative legal maneuvers and uses of detention everywhere, islands are also mobilized beyond islands.

RESEARCHING THE HAUNTING AND THE HIDDEN

How can the death of asylum be documented with the tools of social science, given that it is a nonevent residing in the realm of silence, a crime of attrition, a ghost to study, in Grace Cho's (2009) terms?

> If there is a "discourse," it is a silent and melancholic one in which there have been no lives, and no losses; there has been no common bodily condition, no vulnerability that serves as the basis for an

apprehension of our commonality; and there has been no sunder-
ing of that commonality.... None of this takes place. In the silence
of the newspaper, there was no event, no loss, and this failure of
recognition is mandated through an identification of those who
identify with the perpetration of that violence. (Butler 2004, 36)

Researchers have been assembling databases of border deaths (Weber
and Pickering 2011; Border Observatory 2015; Last et al. 2017). Statistical
data on detention are available from government and NGO sources,
but unevenly so across time and space. Like border deaths, statistics
on detention and interception are often incomplete, if available at all.
Researchers often secure information about interception and detention
through access to information requests, interviews, court transcripts,
press releases, and even media accounts (Burroughs and Williams 2018).
With a dearth of quantitative data, qualitative data offer information
beyond numbers about offshore border enforcement and detention in
sites under study.

Little is known about the detention of asylum seekers on islands, in
part because of their remote and interstitial locations: neither at home
in their countries of origin where they hold legal status and claims to
citizenship are stronger, nor in the asylum process, having their claims
heard by a signatory state to the 1951 Convention Relating to the Status
of Refugees. These liminal locations hold implications for epistemology,
ontology, and methodology; migration-related activities there challenge what we think we know about migration. They require scholars
and citizens alike to improve on what we know and how we know it.
The sites under examination are far from the more powerful central
administration of sovereign territory, legal ambiguity prescribed by
location, and diverse political arrangements and allegiances. And yet
these borderland spaces prove central to understanding global trends
in migration: precarity, exclusion, liminality, and legal struggle. As
such, activities on islands become sources of policy innovation and
experimentation; they simultaneously mirror and inform enforcement
practices in mainland territories and elsewhere.

The empirical work in this book was gathered over several years.
I began with the goal of studying offshore border enforcement that
precluded the arrival of asylum seekers on sovereign territory. Earlier
research on detention and the refugee determination process in Canada

had revealed a community of nation-states that Canadian bureaucrats studied for "best practices." From 2006 to 2008, I researched border enforcement practices undertaken by those nation-states that served as peers with comparable border policies and practices: Australia, the United States, and member states of the EU. In interviews on the policing of borders, respondents frequently discussed actions offshore, the role of islands in migration-related enforcement, and frequent eruptions that emerged repeatedly there. These findings led me to design the Island Detention Project, explained in the following paragraphs.

For several years, I led a team to conduct research with people in and involved in detention, setting out to learn how migrants end up in the enforcement archipelago and what happens once they are there, with particular attention to access to asylum. The research methods included open-ended and semistructured interviews, participant observation, and archival research in the United States (Guam, Saipan, mainland territory), Australia (Christmas Island, Indonesian islands where Australia funds the detention of asylum seekers, and mainland territory), and the EU (primarily on Lampedusa and Sicily, with site visits to Greece and Malta). Owing to the difficulty of entering detention centers and the risks involved with interviewing those detained, most interviews were conducted with those released, representing, advocating for, or visiting detainees. Researchers documented visits to detention facilities in the ethnographic terms of field notes rather than in interviews.

The field and archival research took place between 2010 and 2014 and continued with subsequent archival research. During that time, approximately two hundred interviews with employees from government and nongovernmental organizations, detainees, former detainees, attorneys, authorities, journalists, and advocates were conducted. Interview questions were generally the same across locations, with adjustments to local and national contexts. The interviews sought to understand the journeys of authorities offshore and individuals and families affected by island detention, but also the effects on and responses from local island populations. Fieldwork carried out by a research team of three doctoral students and me also included participant observation in the form of visits to detention centers with advocates and friends of detainees and observation of asylum processes where possible. These methods involved generation of several hundred pages of field notes, interview transcripts, and archives that capture the informal and underreported daily struggles surrounding histories of detention on islands.

There is an important distinction to make when discussing information about enforcement between official and unofficial realms of knowledge, between policy recorded on paper and daily practice. Many of the empirical phenomena discussed in this book fall under the category of practice. These are enforcement practices not often found in the pages of policy or press but in remote field locations hidden from view where authorities carry out work beyond the purview of media, advocates, or human rights monitors. Often, a geographical narrative—such as proximity to interception, necessity of deterrence, or humanitarian rescue of those at risk of dying at sea—stands in as a rationale for remote detention. Although the countries under study are signatories to the 1951 Refugee Convention and/or the 1967 Protocol, some of the practices of civil servants who patrol their borders undermine the responsibilities of the Convention and were often designed to evade the obligations of either domestic or international law through offshore moves. This study therefore draws insight from scholars on daily state practices operating beyond the texts of policy (e.g., Gupta and Sharma 2006; Painter 2006).

The research also aims explicitly to address the issue of strategic concealment on the part of state authorities. All of the sites detailed in this book have, at one time or another in their contemporary use to detain noncitizens, been the subject of political controversy over the concealment of information. Authorities have stopped human rights monitors, activists, visitors, journalists, and clergy from entering facilities at various points in time. The remoteness of sites of detention and the bureaucracy designed to manage them both function to obscure the violence of confinement and the loss of liberty (see Hiemstra 2012; Belcher and Martin 2013). When conducting research on hidden geographies, there is an obligation to press on, on one hand, but also to proceed cautiously, on the other, so as not to render more vulnerable people with precarious status.

One thing has not disappeared, and that is the need and the drive to move. People continue to experience violence, despair, and displacement. They move when conditions become impossible for them to stay. They do not disappear. Recognition of their precarity, lives, and deaths in interstitial spaces is vital. While detention may be construed as a loss of life, for example, it also holds potential as a basis of the formation of political community in Butlerian terms, an idea to which I return in chapter 6. There I probe the life of activism with and for asylum seekers, which is designed to call attention to precarity, a life-affirming response to the death of asylum.

The enforcement archipelago is both a site of enforcement practice and a spatial metaphor for the death of asylum. Everywhere one turns in the field of migration studies, one finds intensifying precarity (e.g., Goldring et al. 2009; Baban et al. 2017). And where there is precarity, there are islands: people isolated not only because they are being detained on an island but because of legal status or remote detention. The island is a material form of exclusion; but the island also operates as spatial metaphor, reconstituted in the form of the jail, the cell, the ship, the liminal status—mechanisms through which people on the move are treated as islands.

PART I

PHYSICAL DEATH

State Mobilities

1

Externalizing Asylum:
A Genealogy

Over the years, scholars have set out to demonstrate the correlation between intensified enforcement operations designed to govern migration offshore and the rise in unauthorized entry and border deaths. They have done so through quantitative (Cornelius 2001; Weber and Pickering 2011; Last et al. 2017) and historical analyses that examine the consequences of changes in enforcement policy (e.g., Boswell 2003; Carling 2007a; Nevins 2010). Suggesting a causal relationship—that enforcement causes death—continues as a source of debate. But there remains little doubt empirically that the geographical extension of border enforcement through the movement of state authorities, infrastructure, and policies offshore correlates with a rise in the physical deaths of people embarking on riskier transnational journeys designed to elude authorities. To be clear, greater enforcement at sea correlates strongly with more deaths at sea (Williams and Mountz 2018).

People take to the sea to get somewhere. But countries with asylum programs endeavor to prohibit potential asylum seekers from landing on sovereign territory where they can make claims. Thus geopolitical standoffs unfold at sea. One need not look beyond the Mediterranean Sea or the plight of the Rohingya fleeing Myanmar and denied landing by Malaysia and Indonesia, both characterized by a sharp rise in 2015. Migrant deaths are morbidly entangled with state investments in the movement of border enforcement offshore—a desire to govern and exclude from within the margins.

Externalization is thus a significant and ongoing part of the securitization of migration (Bigo 2000). While many scholars discuss securitization as the process wherein migrants are criminalized and deemed a threat to national security in discourse (e.g., Ibrahim 2005),

securitization also involves material forms of exclusion that accompany
this shift in discourse. Externalization is one example. By scripting migrants and would-be asylum seekers as criminal and security threats,
the rationale is set forth discursively for their distancing through exclusionary measures or bureaucratic management offshore.

Designed to inhibit access, these extensions of enforcement offshore
also contribute directly to the death of asylum. Political scientists have
been studying these moves under the rubric of externalization since
the 1990s. This chapter traces the history of state mobilities offshore
with a genealogy of externalization. By state mobilities, I refer to the
ways in which states themselves act transnationally to move authorities
and enforcement infrastructure offshore, beyond the physical limits of
mainland sovereign territory. I go back in time to look at key moments
in the past. My genealogy maps a jagged path that ultimately laid the
foundation for understanding the contemporary practices that are the
main subject of this book. Put another way, this chapter explores how
we arrived at the death of asylum.

People often associate the term *externalization* with offshore border
enforcement carried out by the EU, beginning in the 1990s. But a longer
history predated EU externalization practices, leading eventually to the
current situation in which externalization became common practice
of the Global North, politicizing migration events by sea. This chapter
heeds William Walters's (2008) call for researchers to pay more attention to the sites where land meets sea. I develop a genealogy of the term
externalization that spans a four-decade progression of the movement
of border enforcement offshore. The genealogy traces the modern
period of externalization back to U.S. interceptions of Haitians and
Cubans at sea in the late 1970s to early 1980s (Mountz and Loyd 2014;
Loyd and Mountz 2018). Although these measures were interpreted as
obvious efforts to undermine international law (Koh 1994), they moved
gradually into the realm of normalcy in the ensuing decades across a
number of regions. The late 1980s and early 1990s saw the development
and subsequent thickening of immigration control networks offshore.
The 2000s showed the diffusion of externalization as widely accepted
practice to shut down routes to asylum. Within this period, post-9/11
changes to border enforcement brought the movement of externalization
more forcefully into the public geographic imagination, shifting legal
grounds and moral compasses governing the preservation of human

rights, building on fear and premised on national security imperatives (Gilbert 2012). U.S. detention of "foreign enemy combatants" captured during its war on terror catapulted Guantánamo Bay into public discourse as an iconic space of offshore enforcement where domestic and international law could effectively be evaded at the cost of human rights. The years since the 9/11 attacks can be characterized by freneticism around these impulses to move ever farther offshore and deeper into zones of origin and transit routes. These material moves to exclude offshore accompany intensified criminalization as people on the move became caught up in the netting of securitization.

Within this genealogy, the movement of ports of entry proves key. Although generally understood as fixed infrastructure, ports themselves have been set in motion (like borders and detention facilities). Externalization dislodges the port of entry from its original geographical location on the very edge of sovereign territory. As a result, migrants and asylum seekers encounter authorities policing borders earlier in their geographical journey. Ports become politicized sites of designation and exceptionalism where legality and geography intersect, laying the foundation for struggles over and access to rights between migrants and authorities. There enforcement collides with efforts to seek asylum through geopoliticized fields of encounter.

The genealogy of externalization shows the port of entry as a moving threshold where migrants either enter sovereign territory, traditionally along land and sea borders and in airports, or find that they are excluded. Enforcement authorities have recently utilized this designation in fluid ways. In the United States, for example, new rules placed the port of entry anywhere within one hundred miles of the border, enabling authorities to police bus stations and to board trains internally. Under President Trump's administration, this "rights-free zone" was extended to encompass all of the interior. Similarly, in Canada and Australia, military bases, islands, and other sites internal to sovereign territory are designated ports of entry or even excised from sovereign territory for the purposes of migration. In airports, this designation corresponds with microgeographies of liminal zones one moves through en route: from disembarking the airplane into tunnels, hallways, and nonspaces (Makaremi 2009; Maillet 2017). In our entries into sovereign territory, we move through small thresholds as we approach the border, the legal microgeographies shifting with each passage.

In the rest of this chapter, I tell the story of externalization twice through two different, if simultaneous, narratives that operate distinctly across time and space as policies and practices move from place to place. I begin with a brief definition and history of the term *externalization*. Most literature on externalization originates in the EU and addresses the EU context. This relates to the very visible efforts by the EU to open internal borders while fortifying the external border as part of its process of regionalization.[1]

I then trace the evolution of the practice of externalization through a genealogy. The genealogy reveals change that happened in fragmented and eruptive time, through crises that so typically characterize migration events and catalyze changes to policy (Mainwaring 2014; Mountz and Hiemstra 2014).

WHAT IS EXTERNALIZATION? DEFINITION, EMERGENCE, AND USE OF THE TERM

While scholars have endeavored to define the notion of securitization of migration (Huysman 2000, 2006; Ibrahim 2005), fewer have offered much in the way of defining externalization. This is likely because externalization takes many forms: interception, offshore networks of civil servants, increased transit visa requirements, development of detention facilities in transit zones, bilateral arrangements for joint policing and repatriation, and so on. Externalization is one of the mechanisms enabling the death of asylum.

Further complicating any definition of externalization is the degree of informality that these practices and arrangements sometimes entail. Externalization involves enforcement *practice* as well as *policy*. Externalization was often not an explicitly stated policy, particularly in its earliest incarnations, although many proposals were made over the years to externalize through different measures, particularly in the EU context (Schuster 2005). Externalization was therefore not often written into the formal pages of policy but advanced through daily enforcement exercises on land and at sea. These practices—like others in the enforcement archipelago—signal evasion, subversion, and geographical inversions. Over time, informal daily enforcement practices became more formalized as policies and laws designed to externalize.

When I was conducting ethnographic research at Citizenship and Immigration Canada (CIC) in 2000 and 2001 about the federal agency's response to four ships carrying migrants intercepted off the western coast of British Columbia, employees talked about informal exchanges with their counterparts in the United States, EU, United Kingdom, and Australia. They had sent teams to study prosecution of human smugglers in the EU, the boarding of boats at sea by the U.S. Navy, and detention practices in Australia. Civil servants tasked with setting up processing of migrants who had arrived on the boats and their subsequent detention joked about U.S. government boats intercepting ships in the Pacific, refueling them, and then redirecting them north to Canada. They also joked about mimicking Australia's use of islands to detain but conducted actual research into the use of boats as floating detention facilities (detailed in Mountz 2010).

In reality, Canada intercepts very few boats. In fact, following those four interceptions in 1999, only two ships carrying migrants were intercepted in a twenty-year period from 2000 to 2020. But, as I will discuss further in the Canadian context in chapter 5, responses to boat arrivals have proven disproportionately significant in terms of the subsequent restrictions imposed on paths to asylum (Ibrahim 2005).

What I did not understand when conducting ethnographic work in CIC offices in 2000, for example, was the degree to which I was witnessing a pivotal moment in the history of offshore border enforcement. This moment followed decades of criminalization of asylum seekers in which the offshoring of border enforcement to mediate or preclude their arrival happened informally through information-sharing arrangements abroad. These arrangements were in existence since the 1980s but still in the early stages before becoming mainstream—which is to say more common and more politically palatable (if about to "take off").

These ethnographic observations from the Canadian bureaucracy highlight the importance of informal exchanges to understanding the diffusion of border enforcement practices. They raise important analytical and methodological questions about studying the often informal origins of migration-related policies. Many mechanisms of externalization have evolved over time from informal practice to formal policy. Take, for example, the recent trend in the EU toward *mobility partnerships*. These are regional arrangements between states to facilitate the movement of labor by arranging travel documents, for example. They are predated by bilateral arrangements that were usually made behind closed doors, with proceedings and the agreements themselves inaccessible to the public. As Bernd Kasparek (2010, 137) notes, bilateral arrangements like mobility partnerships "aim to regain sovereignty over migration, being able to define the conditions under which migration is supposed to occur."

When much happens in the informal sphere, important questions about methodologies and ontologies of exclusion arise. How do we know what we do about what Aristide Zolberg (1999, 2003) calls "remote control," practices that he argues dated back to early migration policies at the turn of the twentieth century? To answer this question, a brief sketch of the history of the term in existing literature proves useful. The term *externalization* first emerged in writing by political scientists working primarily in a European context and on the case of externalization undertaken by EU member states (e.g., Lavenex 1999; Bigo 2000; Pastore 2001; Brochmann 2002; Boswell 2003; Noll 2003).

Whereas the use of the term can be traced to the late 1990s, when it came into being in association with EU border enforcement and asylum processing, earlier enforcement and security practices show seeds planted—if not labeled externalization. For example, use of the term *external security* preceded the term *externalization* (Bigo 2000; Grabbe 2000).[2] Bigo (2000) tracked the convergence of internal and external measures of securitization while also looking at the successful rhetoric of securitization used by politicians to stir fear and unease (Bigo 2002).

Since shared understanding and usage of the term *externalization* arose in the EU context, the history of externalization in the region is more systematically documented there than anywhere else. Early scholarship documented the erasure of internal and hardening of external borders and the incorporation of migration management into EU external policy (Boswell 2003, 619). As Boswell (2003, 621) observes, though ideas about externalization emerged as early as 1991, the European Council first "formally embraced" the "'external dimension' of EU immigration and asylum policy" in 1999. She identifies two different kinds of external measures: cooperation between receiving and sending states to externalize traditional tools of migration control and more preventive measures "designed to change the factors which influence people's decisions to move, or their chosen destinations" (Boswell 2003,

619–20). Schuster (2005) subsequently mapped plans proposed by EU member states to carry out offshore detention and asylum processing in North African states (an example of an element of externalization that proceeded informally with many plans rejected because they lacked consensus among EU member states). Other scholars studied the geographical expansion of the EU into neighboring regions through externalization (Betts 2004; Salter 2004; Walters 2004; Geiger 2013). At the time, Balibar's (2002) notion that the border was everywhere was gaining currency in border studies, particularly among political scientists. Beyond mere stage or context, the EU proved the driving force behind this idea.

As I will show in the genealogy, some of the early writing on U.S. interception and detention of migrants in the Caribbean (Koh 1994; Noble 2011) can be understood as early practices of externalization before the term came into usage. Yet explicit writing about externalization in the North American context emerged later and dwelled less on the term *externalization*. Coleman (2005, 2007) explored how the United States advanced offshore border enforcement, looking at U.S. border enforcement in Mexico. While Coleman documented U.S. policing in Mexico, another set of scholars and advocacy groups documented Canadian interceptions at sea, informal enforcement of foreign airports, and use of visas to restrict access to Canadian sovereign territory (Brouwer 2003; Canadian Council for Refugees 2003; Mountz 2006; Kernerman 2008).

Australia was also considered a leader in pushing enforcement offshore. Accordingly, scholars there traced earlier histories of offshore border enforcement (e.g., Hugo 2001; Mares 2001; Taylor 2005) (detailed in chapter 4). Some scholars set about comparing externalization carried out by Australia and the EU (e.g., Hyndman and Mountz 2008) and by the EU and North America (Zaiotti 2016).

Externalization intersected with the literature on the securitization of migration (Huysmans 2000; Bigo 2002; Huysmans 2006). While the term could retroactively be applied to the first large preventive offshore enforcement measures undertaken by the United States in the 1980s (which I discuss in the following genealogy),[3] the concept really came into more common usage in the late 1990s in reference to EU measures to shore up external borders while erasing internal borders between member states that were part of the Schengen Agreement.

These changes to border enforcement in the EU coincided with broader anti-immigrant public opinion and discourses that intensified globally throughout the 1990s (Razack 1999; Squire 2009). As asylum seekers were demonized, associated with criminality and security risks, their credibility undermined, paths to asylum shrank in the 1990s and 2000s.

With some exceptions, most of the early literature on externalization was authored by political scientists. To a geographer who thinks spatially, externalization entails three geographical movements of state mobilities to the margins. The first entails the movement of border enforcement offshore (as in interception and interdiction). The second, subsequent component of externalization is the movement of processing and detention to transit routes and regions, holding migrants in transit regions or moving them there once intercepted. A third geographical move entails the use of island spaces to carry out this processing, whether on actual islands or through the creation of the island in forms such as refugee camps and detention centers en route. Essentially, the border is dislodged as a way to thwart progress of those seeking asylum toward sovereign territory where they accrue access to rights (Durieux and McAdam 2004).

Externalization can also be understood as an inversion of the port. Rather than the static infrastructure associated with ports where people arrive and their entry or exclusion is bureaucratically processed, state authorities move this infrastructure offshore to transit regions of migrants, effectively "processing" them closer to home or even at home. As one example, in response to the arrival of some sixty-eight thousand Central Americans seeking asylum in the United States in 2014, U.S. authorities enhanced the capacity to process claims back home, in countries of origin that people had fled.

Externalization relies to varying degrees on the contracting out of these functions and responsibilities to other places and people, whether foreign authorities or third-party contractors who run processing and detention in these sites (Geiger 2013). Externalization is generally premised on the evasion of signatory responsibilities, with a belief that offshore enforcement will slow arrivals and reduce processing. Often, private entities or third parties are required to carry out these functions; they are able to step in at the limits of what states can legally do in their enforcement operations without violating international refugee law and, specifically, the principle of non-refoulement.

A GENEALOGY OF EXTERNALIZATION

While it is tempting to sketch a traditional history of externalization to provide a basic chronological backdrop, this can only be done analytically in the section that follows this genealogy. The genealogical tradition provides an opportunity to tell the story in a mode more akin to the actual development of the phenomenon of externalization, occurring under a particular set of conditions that recur, moving from one place to another frenetically. Like "fast policy transfer" models that Peck and Theodore (2015) track as transnational moves of neoliberal policy across national settings, this genealogy shows an unpredictable trajectory with movement in fits and starts from one significant moment to the next without a precise mapping of *how* these policies and practices moved from one place to another, only recognition that they did. I arranged these events chronologically. Instead of a steady progression of movement offshore, a nice hypotenuse moving steadily and simultaneously across *x*- and *y*-axes of time and space, this history must be told in the terms by which migration and migration-related policy itself progress: in fits and starts and with reactionary moments of dramatic policy transformation associated with migration-related crises. Through a series of high-profile boat arrivals and manufactured crises, rationales emerged that prompted, advanced, and sustained ever more aggressive exclusionary practices to take place offshore. These generally involved extraordinary investments in resources to intercept, detain, or exclude, typically a reactionary response to crisis.

Drawing on the historiographic work of Michel Foucault, genealogy entails no "grand scheme of progressive history"; it is, instead, "the result of contingent turns of history, not the outcome of rationally inevitable trends" (Gutting 2014). I conceptualize key moments or events of externalization as Gordian knots, moments with a particular mix of conditions and elements present. *Merriam-Webster* defines a Gordian knot as "an intricate problem; *especially*: a problem insoluble in its own terms."

In assembling this genealogy, I follow the path of Derek Gregory's (2007) essay "Vanishing Points." In this essay, Gregory traces the operation of U.S. black sites, hidden prisons in the U.S.-led war on terror. He focuses in particular on Abu Ghraib in Iraq and Guantánamo Bay in Cuba, two sites connected for their notoriety in the abuse of foreign enemy combatants held indefinitely during the war on terror. Gregory's tracing shows how vanishing points are produced topologically through the law. He writes,

> I want to contest all these partitions by showing that Guantánamo and Abu Ghraib are connected by the intersections of sovereign and bio-power that are realized through a series of spaces that fold in and out of them. (208)

This folding of spaces is the topological work of sovereign power, productively connecting seemingly disparate sites where sovereign and biopower intersect. This connection that Gregory forges between Abu Ghraib and Guantánamo Bay and the convergence of powers to make die and make live aptly characterizes the loose yet important connections I forge in this genealogy of externalization.

The advancement of securitized rounds of externalization signals a halting series of movements between key moments, crises, and hot spots, and associated patterns. These patterns involve a toxic mix of boat arrivals as manufactured crises, mandatory detention, reactionary policies, production of exceptional sites, expanded capacity to detain, and securitization in the form of antiterrorism legislation post-9/11 that *expanded* legislation and seeds planted during the 1990s period of securitization and criminalization of asylum seekers. Figure 2 lists these key elements. These crises also rely on the production of unruly, racialized people as out of place, threats to the imagined national body.

These times and places can be characterized as moments of hysteria and policy transference. What I am tracking here is not necessarily a thing or a policy but something more ephemeral: a big event, a moment that makes it into international news and captures the imagination and accompanies the memory of a global audience. While they tend to happen along borders where a steady stream of people quietly enter on a daily basis, these moments are international news events. Each contains a particular mix (the Gordian knot) of conditions ripe for high-profile moments of exclusion, listed in Figure 2. These created the conditions for crisis and a public receptive to rapid and dramatic moves in the securitization of migration. Each involved creative interplay between

Boat arrivals and increased marine enforcement, interception

Manufacturing a racialized, classed crisis: the unexpected arrival of undesirables

Ad hoc practice in response or creation of "policy on the fly," "policy on the run"

Production of exceptional sites designed in exceptional circumstances to process and inhibit access

New security or antiterrorism legislation

Mandatory detention

Expanded capacity to detain onshore and offshore (built infrastructure, policy, legal means)

Moment of intense securitization and criminalization (e.g., extensive media coverage)

Creative interplay between jurisdiction and access, geography and legality

FIGURE 2. Key components of externalization events.

jurisdiction and access, geography and legality—equations that result in exclusion.

Figure 3 summarizes key moments in the genealogy of externalization, detailed later. This list is by no means exhaustive.

Event 1: The U.S. Response to Haitians Traveling to the United States by Sea

The origin of the contemporary period of externalization can be traced back to U.S. interceptions and detention in the Caribbean (Koh 1994; Durieux and McAdam 2004; Mountz and Loyd 2014). These interceptions targeted people traveling by sea from the Caribbean on the U.S. mainland in the early 1980s. Noble (2011, 76) writes that 7,387 Haitians arrived in the United States by sea in the 1970s. These arrivals are quietly overshadowed in historical accounts of Caribbean migration by discussions of the more heated and visibly spectacular response to the 1980 Mariel Boatlifts, during which time approximately 125,000 Cubans arrived in Florida during a three-month period (Noble 2011). In 1980, President Jimmy Carter signed the Refugee Act, bringing the United States into line with international law by creating a statutory right to apply for asylum. Many among these arrivals were sent to what were then called "processing centers," which eventually became part

Event number	Year	Event or program	Location	Authority	People moving
1	1981	Haitian and Cuban interceptions: the Haitian Program	United States and the Caribbean	United States	Haitians
2	1991–94	Caribbean crossings: safe haven camps	United States in the Caribbean	United States	Haitians and Cubans
3	1993	Boat arrival: *Golden Venture*	U.S. East Coast: New York Harbor	United States	Chinese
4	1999	Interceptions in BC	Canada	Canada	Chinese
5	2001	*Tampa* incident/Pacific Solution	Australia and islands offshore	Australia	Afghans
6	2006	Boat arrivals	Canary Islands	Spain	Sub-Saharan Africans
7	2007/2009	*Respingimento*	Central Mediterranean	Italy	Sub-Saharan Africans
8	2012–14	Regional Resettlement Agreement and Operation Sovereign Borders	Indian Ocean	Australia	Top source countries: Iran, Sri Lanka, Vietnam, Afghanistan, Iraq, Pakistan
9	2009–10	Boat arrivals	West Coast (British Columbia)	Canada	Sri Lankan Tamils

FIGURE 3. Key moments of "crisis" in the genealogy of externalization.

of the current federal U.S. immigration detention system (Mountz and Loyd 2014).

Shortly thereafter, approximately twenty-five thousand Haitians arrived by boat, prompting a crisis narrative and racialized response on the part of U.S. authorities. The U.S. government initiated Haitian Migrant Interdiction Operations at sea and operationalized the Haitian Program, a predecessor to the wet foot/dry foot policy developed in the 1990s (discussed later) with later arrivals of Haitian and Cuban nationals traveling by boat. Many Haitians traveling by boat were stopped close to Haiti and returned. For those who landed onshore, the Haitian

Program was designed in 1978 to process asylum claims and remove people quickly and en masse, speeding up removal by denying parole once people were detained through creation of an exceptional legal category called the "Cuban–Haitian entrant category." A 1980 court decision found the Haitian Program discriminated against people on the basis of race and country of origin. According to Lipman (2013, 121), none of the four thousand Haitian asylum seekers processed in this program received asylum. Thus we see strenuous efforts to deter, creative interplay between geography and access, and the mobilization of racialized exceptionalism through the law.

For those who did land and were detained on mainland territory, conditions of detention onshore were poor and intended to deter future arrivals. Particularly notorious was the Krome detention facility, a former Nike missile defense base twenty-three miles from Miami where Haitians and Cubans were held separately in the Krome North and Krome South facilities (Dow 2004; Lipman 2013). Dire conditions and poor treatment in this facility led to protests, riots, fires, and legal challenges to unfair treatment (detailed in Lipman 2013). In response, rather than continue to carry out ad hoc detention of Haitians and Cubans arriving by boat, President Ronald Reagan responded to the legal challenges by implementing mandatory detention for all in 1982. Associated expansion of the U.S. detention system began in the 1990s with the next rounds of Cuban and Haitian arrivals (Mountz and Loyd 2014). Though a seemingly exceptional series of responses to boat arrivals scripted as racialized crises, these moves manifested in lasting effects on policy, such as expanded use of detention.

Event 2: The U.S. Creation of a Buffer Zone to Prevent Asylum Seekers from Landing

Things heated up again in this region amid political and economic turmoil in the early 1990s. The situation became more acute with the number of Cubans traveling by sea rising in 1994, adding to Haitian travelers (Noble 2011, 4). As arrivals from Haiti and Cuba increased again, the United States once again stepped up interceptions, deploying its coast guard and navy to intercept with what Harold Koh (1994) called a "floating Berlin Wall." With images on the news of people taking desperate measures to travel, such as crossing the Caribbean on meager flotation devices like rafts and inner tubes, U.S. president Bill Clinton developed what became known as the *wet foot/dry foot policy* (Noble 2011, 4). This policy held that people intercepted at sea (with wet feet) would not have the right to seek asylum, whereas those who succeeded in landing on shore (dry feet) could make a claim for asylum. As a result, cat-and-mouse games of chase between U.S. authorities and people arriving from Cuba and Haiti played out routinely along the Florida coast.

At this time, the United States made arrangements across a number of Caribbean countries to set up "safe haven camps," the most notorious and lasting among them on the U.S. naval base Guantánamo Bay. At their height, approximately forty thousand people were held on U.S. military bases in the Panama Canal Zone, Antigua, Dominica, St. Lucia, Suriname, and Turks and Caicos (mapped in Figure 4) (Koh 1994; McBride 1999).

Over time, short-term detention in these sites gave way to indefinite detention (Koh 1994). These early uses of the U.S. naval base at Guantánamo Bay lay the foundation for subsequent detentions that also managed to evade access to courts and Geneva Conventions during the U.S.-led war on terror that began in 2001. With origins of its modern detention policies in the deterrence of migrants and asylum seekers, Guantánamo Bay eventually became an iconic exceptional zone of offshore infrastructure designed to evade international law, a pattern that would repeat itself time and again there and beyond in the years to follow: a military base functioned as an island, on an island, used to subvert legal responsibilities in a militarized zone. While Guantánamo Bay is now ingrained in the popular geographical imagination, the other offshore sites where asylum seekers were detained in the Caribbean in the 1990s are seldom recalled. In retrospect, these are all early warning signs of the death of asylum. Their construction corresponds with the rise of the neoliberal state and the dramatic expansion of the prison economy in the United States. Whether policies developed abroad or at home under the rubric of foreign or domestic policy, immigration enforcement always collapsed easy division between foreign and domestic through its responses to boat arrivals, uses of mandatory detention, and general expansion of punitive, racialized landscapes.

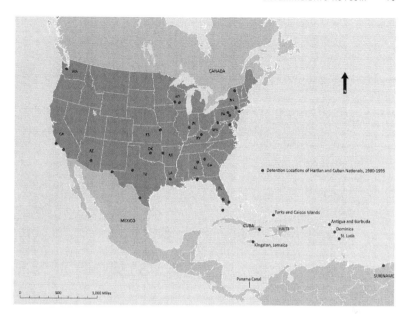

FIGURE 4. Map of U.S. detention of Haitian and Cuban nationals in an onshore and offshore archipelago of carceral spaces that included prisons, jails, and military bases, 1980–95.

Event 3: Boat Arrivals as Crisis in New York Harbor, 1993

In June 1993, a coastal freighter called *Golden Venture* carrying 286 people from the People's Republic of China ran aground within sight of Rockaway Peninsula in Queens, New York. They had been on the ship for approximately one hundred days (Noble 2011, 130). As documented (Chin 1999; Noble 2011), the arrival quickly became a humanitarian rescue operation for New York City police and the U.S. Coast Guard, as people were jumping from the deck of the ship into "numbing water" (Noble 2011, 120). Several people died of drowning, hypothermia, starvation, and cardiac arrest (120).

Scholars of human smuggling demarcate the arrival of *Golden Venture* in the largest U.S. city as a moment when the U.S. public became aware of maritime human smuggling. In response to criticism of its failure to police the coast and pressure to restore a "broken" immigration system, President Clinton set up an interdepartmental task force established to coordinate federal responses to human smuggling.

Event 4: Boat Arrivals in Canada, 1999

If 1993 marked the year that boats arrived—via televised news reports—into American homes, 1999 marked this occasion for Canadian viewers (Mountz 2010). That summer, the Canadian Coast Guard intercepted four boats carrying 599 people from Fujian, China. They were intercepted off the remote western coast of Vancouver Island, British Columbia. Once intercepted, most made refugee claims. These boat arrivals played out as crises in the Canadian media (Hier and Greenberg 2002) and received attention from international news outlets as well. Unmarked boats carrying migrants seeking entry had not approached Canadian shores since the mid-1980s. These arrivals were consistent with an increase in boat travel to other destinations, including the United States. For these reasons, they were of great interest to both Canadian and international audiences.

These high-profile interceptions prompted a securitized response on the part of the Canadian government, discussed in more detail in chapter 5. Whereas Canada did not generally detain refugee claimants, most people intercepted on the second, third, and fourth boats were deemed flight risks and held in detention in a former provincial prison in the remote interior of the province. Women and children were held in the lower mainland, outside Vancouver. The federal government also infused new resources and introduced new measures to address human smuggling in subsequent immigration and refugee legislation passed in 2002 (Ibrahim 2005).

Event 5: Australia's Tampa Incident, 2001

The Australian equivalent of these high-profile boat interceptions that shifted federal policies in the United States and Canada was the 2001 MV *Tampa* incident, which many view as the beginning of Australian externalization—although Head (2005) argues that externalization had already begun in 1999.

By the time the *Tampa* incident occurred, Australia had already required since 1992 a visa for all international visitors and had a policy of mandatory detention for those arriving without a visa. When this interception occurred in 2001, boat arrivals were increasing, and the government was making extensive use of detention on mainland territory. Prime Minister John Howard was up for reelection but not doing well in the polls. When a Norwegian freighter, the MV *Tampa,* assisted 433 asylum seekers traveling on an Indonesian ship in distress, Howard seized his moment. He declared that no more asylum seekers traveling by boat would set foot on Australian soil. The Australian Navy blocked the ship, refusing to allow the captain to land at Christmas Island, the nearest port and Australian territory closest to the rescue.

The *Tampa* incident signaled a turning point in externalization policy and was a catalyst in the politicization of the issue, both in Australia and beyond, as the story attracted international attention. This incident marked the beginning of the Pacific Solution (Hugo 2001; Mares 2001; Magner 2004), whereby intercepted asylum seekers were brought to small islands in the region for processing and detention, including Christmas Island, Nauru, and Papua New Guinea's Manus Island. The Australian Parliament met and retroactively declared thousands of pieces of Australian territory to no longer be part of Australian territory for the purposes of migration (known as the power of excision, and involving excisional legislation). These Australian modalities of externalization have continued and—as detailed in chapter 3—have been among the most draconian and extreme of offshoring practices in the modern history of externalization.

Event 6: Boat Arrivals on Spain's Canary Islands

The erasure of border control in the Schengen Area prompted a geographical draw to entry points across southern European states, including Spain. As Jorgen Carling (2007a, 317) notes, Spain has faced a "complex" migration situation since the late 1990s owing to its proximity to Morocco and to the large numbers of migrants leaving from Morocco and Moroccan-occupied Western Sahara. Carling shows evidence that since 2004, migrant ships have been able to circumvent Morocco. Collyer (2007) and Carling (2007b) have both documented increasing numbers of sub-Saharan Africans arriving in Morocco, with some continuing on the expensive final journey to the Canary Islands and others remaining behind as immigrants.

The period from 1998 to 2003 was a key time of immigration growth, and in 2003, more than one-third of immigrants to the twenty-five EU member states arrived in Spain (Carling 2007b, 8). Geography plays an important role in this story. As Carling writes, "Spain's dual role as a country of transit and destination is mirrored by Morocco's dual role as a country of transit and origin" (9). The interception of unauthorized migrants along Spanish coasts and in Morocco peaked between 2000 and 2003, shortly after the Canary Islands became a key destination. By 2002 and 2003, larger numbers of arrivals were putting strain on local communities, and more than ten thousand sub-Saharan Africans were transferred from the islands to cities on the mainland (Carling 2007b, 21–25).

Carling (2007a; 2007b, 9) outlines the infrastructure set in place by Spain in its attempts to control unauthorized migration from Morocco, including the treatment of Morocco as a "buffer zone." These include intensified border control, stricter visa regimes for sub-Saharan Africans, pressure on Moroccan authorities to thwart human smuggling, and information campaigns in Morocco designed to dissuade potential migrants (Carling 2007a, 322).[4]

In early 2004, three boats arrived carrying more than one hundred migrants each, with combined countries of origin totaling at least ten (Carling 2007b, 26). These increases in arrivals stoked public attention and fear about the potential for arrivals to continue, which they did. Boat arrivals on Spain's Canary Islands marked the arrival of boats on European television screens. Yet marine journeys at that time did not only involve the Canaries. As Frontex formed and joined Spain in intensifying policing in the area, maritime routes shifted east from the Strait of Gibraltar to the Mediterranean Sea.

Event 7: Boat Arrivals on Italy's Lampedusa and the Policy of Respingimento

Subsequent to the boat arrival crises on the Canary Islands were the ongoing arrivals on Lampedusa. Boat arrivals on Lampedusa are by no means unusual: more than 150,000 people landed on the small island between 1999 and 2011 (Cuttitta 2014, 197). As Andrijasevic (2010) notes, however, as the EU expanded, the island transitioned from a site of migrant passage into the EU to one of detention and expulsion (explored more fully in chapter 2). Cuttitta (2014) argues that the island became a stage where Italians and Europeans observed several acts of what he calls the "border play," which reflects broader national and global politics surrounding migration. During this period of transition, the eruption of several crises advanced rounds of externalization in various forms, from islanders themselves using fishing boats to block entry to the port to national policy decisions to implement Italy's notorious policy of *respingimento*—translated colloquially into "pushback" policy—in the late 2000s.

Some of these crises pertained to responses to boat arrivals of relatively large numbers, as in July 2011, for example. Others related to migrant deaths. As Cuttitta (2014, 197) observes, "Lampedusa is the place where hundreds of migrants have touched Italian soil only as dead bodies." Cuttitta observes significant crises in 2009, with the decision of the Italian government no longer to transfer people from the island to other parts of Italy, and 2011, when revolutions in North Africa prompted a mass exodus and arrivals that far exceeded the capacity of the detention center or island. At that time, the island became an open-air camp because of the overcrowding in the facility—what one respondent called "a sort of Guantánamo in the open" (interview, Lampedusa, July 2011). To this, others have added a third crisis in 2013 (Campesi 2014), when a boat sank close enough to be within sight of the shores of Lampedusa and more than three hundred people died (as noted in the introduction). Each of these crises corresponded with advances in externalization in the form of intensified policing at sea.

In 2009 and 2011, this policing implemented Italy's *respingimento,* in effect since 2007, but without resources devoted to its operationalization until compelled by crises. As Cuttitta (2014, 205) notes, in both 2009 and 2011, the number of experts and authorities working on Lampedusa increased significantly, exacerbating the political spectacle of border enforcement as well as its material unfolding at sea. In 2013, humanitarian discourses intensified once again in the aftermath of the disaster close to the island, along with interceptions at sea, under the rubric of Operation Mare Nostrum. The Italian government called this a "military-humanitarian" operation, a classic case of intersecting discourses and actions between humanitarian rescue and securitized interception (Campesi 2014).

Event 8: Regional Resettlement Agreement and Operation Sovereign Borders

Although many Australian schemes made news and raised responses by human rights groups and the UNHCR, one that erupted in international news in 2013 was Prime Minister Kevin Rudd's announcement of the Regional Resettlement Agreement. Although Rudd himself had formally ended the Pacific Solution during his first term in office in 2008, political tides had shifted, and the Regional Resettlement Agreement to process all asylum seekers arriving by boat on Nauru and Manus islands signaled a clear revival of the principles and policies of the Pacific Solution. In this case, however, the two-tier system (with more truncated access to asylum for those held offshore) brought into effect in the Pacific Solution gave way to a more exclusionary system. People intercepted in Australia's excised zones would no longer have *any* access to asylum in Australia, fully outsourcing asylum "management" to other countries and organizations operating in the region.

When Prime Minister Tony Abbott came to power in September 2013, one month after Rudd's announcement, he extended these policies with his own announcement involving a new effort at marine interception called Operation Sovereign Borders. This involved investment of resources in aggressive interceptions at sea, redirecting all asylum seekers to Nauru and Manus with no chance for resettlement in Australia.

As with U.S. naval operations in the Caribbean to intercept and detain migrants offshore, Australia was challenged by Indonesia for its overreach of policing into its territorial waters. Like U.S. officials intercepting in the Caribbean and the Italian *respingimento,* Australian authorities were challenged in their claim that they provided adequate access to make asylum claims during boat interceptions.

Event 9: Boat Arrivals in Canada, 2009 and 2010

After the highly publicized interceptions marked the arrival of boats on North American television screens in the United States in 1993 and in Canada in 1999, things went quiet for a while. Both countries enjoyed and trumpeted brief periods of self-congratulation on their "victories" over maritime smuggling, until they were eventually challenged again with subsequent arrivals. Although there was not another incident with a large number of asylum seekers landing on the U.S. East Coast, in the late 1990s, boats arrived on the Pacific island of Guam, the easternmost U.S. territory and the closest bit of U.S. territory to Asia where an asylum claim can be lodged (Mason 1999).

In Canada, no large groups of migrants were intercepted at sea after the 1999 interceptions until 2009 and 2010. The Canadian government intercepted 76 Sri Lankan Tamils in October 2009 and 492 on the MV *Sun Sea* in August 2010 on the West Coast. These interceptions resonated with the 1999 arrivals, while exhibiting key distinctions. As Sri Lankan Tamils, these claimants were more likely to have harrowing histories of displacement and persecution more widely understood by the public, including flight from internment camps where some three hundred thousand remained after the civil conflict ended in Sri Lanka. Unlike Fujianese migrants, they were welcomed and supported by the Tamil community in Toronto, the largest outside of Sri Lanka—if not by the Canadian government.

As in 1999, the more general Canadian public reacted negatively to the boat arrivals (Cader 2010). Although the number of claimants was relatively small, their visibility and proximity to the border provoked territorial anxiety. Discourse about "bogus refugees" and an overly generous claimant system reemerged. There were other parallels between the 1999 and 2009/2010 interceptions, including blanket detention of claimants. The more recent group of claimants was detained in Surrey, a suburb of Vancouver. They were more securitized than the Fujianese claimants had been, with links drawn in press conferences and media stories to Tamil Tigers and to historically significant protests in Toronto carried out by the Tamil diaspora earlier that year (Canadian Council for Refugees 2015). The possibility of trace amounts of explosives on the ships was announced, bringing forth another round of securitization explained as preventive, to discourage future arrivals.

This interception and the decision to detain were not exceptional responses in the global context. At the same time, for example, other boats of Sri Lankan Tamils were landing in Australia. They nonetheless played out as an exceptional security crisis in Canada and provoked significant legislative and policy changes to Canadian immigration and refugee law and claimant processes (detailed in chapter 5).

As the remaining chapters in this book show, crisis narratives continued to be developed in the extreme in each of these sites: the United

States in the Pacific and Caribbean, the EU in the Mediterranean, and the Australian government working in the Indian Ocean. The terrorist attacks on September 11, 2001, intensified the securitization of migration through antiterrorism legislation and upheavals to immigration departments and enforcement policies across each of these regions.

A BRIEF HISTORY OF EXTERNALIZATION

The development of the externalization literature outlined briefly herein mirrors empirical evidence of nation-states that were advancing border enforcement offshore. A brief and traditional history of externalization might be organized by decades and attempt to map a steady trajectory of these practices and policies as they moved across space and time, from region to region. It would begin with the early history: from seeds planted in the 1970s to the development of the United States as a solo actor in the 1980s. It would look something like the chronology detailed in Figure 5.

The late 1970s and early 1980s saw the early stages of offshore border enforcement practices. While many people today associate externalization with the border enforcement practices of the EU (e.g., Bigo 2000; Boswell 2003; Salter 2004; Walters 2004), contemporary forms of offshore enforcement can actually be traced back to U.S. interceptions in the Caribbean that began in the late 1970s and intensified in the early 1980s with the famous Mariel Boatlifts of Cubans and the concurrent movement of large numbers of Haitian asylum seekers (Stepick 1982; Noble 2011). At that time, the United States led the way in offshore enforcement through its deterrence of Cuban and Haitian migrants and asylum seekers in the Caribbean. Particular large-scale, crisis-riddled events drove major changes to policy, including the investment of resources in marine enforcement to create a buffer zone at sea (Noble 2011), the shift to mandatory detention, the use of widespread detention as a policy deterrent (McBride 1999), and U.S. military bases in the Caribbean (Koh 1994). While legal scholars documented the contravention of international refugee law and undermining of access to asylum with these offshore practices (Koh 1994), these policies nonetheless developed a life of their own and were repeated subsequently by the United States and others. The convergence of alarmist narratives and xenophobic

Decade	Characterized by	Region/activity involved
1970s	Introduction	U.S. marine interceptions in the Caribbean
1980s	Early stages	United States in the Caribbean; Canada establishes ICO network
1990s	Thickening	More resources invested in preventing asylum seekers; growth in detention as deterrent; United States creates safe havens in Caribbean; Five Eyes develop immigration control officer networks
2000s	Diffusion	Offshore enforcement more widely used; Australia and the EU develop offshore processing and policing
2010s	Freneticism	Crossings heat up with crises in the southern EU, on the United States–Mexico border, and in Mexico as a transit zone for Central Americans; Australian offshoring grows more aggressive and extensive

FIGURE 5. Externalization through the decades.

responses repeated itself in this region, leading to the formalization of externalization in policies such as safe haven and wet foot/dry foot, the latter announced by President Clinton in 1994. Eventually, similar policies have appeared in other regions and other forms in the time since.

The 1990s saw a *thickening* of externalization measures, with increased investment in their general extension globally. While the United States boarded boats on international waters and detained throughout the Caribbean, Canada developed the first formal network of immigration control officers (ICOs), civil servants who practiced informal policing through collaborative measures like training airline personnel and sharing information with local authorities abroad. Andreas and Nadleman (2006, 116) discuss the importance of informal forms of policing in the development of "global prohibition regimes," and their contention bears out in the case of offshore enforcement of migration. With Canada's ICO network established, other countries followed suit, with the United States, the United Kingdom, Australia, and New Zealand—the Five Eyes or Five Country Conference—also developing offshore border policing networks (and recently collaborating to expand data sharing; MacCharles 2015).

The 2000s were a period of widespread *diffusion* of the very idea of externalization, beginning with Australia's introduction of the Pacific Solution and continuing with the 2004 establishment and first operations of Frontex in 2005, the coordinating border enforcement agency of the EU whose history is one of crisis response (Campesi 2011, 2014). The 2000s also saw many bilateral arrangements put into place by Australia and the EU with source countries to cooperate and ease processes of repatriation, including the issuing of travel documents. As migration heated up across the southern frontier of the EU, a succession of crises moved from east to west and back again, with migration struggles amplified in Spain's Canary Islands in 2006, then moving west to Lampedusa, Malta, Cyprus, and Greece (Carling 2007a, 2007b; Lutterbeck 2009). This decade saw the operationalization of Italy's *respingimento,* or pushback policy, as well as the EU imagining and investing in offshore detention camps in northern African states. As Frontex coordinated policing at sea, infrastructure to thwart and detain moved farther offshore, deeper into transit routes—a geographical move that has been well documented (Médecins Sans Frontières 2011b; Campesi 2014).

With thickening and diffusion, externalization moved from creative measures to formalized policies. The 2010s proved to be a period of *freneticism,* particularly evident in Australian offshore enforcement practices (characterized in more detail in chapter 3, which focuses on the use of islands). This particular hysteria in Australia involved the shutting down of the Pacific Solution in 2008 and its reestablishment in 2012. It involved opening an AU$398 million facility on Christmas Island in 2008 (Hawke and Williams 2011), followed by a shifting of detainees to Darwin (onshore) and then to Nauru and Papua New Guinea's Manus Island. The freneticism involved legal challenges and high court rulings that declared two-tiered, differentiated asylum processes for those landing onshore and offshore to be illegal and the subsequent removal of all intercepted first to two small Pacific islands and then farther offshore in the region, with the contracting out of detention, asylum processing, and resettlement to Indonesia and Malaysia. The Pacific Solution (Hugo 2001), the Indian Ocean Solution (Marr 2009), the Indonesian Solution (Nethery et al. 2013), the proposal of East Timor (*West Australian* 2010), and the financial deal with Malaysia all happened in quick succession.

It is easy, only in retrospect, to narrate externalization through recent decades of post–Cold War securitization and the rise of neoliberalism and technocratic forms of "migration management" that amount to their depoliticization (Pécoud 2014). A more accurate depiction of seemingly gradual changes to border enforcement, however, shows the central role of migration-related crises in changing how civilians and civil servants understand and react to change. The crisis-driven realm of immigration and border-related policy making means that a single event can change policy rapidly and dramatically. The genealogy therefore foregrounded these events, showing them to be highly publicized and politicized. Spectacular events like boat arrivals capitalize on fear and change the ways that people geographically imagine what is possible in border management offshore. While I have argued in this chapter that externalization policies advanced in fits and starts *through* these crises, I have also shown in this section that when analyzed in retrospect, externalization can be imagined to have progressed steadily through the decades until we arrived at the death of the enforcement archipelago. This death was not sudden, nor was it unpredictable.

CONCLUSIONS AND CONSIDERATIONS

Additional kinds of places also fit into a broader typology of sites that render people stateless by geographical design (Mountz 2010), including the development of airport waiting zones and detention centers (Makaremi 2009; Maillet 2017). Externalization is happening in these places as well, and a fuller genealogy would include them in the historical development of offshoring immigration enforcement. While I include these sites in the typology designed to understand places that render people stateless by geographical design, I do not include episodes in these sites as key moments in the broader genealogy. Events in these sites have not catalyzed public attention and policy shifts at the scale of the migration events included in the genealogy. In this chapter, I have focused, instead, on spectacular events that propelled forward rounds of securitization that advanced offshore enforcement. An expansion of the genealogy would include the dramatic storming of walls around the Spanish enclaves Ceuta and Melilla in Morocco (Carling 2007a). As Andersson (2014) demonstrates, a spectacular enforcement response unfolds in Ceuta and Melilla, as it did on the Canary Islands.

The chapter's genealogy of externalization drew together the recurring spatial logics of this constellation of sites, a Gordian knot that emerges out of seemingly unique and generally crisis-riddled circumstances—situations that repeat the same patterns of exclusion, including the creative interplay of geography and law, jurisdiction and legal status.

A clear pattern appears across the events included in this genealogy, not only in terms of the elements present when migration events transpire and rounds of securitization advance but also in terms of the sequential relationship between manufactured crises and changes in policy. Typically, the narrative of boat arrivals as crises engenders reactionary policy responses, enhanced resources invested in enforcement, and the movement of the exceptional into the routine (Mountz and Hiemstra 2014).

These moments planted seeds nourished in the decades that followed with xenophobia, political mobilization of fear to advance exclusionary agendas, and periodic economic crises. Neoliberalized growth in economic asymmetries and conflicts continued to fuel the need to emigrate, even in the face of the barriers constructed and the exclusionary politics of asylum in which claims would be received.

I refer to these externalization events as Gordian knots because they are intricate and insoluble in their own terms. Most externalization policies function as superficial dressing to stop the hemorrhaging from deeper wounds. Naval blockades, walls, fences, and even the destruction of smuggling boats planned by the EU in response to the recent, sharp rise in Mediterranean crossings simply do not address the deeper causes of displacement—poverty and conflict—and the kinds of meaningful, longer-term solutions that might begin to address them. These would include legal avenues to migration that aligned labor market demands with the need to migrate. These solutions would also shift resources from enforcement to development at home.

A spate of recent books called attention to the futility of walling in wealth and fencing out poverty: Wendy Brown's (2010) *Walled States, Waning Sovereignty,* David Carr's (2012) *Fortress Europe,* and Michael Dear's (2013) *Why Walls Won't Work.* Empirical research continues to show consistently that deterrence strategies—including externalization, interception, detention, and material barriers—do not work (Williams 2018). Still, their popularity continues, as witnessed in late 2015, when several European states erected barbed wire fences to deter asylum seekers from entering their territory. To fearful or frustrated publics and policy makers, they demonstrate spectacular shows of an emasculated nation-state flexing its muscles in the face of globalization. For Brown (2010), these walls symbolize failures of sovereignty. To the security industries that build and run detention and border enforcement, they signal profit.

As demonstrated by this chapter's genealogy, spaces of asylum have been shrinking and routes to protection foreclosed upon at a global scale for over three decades, beginning in the early 1980s, ballooning in the 1990s, and accelerating from 2001 onward with the MV *Tampa* incident and the attacks on 9/11. There is no doubt that a group of wealthy, Western, immigrant-receiving states in the Global North are leading the way (Australia, the United States, Canada, EU member states).

While it is difficult to trace exactly how policies move from one region to another, many scholars have tried to track their diffusion and transfer (e.g., Peck and Theodore 2015). Did Canada mimic U.S. policies in the Caribbean or Australian policies in the Indian Ocean when intercepting people arriving by ship and detaining en masse? Camp X-ray was constructed to hold "foreign enemy combatants" without access to U.S. courts with the use of indefinite detention on the Guantánamo Bay U.S. naval base. When construction was well under way on the high-security Northwest point detention facility on Christmas Island in 2006, many Australians I interviewed compared the site to Guantánamo Bay and hoped that this would be a finding of my research. Was this the global diffusion of policy from Guantánamo to Christmas Island? More recently, there have been many assertions that Canada is following Australian policies. Because this offshore infrastructure is often hidden, the precise spaces of diplomatic exchange and details of bilateral arrangements often remain unknown and budget lines and funding transfers difficult to track (although WikiLeaks has provided important interventions). Often externalization is not formalized in written policy or law but instead is established through daily practice, making research on everyday geographies of enforcement important (e.g., Pratt 2005). To date, the best evidence of their correspondence occurs in public discourse when officials such as former Canadian ministers of citizenship and immigration, Jason Kenney, and of public safety, Vic Toews, raise the Australian example.

In this chapter, I have shown the conditions that set the stage for what can best be understood as the late stages of the death of asylum.

The reactionary policies designed after migration-events-as-crises (laid out in the genealogy) involve the production of further exceptional sites designed in exceptional circumstances to process and inhibit access. Over time, these exceptional and ad hoc responses become the norm, from mandatory detention in the United States to pushback undertaken by Italy. Rather than retreat from these measures to externalize once crises end, states have invested in normalizing and institutionalizing exclusionary measures.

In this chapter, I have pulled these stories together to trace the vanishing points that constitute legal geographies of exclusion. But as if peeling the layers of an onion, I will continue to tell the story again and again, in other ways and from other places. These stories will be revisited in this book, when past crises haunt the asylum seekers in the present.

2

The Border Becomes the Island

Scholars in migration, mobility, and border studies have located the border itself as in motion relationally to migrants and authorities. On land, at sea, and in the geographical imagination, the border accrues and attracts migrants seeking entry as readily as it does enforcement resources. The border itself becomes a flashpoint, an assemblage, a simultaneously magnetic and repellant topological infrastructure on the move. On one hand, authorities themselves travel great distances to police and detain; on the other, the collection of biometric data distributes bordering around the globe with the collection and integration of big data. Bodies and borders are thus in motion relationally. The biometric border (Amoore 2006), for example, collects fragmented biometric data about the body, and authorities move, using these data to exclude those very bodies. Chapter 1's genealogy of externalization featured this mobile border as central protagonist, demonstrating the productive and prolific nature of its shape-shifting form that adheres closely to the movement of racialized bodies.

In this chapter, I argue that the spatial form of the border has changed from line to island. If entry was ever characterized by crossing the line, it can now be characterized as a proliferating series of islands where migrants en route experience multiple spaces of confinement along the way. The topological border plays with law and jurisdiction to undermine access as the border spreads offshore. This transformation of the spatial form of the border from line to island is driving the topological formation of the enforcement archipelago. As a result, as explored here in the case of Lampedusa and on Australian islands in chapter 3, island spaces of confinement proliferate, and islands themselves are produced and remade as carceral spaces.

Once conceived of as boundary lines drawn by cartographers to demarcate sovereign territory, borders have undergone dramatic spatial and conceptual transformations. They are increasingly transnational (Salter 2004; Bialasiewicz 2012; Mountz and Loyd 2014), biometric (Amoore 2006), contracted out, and policed onshore and offshore. Local enforcement officials internal to sovereign territory take up the work of border enforcement, and federal authorities travel abroad to police borders in foreign territory (Coleman 2007; Bialasiewicz 2012). These vertiginous spatial logics repeat themselves time and again until the location of the border bewilders and people find themselves suspended in temporal, spatial, and legal limbo, unable to escape border policing. Borders follow migrant bodies through interception, and border movement therefore follows a specific spatial trajectory offshore.

Two key geographical trends in border enforcement involve the repelling of borders and people trying to reach sovereign territory and the confinement of people on the move in remote locations. Both trends are well established in existing literature in what is often referred to as externalization of enforcement (e.g., Coleman 2007) and the growing field of carceral or detention studies (e.g., Moran et al. 2013). Research in the enforcement archipelago shows the convergence of these two trends. People are not only thwarted offshore but detained en route. In other words, border enforcement has not only moved offshore but is deployed to enclose, contain, and confine people far away from aspirational sovereign destinations where they seek entry and asylum. Readmission agreements between countries, for example, facilitate the return of people to countries of origin, eroding the right to seek asylum. As a result of these trends, political asylum is in crisis, and islands have come to the fore as sites of struggle over entry and exclusion.

These spatial transformations of the border are part of the "securitization of migration" (e.g., Huysmans 2006; Amoore and de Goede 2008). While many scholars write about securitization of the border as a shift in discourse (e.g., Ibrahim 2005), securitization also involves material changes in the landscape. In this chapter, I chart this shift in geographical terms. Movement of the border offshore forms the architectural foundation of the enforcement archipelago. As shown in chapter 1, states began to reach beyond land borders in efforts to manage migration in the 1970s and 1980s (Coleman 2007; Mountz and Loyd 2014), stopping unauthorized migrants from reaching sovereign territory long before they boarded a boat or airplane. Throughout the

1990s, the border continued outward as uses of interdiction and remote detention in legally and jurisdictionally ambiguous zones became standard practice. In my own research, mapping these mobile borders led me to sites where management of migration takes place and struggles over access and exclusion unfold offshore. The archipelago engulfs migrants in the borderlands between regions, transferring the border from frontier to the intimate spaces of the body (see Anzaldúa 1987; Wright 1997; Vaughan-Williams 2015). Ultimately, the body is the finest island produced through carceral spaces of the border.

By enacting enforcement in extraterritorial locales, states use geography to subvert international refugee law to which they are signatories. The use of remote locations to regulate access involves practices in effect for many years but exacerbated in the post-9/11 securitized climate that conflates people moving for different reasons (Bigo 2002; Sparke 2006). The 1951 Convention Relating to the Status of Refugees and its 1967 Protocol guide signatory states to implement policies that provide access to an adjudication system for those who reach sovereign territory to make an asylum claim. Beyond sovereign territory in "grayer" zones offshore, however, states may not act on any such obligation. This issue is subject to legal debate, and Gammeltoft-Hansen (2011) argues that states are still under obligation to protect.

This chapter moves between these perspectives to juxtapose the mobilities of state enforcement infrastructure and migrants. Amid global conditions of acute displacement and extreme confinement, the co-constituted spatial forms of state border enforcement and migrant border crossings have shifted. If international migration ever involved the spatial metaphor of a crossing—as in crossing the line—this metaphor has now been replaced by a proliferating series of spaces of confinement experienced along circuitous and precarious transnational routes. People on the move in search of protection and livelihood are likely to cross multiple borders and experience multiple periods and spaces of confinement throughout their journeys, across national contexts, at sea, and on land. The geographical metaphor of the crossing must therefore be replaced by that of the island: border as island. This reimagination of the spatial form of border enforcement is a conceptual response to empirical evidence. A key finding about migration enforcement on islands is the reproduction of the form of the island. In other words, people are not only detained remotely on islands but detained remotely and isolated within islands in high-security facilities or solitary confinement. My research findings showed the proliferation of the spatial form of the island beyond the island itself. Together, these two trends—the use of islands and the reproduction of the spatial form of the island—constitute the transformation of much border enforcement from a focus on the line to the island. The border has not changed in every way, nor are borders ubiquitous. Rather, the dispersal of enforcement takes different forms in different countries (Bloch and Schuster 2005; Welch 2002) and extends offshore. It is possible, however, to trace spatial patterns of exclusion across distinct national contexts.

Designing spaces of confinement to detain migrants is not new; the detention industry has been well established since the 1990s, in some countries more than others (Flynn and Flynn 2017). However, the contemporary proliferation of confinement results from intensified investments by governments and precipitous growth in business of the global prison industry (Conlon and Hiemstra 2016). This proliferation and intensification fuel new state practices: unprecedented investments in material and human resources (including government authorities and third parties such as the IOM). In research on islands, I found that this intensification contributed to the reproduction of the form of the island.

In this chapter, I follow the mobility of state actors and exclusionary infrastructure to places that are simultaneously hypervisible and hidden. There, operating through this opacity, sovereign power haunts migrants through the displacement and relocation of border enforcement. I proceed by first tracing the development of the EU archipelago offshore in policy and enforcement practice. This development set the stage for the spatial transformation from border to island in the region. I then examine the border as topological form to understand *how* the border moves offshore. In addition to mapping the broad policies that set the stage for the transformation of European borders from lines to islands, I examine these specific processes at work on the Italian island of Lampedusa. I visit the microgeographies of sites in the enforcement archipelago where these exclusions transpire, where migrants enter into extended periods of spatial, temporal, and legal limbo and deathly living. Viewing the governance of migration through the lens of the island, we can trace not only the offshoring of the border but its transformation to the confining form of the island.

THE DEVELOPMENT OF THE EU ARCHIPELAGO IN POLICY AND ENFORCEMENT PRACTICE

Major policy developments that advanced the offshoring of EU borders are too numerous to explore in full but are listed—in summary fashion, not in totality—in Figure 6. I discuss these developments in brief in this section to set the stage for the spatial transformation of the border from lines to islands, viewed from the vantage point of southern Europe. EU states collaborated to harmonize border enforcement—to police the external border and erase internal borders—yet have struggled over harmonization of asylum seeker arrivals. Multiscalar struggles between state and suprastate institutions result in perpetual tension. With displacements and mass migrations in 2015, tensions related to asylum seeking erupted and threatened the cohesion of the EU, fueling the rise in popular nationalism that had already been percolating. In practice, authorities and migrants continuously shift routes and police new "hot spots"—sometimes islands, other times metaphorical islands—resulting in geostrategic investments in enforcement (see Vradis et al., 2019). In response, some began the process of rebordering, while others (Germany and Sweden) accommodated asylum applications.

KEY POLICIES OF THE EUROPEAN UNION TO EXTERNALIZE THE BORDER, 1985–2015

Most recently, in response to the 2015 arrival of asylum seekers, the EU has incorporated the language and geographical logic of "hot spots" into its mobile policing of the border, setting up checkpoints in sites that have become heavily trafficked routes (European Commission 2015; Pallister-Wilkins 2017a), thus incorporating islands into the logic of internal policing. In a report commissioned by the EU Parliament (2016) on the subject, hot spots are described as follows: "Located at key arrival points in frontline Member States, hotspots are designed to inject greater order into migration management by ensuring that all those arriving are identified, registered and properly processed" (8).

In the EU, policies, authorities, and migrants have followed a clear

Year	Policy	Explanation
1985	Schengen Acquis	Created unified EU security policy
1990	Inception of the Dublin Convention	Delineated a unified refugee system, delimiting rights to seek asylum geographically
1993	Establishment of the Schengen Area	Established common visa area, thereby shifting enforcement to the "external border"
1993	Common EU expulsion policy	Created standard travel documents and procedures for expulsion, extended over time
1994/1995	Formalized third-country cooperation	Enacted third-country cooperation and aid for the purposes of migration control; formalized in the Mediterranean through partnerships
1997	Treaty of Amsterdam	Formally established the Justice and Home Affairs (JHA) powers, including authority to legislate on immigration
1997	Inception of the EURODAC system	Constructed fingerprint database to biometrically measure migrant identities, particularly for enforcement; biometrics formally introduced elsewhere in 1998
1997–2001	Odysseus Program	First joint programs; first fully funded program to enforce external border
1998	Creation of EU expert missions on border enforcement	Sent to third countries to survey border enforcement systems and provide assistance
1999–2003	Tampere Program	Plans for external border enforcement and funding
2000	Third-country processing of visas	Moved migration processing out of the EU for specific classes of visas and geographies
2001	Inception of Frontex	Unified EU border guard in policy

FIGURE 6. Key policies designed by the EU to externalize the border, 1985–2015.

2002–6	ARGO Program	Major funding program for enforcement of external border; source of first large-scale maritime interdiction operations
2004–8	Hague Program	Laid out JHA plans for external border enforcement and funding
2004	Common European Asylum System	European Council creates plan to have this system in place by 2010
2005	Inception of the External Borders Fund, 2007–13	First permanent, obligatory fund for enforcement of external border; many times larger than previous funding
2005	Inception of the European Patrols Network	Established permanent maritime interdiction operations on a EU scale
2006	Inception of joint return flights	Made EU-wide scale through Frontex
2008	Inception of EUROSUR	Established unified surveillance system across the EU; by 2012–13, Frontex attributed tracking of nearly all boats; established in 2011
2008	Pact on Integration and Asylum	Rearticulates EU cooperation on migration and asylum; pushes deadline for common asylum system to 2012
2009	Schengen Information System and Visa Information System created	Centralized biometric, visa, and other migrant information under EUROSUR
2009–14	Stockholm Program	Laid out plans for external border enforcement and funding
2015	EU Action Plan against Smuggling, 2015–20	EU-wide policy and funding to increase interdiction and prevention, positioning smuggling as threat against which securitization proceeds
2015	Formalization of "hot spot" approach to migration management	Multiagency collaboration to establish checkpoints to bring order to migration and return, particularly in Greece and Italy

spatial pattern: reaching the outer edges of the EU and attempting to enter the region as borders are pushed progressively farther offshore. As more countries joined the EU, the edges of its territory expanded, and migrants accumulated farther outward, gathering in cities and entry points along the margins in Turkey, Greece, and across the Mediterranean in North Africa. Struggles over entry transpire in these transit zones where many aim to enter the EU and others aim to block their entry. Member states also spatialize their enforcement practices in a fashion consistent with the genealogy of externalization. They move borders outward, focusing on policing the margins of the EU as internal border crossings are minimized for the purposes of integrating labor migration.

The 1985 Schengen Acquis and subsequent creation of the Schengen Area in the EU effectively removed borders internal to the EU, allowing for free circulation of people internally and eradication of border friction for those moving among EU member states. This attempt at internal boundary erasure set the stage for a related move to pool resources to shore up the perimeter and externalize borders. Drawing from anatomical studies and likening the region to a body whose blood flows to the site of injury, Cetta Mainwaring (2012b) calls this concentration of enforcement resources along outer edges the "distalization effect." These efforts were pronounced and tested along the southern frontier with the Mediterranean Sea. There islands emerge as interstitial zones of transition in migrants' transnational sojourns between northern Africa and southern Europe. Following the establishment of the Schengen Area, unauthorized migration was identified by the European Commission as a problem and a population frequently produced and targeted for "management" (Maillet et al. 2018).

The Dublin Convention was signed in 1990, followed by the Dublin Regulation (often referred to as Dublin II), and eventually Dublin III. The Dublin regulations shaped the Common European Asylum System, requiring asylum seekers to request protection in the first country where they land and where asylum processes exist. They were not allowed to undertake what policy makers frequently call "asylum shopping" by moving to destinations desirable for improved chances perceived there to acquire work, asylum, or both. Migrants intercepted crossing one country to make a claim in another are turned back under Dublin II. This edict benefited the older, central, core EU members, causing considerable tension among EU member states and the EU Court for Human Rights, explained in more detail later. Dublin II intensified pressure on southern border states where arrivals were greater. In addition to carrying what they often narrate as a "burden" of enforcement, these states must process asylum seekers rather than serving as transit countries en route to other destinations. Thus Italy, Greece, and Malta have—in recent years—borne a disproportionate share of the work of reception and processing of newly arrived asylum seekers.

The spatial logic governing migration along the peripheral zones of the EU involves the deterrence of would-be migrants and asylum seekers by pushing enforcement and authorities ever farther offshore (Carling 2007a; Andrijasevic 2010). Key to the institutionalization of EU territorial expansion through border enforcement was the 2004 creation of Frontex. Frontex serves as the collaborative agency that oversees joint policing efforts along the southern sea and land borders that conjoin highly asymmetrical terrain surrounding the Mediterranean. From its operationalization in 2005, the agency played a key role, guiding member states in collaborative policing, not only along the edges of the EU, but in third countries. As joint policing operations and bilateral arrangements for return moved the border offshore, islands emerged as hot spots of struggle over entry and exclusion: the Canary Islands, Lampedusa, Malta, and Greek islands.

A key element of securitization of migration in the EU involved the "externalization of asylum" (e.g., Betts 2004; Schuster 2005). As EU states harmonized citizenship policies and eradicated internal borders to facilitate labor migration, they struggled to find common asylum policies. While harmonization of labor migration proved central to the project of easing internal mobility within the EU, the design of a common asylum policy proved a trickier endeavor. In 2004, the European Council prescribed the creation of a Common European Asylum System by 2010. In 2008, EU heads of state and government signed a Pact on Integration and Asylum intended to rearticulate EU cooperation on migration and asylum. The Pact pushed the deadline for the common asylum system to 2012. The Pact included language that has become endemic to current efforts to manage migration by state and suprastate entities, including endeavors to "organize legal immigration," "control illegal immigration," improve border controls, construct a collaborative asylum process, and "create a comprehensive partnership" to "encourage synergy between migration and development" (Council of the European Union 2008). The Pact established guidelines meant to direct member states while respecting their autonomy and disparate needs and capacities in the arena of migrant reception, processing, and integration.

Collaborative policies and practices subsequently moved asylum seekers beyond sovereign territory and closer to regions of origin (Boswell 2003; Schuster 2005). As enforcement resources were consolidated at sea and in North Africa, people encountered the proliferation of spaces of confinement onshore and offshore. They attempted multiple journeys to reach Lampedusa to enter the EU, spending years en route, stuck somewhere in the borderlands, awaiting a chance to enter, or propelled through "revolving doors" in the archipelago. Still others made it in, either moving through Italy and on to other parts of the EU or staying in Sicily or elsewhere in Italy.

Generally, struggles over EU integration and individual sovereignty have been repeated sources of tension in the design and implementation of EU policies: common objectives and national solutions come into conflict in negotiations to share responsibilities. In practice, rather than working in communal fashion as equal partners in the design and implementation of asylum policies in the EU, states work in their own interests and join forces with other member states with common interests (Parkes and Angenendt 2009). They work both within their own sovereign territories and beyond in third countries, from which the management of migration and asylum is managed, de facto, offshore.

When assumptions of internal harmonization collide with the geographical realities of migration across southern borders, the pronounced contradictions reveal tensions around renationalization among member states struggling over regional boundaries and their right to process—or not process—migrants and asylum seekers. Italy and Malta, for example, have long bickered over their respective search-and-rescue areas and the fate of migrants caught at sea in between, sometimes playing geopolitics with precarious lives and prolonging trauma among migrants on boats desperate to land on nearby islands. One such case occurred in April 2009. The captain of the *Pinar E,* a Turkish flag freighter, rescued 140 migrants from a vessel in distress. The captain of the *Pinar E* wanted to disembark at the nearest port. Italian authorities argued that the interception occurred within the search-and-rescue zone administered by Malta, whereas Malta maintained that the ship should travel to the nearest port, which they claimed was Lampedusa. It was only after the president of the European Commission appealed to both countries for a solution to a four-day stand-off that Italy accepted the migrants (Frelick 2009, 38).

Bill Frelick (2009) documented the human cost borne by migrants for these geopolitical squabbles in his report for Human Rights Watch. He interviewed unaccompanied minors stranded on the Zodiac inflatable boat during the episode. One adolescent boy recounted,

> We were calling for people to rescue us. We waved our shirts to passing ships. Some passed us. Others gave us food and water, but did not rescue us. We had no fuel and the waves were carrying us. People were crying. We prayed to God to save us. . . . After four days a big Turkish ship came and threw a rope to us. We climbed into the big boat. They gave us water to drink. They gave us food, even though it wasn't enough. We spent three more days on the Turkish boat. (39)

The devaluation of life in geopolitical stand-offs gave way to greater collaboration and remarkable investments at the nexus of humanitarianism and exclusion at sea across the archipelago (Aas and Gundhus 2015). The *Pinar E* incident foreshadowed what would grow over the next several years into a tragic but common plight. As thousands took to boats to cross the Mediterranean, the *Economist* (La Guardia 2015, 77) estimated some one million migrants awaiting departure along the northern coast of Africa. In response, the EU devised various strategies under the guise of humanitarian rescue to intercept migrants at sea. Following the tragic deaths of more than three hundred people when their boat sank close to Lampedusa in October 2013, Italy initiated Operation Mare Nostrum. This was followed in 2014 by Frontex's Operations Hermes and Triton. These eventually culminated in the creation of Search-and-Rescue Areas that extend well beyond territorial waters surrounding EU member states and close to the coast of Libya (Williams 2018). These operations applied and extended the now well-established humanitarian rescue–security nexus with interception as a form of deterrence (Williams 2014; Pallister-Wilkins 2017b). Migrants bear the largest burden of failures of policy and geopolitics, in the form of drowning, detention, and exclusion, all material expressions of the social death of asylum seekers.

The Stockholm Program also laid out a process that would run from 2010 to 2014 and involve significant changes and a renewed commitment to common European asylum policies. The Program institutionalized the spatial logic of offshore management through its emphasis on "prefrontier border control" and plans for cooperation with third countries. "Front-end" measures included more security checks before visas were granted to third-country nationals. Also assumed by the Treaty was a geographical likelihood that new member states in eastern and southern Europe would continue to manage the bulk of migration and asylum claims. As a result, those countries that were once regions of transit—Spain, Italy, Malta, and Greece—increasingly became sites of destination and detention.

As the EU expanded, new members also took measures to collaboratively and creatively push the border away from sovereign territory to preemptively govern migration flows. Geographical fortune and the economic asymmetries between regions of origin and destination set the stage for confrontation between states. The borderlands between southern Europe and northern Africa and between eastern and western Europe became transit zones and enforcement landscapes. The enforcement measures put into place as barriers to entry in these locations include policing at sea, pushback policies, bilateral arrangements to return migrants intercepted to regions of origin, and detention of those making unauthorized entry either to work or to claim asylum. This was the context in which we began research on Lampedusa and the time when scholars began to document the transformation of the island (Andrijasevic 2010; Cuttitta 2014).

The assumption that protection and processing would happen among all EU member states set the stage for geopolitical struggles over accountability to people seeking asylum. Dublin II and the assumption that protection would be granted evenly was criticized by the UNHCR and tested with decisions in two human rights cases rendered in 2011 and 2012. These decisions challenged Dublin II by declaring that the same measures of protection were not available evenly across EU member states. In January 2011, the European Court for Human Rights ruled in favor of an Afghan asylum seeker who had entered Europe through Greece. His counsel argued that conditions of detention in Greece were so poor that the country could not be considered a safe place to seek asylum (Euractiv 2011). This decision raised once again the concept of "burden sharing" and power struggles over which states face a higher share of the burden of processing. Mainland EU states appeared to want extraterritorial processing, alongside access to asylum and protection of human rights in principle, if elsewhere. This decision threw into question the application and viability of Dublin II, with faith and practice deteriorating as unauthorized entry has increased over recent years.

The legal infrastructure and policies outlined thus far were designed to harmonize asylum processes on paper but did not account for the highly uneven geographical contexts in which they were implemented across member states of the EU with distinct resources, geographical locations, infrastructure, and politics associated with the processing of migrants and asylum seekers. As a complex experiment in regionalization, the EU faltered for years in the design of a common approach to asylum and all but abandoned the Dublin system with the surge of asylum seekers in 2015. This faltering played out first along external borders and islands where fault lines emerged, and subsequently within sovereign territory of EU member states that had once agreed to eliminate the national borders that divided them, culminating in 2015 when Germany stopped enforcing Dublin amid the influx of more than one million Syrian nationals. Residents and authorities in the southern European states of Italy, Greece, and Malta, which do the majority of processing and enforcement on behalf of the EU, frequently articulate the feeling of being abandoned by wealthier, northern EU member states, which they accuse of not partaking in "burden sharing." Landlocked, northern member states do not want those granted asylum to have free mobility to leave the country where they were originally granted asylum. As shifting migratory corridors through the EU showed in 2015, these movements are relational. People changed paths as they migrated, in relation to border closures and openings (Pallister-Wilkins 2017; Popescu 2017).

By 2015, decades of policy and legal infrastructure designed to govern orderly migration into and through the EU began to crumble under the weight of fiscal and political crises and the increased number of people seeking asylum following displacement from Syria (Kasparek 2016; Popescu 2017). Nationalism and related claims to state sovereignty were rekindled amid the continuous politicization and bureaucratic "management" of human migration. Geographical and geopolitical tensions emerged in the stark terms of crisis, with Germany receiving more than one million migrants and asylum seekers in the same months that Hungary closed its borders and others, such as Austria and the Balkan states, fortified theirs.

Tracing the routes of EU enforcement efforts alongside the routes traveled by individuals attempting to navigate this ever-expanding southern archipelago suggests that protection of migrants is not being achieved. Instead, precarity grows in close correlation with intensified enforcement, and more people find themselves in revolving doors, intercepted and sent back repeatedly from Greece to Turkey and from the Mediterranean to detention in Libya, and lost at sea (Médecins Sans Frontières 2011b; Williams and Mountz 2016). Research conducted by Médecins Sans Frontières (MSF) on the border between Libya and Tunisia found direct links between the return of migrants from the EU and systemic physical abuse as both a deterrent and a form of sexual and economic exploitation in detention facilities (both formal and informal) in Libya:

> There is compelling evidence that the system of migrant capture, detention and deterrence has facilitated the creation of an economically-driven machine that involves not only detention but also the systematic torture and extortion of ransoms from vulnerable migrants and their families. (Médecins Sans Frontières 2011b, 4)

Meanwhile, new rounds of externalization, such as cooperative policing and other bilateral arrangements for return, continue to unfold. In March 2016, twenty-eight heads of member states signed a deal with Turkey to stem the arrival of migrants crossing the Aegean, from Turkey to Greece. All "new irregular migrant arrivals" would be returned, and EU member states would increase financial support for refugees in Turkey and their own resettlement of Syrians via Turkey (Collett 2017; van Liempt et al. 2017). This was one of the largest, most public readmission agreements ever signed. Its legality was questionable, particularly pertaining to human rights records in Turkey, and it essentially amounted to displacement of the problem of the displaced (Collett 2017). The EU's New Migration Partnership Framework—signed in June 2016—lay the groundwork for bilateral agreements to arise out of its fluid "compact" structure and included a third-country agreement to block Syrians. In 2017, the Italian prime minister signed a Memorandum of Understanding to reenter bilateral arrangements with the conflicted Libyan leadership to control migration with additional funds, training, and equipment (Euronews 2017). Mass migration into the EU in recent years has frayed the unity of EU member states and threatened dissolution of the EU and the infrastructure of the Schengen Agreement. Whereas readmission agreements have been historically secret, there was a public appetite in the EU for pushback to mass migration. EU borders were set in motion, yet again.

Most recently, the EU has moved to expand the archipelago to control human mobility well beyond the Mediterranean and surrounding border states. Martina Tazzioli (2019) argues that the EU uses mobility to govern mobility in European borderlands, while Loren Landau (2019) locates new forms of governance across the African continent.

BORDER AS TOPOLOGICAL FORM

As externalization policies unfolded, enforcement did not *only* move outward in concentric circles like the movement of a wave. Additionally, resources accrued and affixed to certain bodies and islands as sticking or focal points. What accounts for the spatial transformation of border from line to island? The answer requires an understanding of what scholars are increasingly identifying as the topological border (Martin 2013; Hepworth 2015). The topological border is dynamic, an "emergent process" (Belcher et al. 2008; Marr and Secor 2014). As Lauren Martin (2013) has argued, borders themselves constitute an emergent topology that blurs lines around jurisdiction, inclusion, and exclusion. Borders have historically always been emergent, in a process of becoming that involves interplay between spatiality, sovereignty, and legality and the ability to exclude on the basis of identity (Ngai 2008). In the United States, for example, the Bracero Program of the mid-twentieth century reached deeply across Mexico to recruit short-term, seasonal agricultural workers subjected to particular legal and extralegal socioeconomic configurations (Nevins 2010). Once demand for this labor subsided, the program ended, and resources were shifted to efforts to send workers back to Mexico. The 1965 Border Industrialization Program emerged inside Mexico, a precursor to NAFTA and maquiladoras, both efforts to keep workers in Mexico. More contemporary forms of offshore activity similarly enact these contradictions, juxtaposing the facilitation of labor with aggressive rounds of exclusion. Such contradictions require dynamic enforcement methods to move resources. Through their immigration policies, societies often imagine migrants as temporary workers with malleable mobility, recruiting and admitting those whose labor is desired while repelling others. This spatial imagination requires mobility and dehumanization. The spaces, states, and categories of movement in between constitute thresholds where migrant workers and asylum seekers enter into long periods of legal, spatial, temporal, and psychological limbo. For these reasons, the oceanic turn foregrounds movements at sea (e.g., Peters 2010; Perera 2013; Sharpe 2016; Stierl, 2020).

Migration-related border enforcement is topological: the infinitely evolving "emergent process" (Belcher et al. 2008) through which exclusionary infrastructure develops new topographies designed to fix workers and their mobility in place. Other infrastructures have been set in motion by the topological border. Indeed, everywhere one turns to understand contemporary border enforcement, immigration policing, and detention, one finds the ad hoc, temporary, crisis-driven, provisional nature of enforcement. Administrative discretion abounds. Nearly any place can become a provisional detention center: a hospital room, a school, or an island. Most places can also be rescripted as ports of entry, and existing scholarship explores the shift from exterior to interior policing (Coleman 2007; Varsanyi 2008).

While scholarship in the wake of the 9/11 attacks on U.S. soil returned repeatedly to Guantánamo Bay and Abu Ghraib as iconic liminal sites of Agamben's (1998) bare life (discussed in the introduction), nowhere is the topological more evident than in border enforcement—a field forever evolving to meet migrants wherever they move—and in its haunting lethal resonance at sea (Sharpe 2018; Stierl 2019). As the border extends outward, certain thresholds become highly productive sites where sovereign power is worked through, islands among them. Borders are reconfigured through this dispersal, moving to the body of the migrant or asylum seeker, where the body becomes isolated, a ground of policing and legal and political contestation. Offshore detention also productively blurs lines between human and animal, inside and out, life and death, and sovereign and biopower (Butler 2004; Gregory 2007; Vaughan-Williams 2015).

In recent years, Zolberg's (2003) concept of "remote control" has grown *more* remote and mobile, with distant measures of enforcement that immobilize potential migrants by policing more deeply transnational routes of transit and even countries of origin (Landau 2019). The seemingly fixed materiality of state architecture (the port, the processing facility, the detention center) is moved closer to mobile bodies, shrinking routes to protection. The port is inverted, moved and moored offshore. Islands near mainland territory once functioned as iconic ports of entry and sites of exclusion: Angel Island, Ellis Island, Canada's Pier 21 (which is in Halifax and implemented quarantine on a small island), the sites where migrants first encounter agents of the state. These ports of entry are now more geographically distant, ironically in a world characterized as more proximate with time–space compression (Harvey 1989). These first moments of encounter have now moved much farther offshore, transpiring instead at high seas and around island territories in Caribbean, Pacific, and Indian Ocean regions. The topological border drives the expansion of the enforcement archipelago with an endless cycle of proliferating spaces of isolation. As migrants encounter border enforcement earlier in the journey, they also experience proliferating spaces of confinement in multiple countries as the border takes on the spatial form of the island.

As the enforcement archipelago evolves offshore, it alters the social and economic fabric of places with material infrastructure and detention industries. As the topological border remakes geography with proliferating islands, island communities are themselves exploited and transformed from zones of passage to carceral spaces with construction of facilities, separation of islanders and migrants, and islanders employed in or in support of the detention industry (discussed in chapter 3).

A spatial pattern repeats itself; borders are becoming in specific ways across the enforcement archipelago, patterns that capture and capitalize on and exploit particular kinds of people and places. As topological borders manipulate law and jurisdiction to undermine access, authorities move the border to mobile bodies, engulfing migrants in the borderlands, transferring borders from frontier to global intimate (see Anzaldúa 1987; Wright 1997; Vaughn-Williams 2015). As the enforcement archipelago remakes the island as carceral space, the carceral also becomes corporeal. In the next section, I detail this pattern with discussion of transformations on Lampedusa. Findings on Lampedusa over time show that the topological form is not only the outcome of enforcement decisions but also an outcome of shifting migration patterns, smuggling routes, and responses from local communities. In this sense, the archipelago functions as assemblage, a dynamic interaction of many entities and materials: mobile people and infrastructure, constructions of the geopolitical on the racialized, classed, and gendered bodies of asylum seekers on land and at sea.

Enforcement archipelagoes develop through encounters and negotiations between authorities and migrants, each responsive to the other in a recursive relationship. Owing to this interplay, various places become sites of border enforcement across the enforcement archipelago, whether through official policy or unofficial practice. Migrants sometimes encounter borders "at home" in regions of origin, sometimes before (traditional) border crossings are even attempted. Those traveling by boat often meet the border in the form of enforcement at sea. Those who are not returned often find themselves in interstitial sites located somewhere between country of origin and desired destination, in aquapelagic places of land and sea (Stratford et al. 2011; Pugh 2013). These sites function as islands to contain, exclude, and "manage" people and their mobility; some *are* actual islands. Migrants can end up in detention facilities, themselves places where borders proliferate both within the facility and in the surrounding area. After carceral spaces to detain migrants proliferated on mainland and island Italian territory, including Sicily and Sicily's Lampedusa, Italy also moved to thwart mobility at sea and through bilateral arrangements in Libya and Tunisia. Nearby, in the marine routes surrounding these islands, EU member states developed sophisticated infrastructure to eventually boast the ability to track all boats crossing the Mediterranean. This capacity did not result in the ability to rescue migrants, although large-scale operations were often narrated in the dehumanizing terms of humanitarian rescue (Vaughn-Williams 2015). This extended surveillance capacity *did* result in the ability to exercise more control over vessels, with boats themselves becoming carceral spaces, as in the case of the Left to Die Boat, known to be adrift and in distress but never rescued.

GEOGRAPHICAL ROUTES AND ISLAND PERSPECTIVES: APPROACHING LAMPEDUSA

Migration routes and enforcement strategy operate as relational geographies. Tracing their shifts and growth alongside one another places islands as flashpoints in the borderlands. There migrants and enforcement authorities struggle over entry into and exclusion from the EU from western to eastern points where boats approach European islands. Up until the early 2000s, Lampedusa functioned as a transit zone or space of passage within longer corridors into Italy and the EU; it was the closest bit of sovereign territory that people traveling by boat could reach in their efforts to enter. People who landed on Lampedusa and made an asylum claim were transferred to a reception center on the island of Sicily (Andrijasevic 2006). Many eventually made their way to other parts of Italy or other European countries to work and seek asylum. In 2002, the conditions of work and management of migration shifted when Misericordia employees replaced Red Cross volunteers who ran the shelter on the island (Cuttitta 2014, 203). In 2004, amid pressure to tighten security and improve enforcement, Italian authorities increased policing at sea and reduced the transfers to Sicily and mainland Italy. Conditions in the increasingly crowded detention facility on Lampedusa deteriorated. Italian authorities began to send migrants back en masse on chartered flights to Libya without processing their claims and—reportedly—without adequate time to establish their identities and assess their well-being if returned to and through Libya (Médecins Sans Frontières 2004). These issues of identification and processing have been sources of tension for over a decade as Italian authorities sometimes endeavor to misidentify people as being from the wrong country of origin—from countries understood as non-refugee-producing—to expedite their removal. Migrants we interviewed reported being misclassified as Tunisian to mediate their access to asylum and expedite their return, even when they explained their attempts to correct the misidentification by authorities.

Between 2004 and 2008, Italy's Lampedusa and Spain's Canary Islands proved the most popular backdoor entrances to the EU from western and northern Africa and, subsequently, sites of increased enforcement (Andrijasevic 2006; Carling 2007a). Intensive migration activity by sea captured the attention of the global community, this time off the western coast of Africa on the shores of Spain's Canary Islands in the early 2000s. During summer holidays on Lampedusa and the Canaries, once privileged European mobility abutted the forced displacement and subsequent immobility of those attempting passage through the Africa–EU borderlands. Migrants traveled land routes through Mauritania, Morocco, and Algeria before crossing the sea (Carling 2007b). In 2006, at the height of boat arrivals there, the media frequently reported stories of tourists watching as the human drama of African migrants arriving on beaches unfolded before them. Like other countries responding to marine arrivals, Spain sought to balance international obligations and national agendas in relation to broader EU efforts to harmonize migration and enforcement and protect human rights. In Spain, however, asylum seekers spent less time in detention due to national policies that sought more humane solutions by limiting time in detention and processing. Between 1999 and 2011, 95,907 migrants arrived on the Canaries by boat, reaching a peak in 2006 with 31,678 and then declining dramatically (Cuttitta 2014, 197).

This decline resulted from Frontex's intensification of policing of the archipelago during this period of heightened arrivals in 2006. The interceptions drove human smuggling elsewhere (Carling 2007a, 21). As Frontex increased enforcement around the Canaries, migrant routes shifted east along the Mediterranean. As Carling suggests, the movement of enforcement outward in increments also shifted smuggling operations farther offshore, first away from the mainland, then away from the Canary Islands, and finally into Morocco (Collyer 2007). This movement also contributed to an increase in arrivals on and interceptions near Lampedusa. Between 1999 and 2011, more than 150,000 migrants arrived by boat on the Italian island.

Frontex and Italy also intensified policing, resulting in another geographical shift and increased boat arrivals on Greek islands and the island state of Malta; these boats had departed primarily from the coast of Libya and Tunisia. According to Lutterbeck (2009, 119), modern migrant arrivals by boat on Malta began in 2002. Before Malta joined the EU in 2004, it had been a space of passage en route to the EU. Once joining, Malta became responsible for slowing migration, increasing detention and carceral spaces on the island. Peaking at 2,775 migrants in 2008, the number of arrivals was much more modest than on Lampedusa and the Canaries, which both received tens of thousands during this time period. Maltese authorities argued, however, that given its small population, it had processed the highest number of asylum seekers of any EU state per capita (Lutterbeck 2009). Malta has repeatedly called on the EU to take on a greater share of the "burden" in its migration crisis (Mainwairing 2012a). In a symbolic move, the EU opened the European Asylum Support Office there in 2011 with Asylum and Migration funds.

Greece also experienced increased arrivals, leading to geopolitical tensions over responsibility along its shared border with Turkey and within the rest of Europe. Greek asylum processing and acceptance rates remained extraordinarily low, significantly lower than rates in other EU member states, prompting questions as to whether Greece was honoring the Dublin Conventions and whether return of asylum seekers to Greece as the first country of landing was legal.

In contrast with Greece, and largely in response to the rise in Syrian asylum seekers migrating to Europe as a result of the civil war, Sweden opened borders in early 2015, and that fall, Germany opened doors to Syrian asylum seekers. During this period of openness, tension unfolded among member states as others sought to close off their borders and migratory routes to Germany. Migrants changed routes as states fortified borders and checkpoints (Popescu 2017). Eventually, both Sweden and Germany once again restricted entry, coming into line and no longer functioning as outliers to EU member state policy.

In 2014 and 2015, as Mediterranean crossings increased significantly, this increase was reflected in arrivals on Lampedusa (and in Turkey and Greece). Figure 7 shows the disembarkation of a boat on Lampedusa, as people are received by the Italian Coast Guard, Red Cross, and volunteers. While changes in geopolitics and conflict—as well as border enforcement—have caused the number of boat arrivals to fluctuate dramatically over the years on Lampedusa (Cuttitta 2014), the island has remained a significant entry point. This makes the island an ideal place from which to examine what happens on a remote island as borders shift and are externalized and as the enforcement archipelago expands to engulf the island in shifts offshore.

FIGURE 7. Boat arrivals on Lampedusa. Photograph by R. Tina Catania.

VANTAGE POINT LAMPEDUSA: FROM PASSAGE TO CONFINEMENT

As processing and enforcement were pushed offshore, certain entry points became hot spots where migrants frequently attempted to enter by sea. Countries where these hot spots are located struggled to balance national interests and international responsibilities. Italy's Lampedusa proved a popular entry point to the EU from northern Africa and, subsequently, a site of increased enforcement (Andrijasevic 2006, 2010). Lampedusa is a small island southwest (though administratively part) of Sicily, not far from Tunisia. More than fifty thousand African migrants arrived by boat on Lampedusa between 2005 and 2007. Arrivals increased steadily until reaching an apex in 2008, then dropped precipitously in 2009 and 2010, only to skyrocket again in 2011 with the Arab Spring (Cuttitta 2014, 202), drop again, rise again in 2014 with increased Syrian displacement, and drop again (Williams 2018). As Williams shows, arrivals rise and fall annually in a seasonal cycle, with the single most influential factor in their fluctuation being enforcement operations. Related struggles over entry raised governance issues throughout this cycle, as Italy sought to balance its own agenda in relation to broader EU efforts to harmonize migration and enforcement and protect human rights. Islanders and migrants, connected by the sea, lived out the consequences of national and supranational policy and geopolitical arrangements.

The main contours of the externalization of EU borders discussed earlier can thus be mapped through the history of Lampedusa. As Paolo Cuttitta (2014, 198) has observed, Lampedusa functions as "observatory for the globalized governance of migration." The island is significant not only for its geographically remote location and proximity to Tunisia but for the politicized responses to migration that transpire on the island and across Italy and the EU, "transforming it into the quintessential embodiment of the Euro-African migration and border regime" (Cuttitta 2014, 199). Central to externalization is the collaborative policing of boat migration in the region by Frontex. Also central to the story of externalization as it affects Lampedusa is the collaboration between Italian and Libyan officials, who put their first bilateral agreement for policing in place in 2000 (Cuttitta 2014, 202) and, in 2017, signed their most recent Memorandum of Understanding—despite the fractured nature of Libyan leadership at the time.

As Andrijasevic (2010) writes, for many years, Lampedusa functioned as a zone of passage to Italy and the EU. But the island changed quickly from being a safe haven of entry and transit to a site of detention and expulsion as Italy pushed enforcement outward. Over the course of this transformation, with enforcement increasing in the early 2000s, authorities at times attempted to inhibit the access of human rights monitors and Italian authorities. This illustrates efforts to use islands to hide asylum seekers from view while restricting access. As on Nauru and Manus islands, advocates and human rights monitors were restricted from viewing the center, compounding the isolation of migrants inside. In the case of Lampedusa, the UNHCR became vocal in criticizing early decisions to repatriate en masse and also expressed concerns about conditions in what was then called the Temporary Holding Centre, where authorities had successfully blocked entry of human rights monitors for several months after beginning its more aggressive deportation campaign (UNHCR 2005). As pressure mounted, Italian journalist Fabrizio Gatti went undercover and entered the center as a migrant intercepted at sea and reported on the poor conditions he witnessed. Subsequently, the European Parliament succeeded in sending its first delegation to tour the center in June 2005 (European

United Left 2005). According to human rights advocates I interviewed in Rome and Geneva in May 2006, the Italian government deported a large charter flight of detainees the night before the advocates' arrival and improved conditions by adding mattresses and painting the center.

MSF is one organization that succeeded, for a time, in working within the center. After issuing a report that criticized conditions inside the facility, however, MSF was no longer allowed inside. Instead, it was reduced to servicing the medical needs of detainees with brief triage outside the center in a tent on the dock where migrants were brought ashore following interception.

In 2007, Italy took further steps to extend enforcement offshore with the Protocol of Joint Patrol of the Mediterranean with Libya. This initiative involved more collaboration with Libyan authorities to intercept and return boats with enforcement of its pushback policy *(respingimento)*, designed to capture and repel migrants intercepted at sea rather than allowing them the rights that one accrues to seek asylum once landing on sovereign territory (Tazzioli 2011). With increased interception and return, smuggling routes for migrants shifted again. The number of arrivals dropped precipitously on Lampedusa, as smugglers moved routes and arrivals again swelled in both Greece and Malta. As Lutterbeck (2009, 123) suggests, "plugging one hole in the EU perimeter quickly leads to enhanced pressure on other parts of its external borders."

As a result of intensified implementation of *respingimento,* few ships arrived at Lampedusa by sea in 2009 or 2010, resulting in some confidence that the problem of migration to the island had been addressed. As I traveled through Sicily with research assistant Tina Catania en route to our first visit to Lampedusa, we were told along the way that boat migration had ended. This turned out not to be true. We found that boats *were* landing, but those onboard were being shuttled quickly and quietly to other parts of Sicily to keep numbers low and craft the appearance that the highly politicized problem of migration to Lampedusa had been "solved."

Then, in 2011, the eruption of political unrest related to the Arab Spring in Tunisia, Egypt, Libya, and elsewhere again threw Lampedusa into the spotlight. By the end of February, some five thousand Tunisian and Egyptian migrants had landed on the island, calling attention once again to the role and ramifications of offshore interventions (*Spiegel Online* 2011). By June, this number had increased to approximately forty-four thousand (Migrants at Sea 2011), with estimates eventually exceeding fifty-one thousand (Ministero dell'Interno 2011).

In 2011, bilateral arrangements between Italy and Libya fell apart as then Libyan president Muammar Gaddafi was ousted. Whereas 2010 had seen almost no migrants detained on Lampedusa, the number exceeded fifty-one thousand in 2011 (Ministero dell'Interno 2011). With the political crises unfolding daily in February 2011, Italy called on the EU to hold a meeting to design a concerted strategy to respond to migration. As the EU panicked about the potential arrivals and a crisis developed along Libya's borders, the unsettled African states turned away from previous development deals and readmission agreements that allowed entry of European authorities to "stem the tide" (*Spiegel Online* 2011). During the 2011 crisis, the port at Lampedusa was officially closed (Tazzioli 2011). Many migrants were carried away from the island on commercial cruise ships, held in the port of Palermo, and eventually returned to Tunisia. Thousands more moved through what many characterize as a "revolving door" (Human Rights Watch 2008), attempting to migrate to the EU, being returned, trying again, spending time in detention, and thus making their way slowly through the enforcement archipelago.

Meanwhile, as the detention industry took hold on the small island, residents and authorities lived out cycles of resistance and complicity to this unwelcomed influx of people and jobs. Lampedusans vacillated over the years between the impulse to rescue and support people crossing the Mediterranean in desperate circumstances and to close off the island to further arrivals and cast blame on federal and international authorities for these circumstances. The small year-round community of approximately six thousand residents was, at times, overwhelmed, receptive, and hostile toward migrants and asylum seekers. It is a small fishing community that increasingly makes its livelihood from tourism, as fishing licenses have been reduced to prevent overfishing. Like other island communities, Lampedusans have a history of welcoming migrants, providing food, shelter, and other kinds of assistance during times of crisis. At other times, they have protested the Italian government's use of the island and failure to provide ample resources in its response to migration and taken matters into their own hands by blocking the port with private boats, primarily fishing trawlers. They engaged with authorities, hoping alternately for more humanitarian assistance when boats drowned or for an end to detention when the island was overwhelmed.

Like islanders, authorities expressed contradictory responses to newly arrived migrants whom they were tasked with policing through interception and detention. Sometimes they shared the futility and feeling overwhelmed by the journey and their encounters:

> Basically they are returned to Libya even if they are Somalis or Nigerians. So it may happen that these people are coming from Somalia.... The "journey of hope," as they say, doesn't entail only crossing the Mediterranean Sea from Libya to Lampedusa. Actually the journey of hope is two years long because those who leave from Somalia have to cross the whole of Africa, through the desert, only to arrive in Libya and wait before they can leave. Then they leave, and once they have left, they are carried back again. You can see how that's a sheer madness. (interview, CPT worker, Lampedusa, 2011)

In an interview in July 2011, one manager of the detention center explained the international attention in his depiction of the crisis that unfolded during the 2011 uprising: "We had all of them—BBC, CNN, *New York Times*. All of them!" In a separate interview, one of his employees crafted a different narrative: "These people leave no mark, actually. Because they're nothing, they're ghosts. They're nonentities. In our system, they're nothing. And they're still nothing" (interview, Lampedusa, July 2011). These two perspectives affirm the juxtaposition of hypervisibility and invisibility that befalls the small island, local residents, and migrants who land there. Most times, they are quietly forgotten, until another migration episode pushes them back into the national and international spotlights.

How can we make sense of these two statements made by employees working at the same detention facility at the same time on Lampedusa? One speaks of hypervisibility of migration crises: there is a sense that the world is watching. The other renders detainees invisible: ghosts who haunt public discourse and domestic politics. Still hidden by these narratives are the lives, identities, and emotions of those detained. Clearly articulated in these statements are forces of hypervisibility and invisibility. To return to Butler, what constitutes a grievable life? What is a life deemed "nothing" in this context, and where do those people

FIGURE 8. Boat cemetery on Lampedusa, where ships are brought once they have been intercepted and offloaded. Photograph by the author.

living out ungrievable deaths end up, whether in life or in death, in the extended limbo of the revolving door?

Paolo Cuttitta (2014) maps the arc of this history and argues that the rise and fall of arrivals on Lampedusa function as a stage on which the "border play" or spectacle of migration politics unfolds (see De Genova 2002), both reflecting and refracting broader national politics surrounding migration. Time and again, competing political agendas, fears, and desires have played out on the small island. At a smaller scale, these competing forces to govern, identify, contain, hide, and disappear can be seen in conflicts over the boat cemetery (depicted in Figure 8), a place that researcher Tina Catania and I found after inquiries during our first visit to the island to conduct research in 2010.

Located in a cordoned-off section of the island dump, the cemetery had come to represent the lost lives and myriad emotions and memories associated with the boat arrivals: fear, shame, sadness, and anger. In 2010, a small group of young activists were sneaking into the cemetery to do what Divya Tolia-Kelly (2006) calls "emotional recovery work."

They were collecting personal effects that had been left behind after interceptions, such as shoes, clothing, photographs, Korans, letters, poems, and cooking oil. Knowing that the boats are eventually destroyed and migrants sent away, they wanted to memorialize the lives that had passed through the island in a museum.

This was the same summer when very few individuals were recorded as having arrived on the island, which was largely attributed to the pushback campaign. Many, however, criticized Italy for moving arrivals by boat along so quickly to other places precisely so that they would not be recorded. These moves demonstrated the mobilization of bordering in the form of the island: a desire to manage migrants and their mobility through containment and confinement to small spaces within the island and beyond it, on boats, in ports, and in detention facilities elsewhere.

After Lampedusa's Mayor De Rubeis announced plans to have the boats destroyed by a company that would be contracted and brought to the island to do the demolition, activists protested the plans. In September 2010, shortly after our first visit to the island, the cemetery was mysteriously burned down in a fire ruled to be arson. Fierce contestations over the politics of representing migrants unfolded. In 2011, Italian authorities were accused of returning people without first properly ascertaining their identities. The politics of representation, identification, and exclusion resurfaced again in 2013 when Italy was criticized for granting postmortem citizenship to those who had drowned near Lampedusa, while detaining those who had survived. Italy benevolently allowed political subjectivity as a replacement for biological life, substituting one death for another in Butlerian terms of recognition.

Arrivals on Lampedusa also fluctuated in relation to EU-wide investment in resources in response to migration. Following the high-profile boat wreck of October 2013, Italy and Frontex initiated large-scale marine enforcement operations, beginning with the Italian initiative Mare Nostrum from October 2013 to October 2014, followed by Frontex's Operation Triton, and advancing development of search-and-rescue areas. Frontex mapped jurisdictions for policing and interception on the Central Mediterranean through these Search-and-Rescue Areas (Williams 2018). Each of these operations and the Search-and-Rescue Areas elided notions of humanitarian rescue and border enforcement (Williams 2015; Tazzioli 2016). This tension between humanitarian and enforcement responses characterizes not only the large-scale operations at sea but also the more localized responses of island residents to migration influxes.

As detention increased on Lampedusa, *forms* of confinement shifted (Andrijasevic 2010). As in 2011, capacity was so overwhelmed that migrants were sleeping all over the island, and particularly on a hill that came to be known locally as the "hill of shame." At these times, the entire island became a carceral space, what one resident referred to as "Gitmo," a reference to Guantánamo Bay (interview, Lampedusa, July 2010). Islanders fluctuated between forms of volunteerism and protest of boat migration and detention in their small community, particularly when arrivals spiked precipitously in 2011:

> Things really became unmanageable, unsustainable, because we had seven thousand to eight thousand people in the streets, with not even their most basic rights guaranteed. I mean, they were sleeping outdoors, they were relieving themselves outdoors, they had nothing to eat, they had no clothes.... Therefore, our organization, together with the parish church and another organization— and lots of Lampedusans, too—began doing all we could: cooking, giving clothes. (young male activist, interview, Lampedusa, June 2011)

Over time, detention capacity was increased and groups separated from each other, women and families from single men. Based on her research findings in detention centers in the United Kingdom, Mary Bosworth (2014) argues that most people involved in detention in some fashion— as employees and detainees—express ambivalence about these institutions, understanding their existence as better than some alternatives, but also not as peaceful or productive for those on the inside. Similarly, people we interviewed on Lampedusa and across Sicily in detention facilities as employees, detainees, and community residents expressed deep ambivalence and contradictory opinions about detention. For example, we spoke with one young man detained in the largest of eight facilities in Sicily who expressed this experience of languishing:

> There had been some boys staying there for a year and a half and they had no papers.... Staying there for a year and a half, doing

nothing, that's heavy. Then they moved me here. I waited one year. . . . During that time, I could have done a lot of things. One year just went by like that. . . . I couldn't attend any training courses, that year. . . . I couldn't do a lot of things. (young male detainee, interview, Mineo, Sicily, July 2011)

Another man we interviewed had also been detained and later, when we interviewed him, was volunteering at the facility. He too narrated the stress of limbo:

> They want to live within the law. Because it's not good to live like you're a criminal. Nobody likes that. Especially when . . . you are willing to work . . . for you, your family, for the place where you're living. But you can't. I mean, they're kept in this uncertain situation, always worried about it: how is this going to end up? Will I become a criminal just because . . . ? You're always worried. I mean . . . that's an inner turmoil . . . for anyone. For any human being. (former detainee and current worker/volunteer at center, interview, Mineo, Sicily, July 2011)

Many people landing on Lampedusa over the last several years traveled across multiple international borders and treacherous desert landscapes to reach the African coast. Many spent years in limbo or detention in Libya or Tunisia. Recent bilateral arrangements for policing and return between EU and African states made it even more difficult for them to travel any farther on their transnational journeys. As Andrijasevic (2010) and Bialasiewicz (2012) show, Italy increasingly policed borders on Libyan soil, deporting and supporting detention there to prevent departure by sea. With Italy policing to prevent departure and expedite return, few migrants arrived on Lampedusa in 2010. Once arriving, the journey does not end but continues in the form of spatial and legal limbo and the stress of uncertainty. While those migrants making the journey experience trauma, those working on the front lines experience secondary forms of trauma and detachment on display in interviews quoted here. If the island provides a window into the management of global governance, Lampedusa shows that the issue of response to mass displacement is far from resolved.

CONCLUSIONS: ONTOLOGIES OF EXCLUSION AND LOSS

In this chapter, I have discussed the topological border and its role in producing the enforcement archipelago. Within the archipelago, the border has been transformed spatially into a proliferating series of islands that exploit and remake actual islands—including Lampedusa—as carceral spaces. I developed this argument by first tracing the legal and policy architecture of border externalization in and around the EU and then moved to Lampedusa as one site from which to observe externalization and associated shifts in migration routes over time, as well as local responses to nationally articulated migration "crises."

In the enforcement archipelago, the spatial forms of borderlines and borderlands have been supplanted by islands, with proliferating spaces of confinement becoming the primary spatial form of exclusion: border becomes island, border surrounds body. Transnational journeys across borders have shifted from the spatial metaphors that iconoclast border studies scholar Gloria Anzaldúa (1987) once wrote about: the line as crossing or hybridity, which involved violence but also something new and hopeful in the form of hybrid identities. For Anzaldúa, living close to the line in the borderlands meant hybrid forms of identity, incorporating self and other and multiple languages and cultures. Borders and transit corridors are increasingly experienced as a proliferating series of spaces of confinement. Instead of a crossing, people encounter remote detention and lack mobility in transit, in detention, through legal systems and asylum procedures.

The enforcement archipelago is a topology with emergent and overlapping forms of mobility and stasis: it comes into being through the spatialized securitization of migration. This securitization also entails the distancing of detainable populations from mainland territory. As migrants illegalized (Andrijasevic 2010, 94) and contained farther offshore on remote islands in the enforcement archipelago, they are both geographically distanced and discursively othered. The containment of racialized others in remote locations plays on the politics of threat and fear, protecting and securing an imagined nation at home from dangerous threats elsewhere (Razack 1999). As the enforcement archipelago expands, states shrink routes to livelihood and protection.

Spatially remote forms of detention and policing on islands—and on metaphorical islands elsewhere—inhibit people from accessing advocacy and claimant systems. They also serve the purpose of hiding detainees from public view and mediating access to asylum through various means of geographical distance, dispersal, and isolation.

Boltanski (1999) argues that distancing operates through humanitarian discourses to create sympathetic publics: a return to Hannah Arendt's "politics of pity." Conversely, the politics of fear are well-rehearsed discourses of migration: fear of invasion and "yellow peril," for example (Anderson 1991). As Boltanski's distant problems approach, migrants become dangerous. Rather than strategic visibility, then, detained asylum seekers and migrants are simultaneously invisibilized as potential victims and hypervisible as potential security threats. This sleight of hand does the work of distracting the public, calling attention to processes and infrastructure of securitization (e.g., highly visible boat interceptions, high-security detention centers), while hiding from view people contained therein and the transnational communities, geopolitical relations, and colonial histories in which they are embedded and embroiled. Within the enforcement archipelago, the violence of detention and border enforcement is obscured from the view of publics. The creation of fear through processes of securitization proves central to the disappearance of protection and safe haven. This same contradiction can be witnessed in the diametric narratives of islands.

In the next chapters, I show that ontologies of exclusion involve understanding life and death as forms of being in remote sites of detention. The racialized dehumanization and exclusion of mobile bodies become mundane forms of state violence. Those who are hidden from view at moments of interception and offshore detention also face the active obscuring of their identities, histories, and causes of displacement. Blocked entries into sovereign territory are not counted in nationally based censuses or other statistical measures. Preemption makes such blocking possible, maneuvering geographically around international law and EU edicts. Media outlets are more likely to report big events— the literal and tragic losses of life at sea—than the routine returns that follow interception.

Migrants are governed or "managed" in the enforcement archipelago through their disappearance as states shift preemptive border enforcement strategies regularly. Those who attempt to enter with permission disappear, and many who attempt to enter without authorization also disappear. They are scripted as "undeserving," racialized others and security threats, detained remotely and therefore removed quietly from support, access, and rights in the form of interpreters, refugee advocates, and communities. At times construed as security crises, states exploit such contradictions productively to undermine access to legal representation, human rights, and avenues to legal migration and asylum (Mountz 2011). These exclusionary episodes play out in highly public fashion, broadcast by the largest media outlets in the world to a global audience. Simultaneously, many dimensions of the transnational journeys and sovereign undertakings remain hidden from view. Most hidden are the lives, identities, survival strategies, and emotions of those detained.

As topological borders manipulate law and jurisdiction to undermine access, authorities move the border to mobile bodies, engulfing migrants in the borderlands, transferring borders from frontier to global intimate (see Anzaldúa 1989; Wright 1997; Vaughn-Williams 2015). As authorities and migrants shift routes relationally, the border is transformed from line to island. As the enforcement archipelago remakes the island as carceral space, the carceral also becomes corporeal. This chapter's movement has traced borders to bodies, finding islands in the form of spaces of confinement created to contain human mobility. The topological border moves islands everywhere, and chapter 4 explores the use of remote detention internal to sovereign territory as a form of island making through bordering in the interior.

PART II
ONTOLOGICAL DEATH
Shrinking Spaces

3

The Island within the Archipelago

> The detention camp is a small jail and the island is a big jail. All of the island, same jail. I want to get freedom.
> —MONAWIR AL-SABER, recounting his prolonged detention on Nauru (Gordon 2006)

> We are just surviving. We are dead souls in living bodies.
> —ANONYMOUS WOMAN detained on Nauru to Human Rights Watch Researcher, 2015

Although islands are often geographically imagined as peripheral or marginal, distanced from mainland territories in various ways, they are far from remote. In fact, islands prove central to understanding contemporary trends in global migration, including the death of asylum. Islands become sites of remote detention within the archipelago: physical landforms predisposed in the geographical imagination to what Moran, Gill, and Conlon (2013) call carceral spaces. Islands are themselves proliferating, pervasive. *Could the island be the new camp?*

For those who reside on islands, whether by choice or by force, they lie at the center of daily life, not its periphery. In 2010, Australian news outlets showed footage of a detainee in the North West Point Immigration Detention Centre on Christmas Island who dug his own grave and slept there nightly, a poignant expression of deathly living and living death in the archipelago, or "dead souls in living bodies." On islands, migrant bodies become sites of territorial control, conflict, and contestation, where political value is lost and regained. There, politicians and migrants negotiate exclusion and citizenship as they move through the spectrum between life and death in the archipelago.

This chapter posits island detentions as a key element of the "securitization of migration," key sites within the archipelago where national security is prioritized over human security, where access to sovereign territory is mediated in ways that foretell the death of asylum. In research

I conducted on offshore border enforcement from 2006 to 2008, islands emerged as spatially significant sites of exclusion in the geographical landscape where migrants tried to access asylum processes and where nation-states invested significant resources in enforcement to manage their entry. This led to subsequent field research from 2010 to 2014 on islands as sites of enforcement. Australia is an island state with a history of settler colonialism that resonates with contemporary carceral landscapes (Perera 2009; Coddington 2017). Australia is a proven leader in offshore enforcement and detention on islands, and I draw on its recent history in this chapter. By detaining migrants on islands within the enforcement archipelago, states and third parties—such as organizations contracted to run detention facilities—hide asylum seekers from view of media, human rights monitors, and publics at large. As a result, the perspectives of those involved in island encounters—civil servants, migrants, attorneys, and advocates—are underrepresented in contemporary debates on immigration and border enforcement in public discourse and scholarly literatures.

Within the archipelago, the island functions simultaneously as border, prison, and refuge. Islands are sites where migrants land and nation-states exercise power through the management of global migration. As such, they are sites ripe for investigation of how sovereign and biopolitical power converge offshore to create Gregory's (2007) "vanishing points" (Sparke 2006), where nation-states exploit legal ambiguity, economic dependency, and partial forms of citizenship and political status to advance security agendas. In the field of island studies, scholars map broad patterns and variations in jurisdiction and governance to situate activities on islands (Baldacchino and Milne 2006). Migration scholars, meanwhile, have identified forms of precariousness encountered by people on the move (e.g., Goldring et al. 2009; Vosko et al. 2014). These two trends converge as detention facilities proliferate on islands: growth in migrants' precariousness and exploitation of islands as sites of creative exercises in power.

The islands that pepper the archipelagoes of this book are distant and distinct from each other historically, geographically, culturally, economically, and politically. Yet important patterns connect them and fuel examination of emergent topologies of sovereignty there. For example, islands play key roles in military strategy, resulting in violent colonial histories and militarized landscapes, such as large naval bases in small territories where local communities have been dispossessed of land (Kaplan 2005; Vine 2009) as imperialism sows its roots.

These residual material landscapes then become sites where past usage haunts present occupants as built structures are repurposed for detention and processing. David Vine (2009) writes about U.S. military use of islands as sites from which states exercised regional influence during decolonization. He does this with archival and ethnographic work on the forcible removal of Chagossians from British island territory of Diego Garcia in 1971 to make way for one of the biggest U.S. naval bases in the world. Today, some of these same islands once envisioned as ideal locations for U.S. military bases to influence regional control—the "strategic island concept"—are now used to regulate human mobility through capture of liminal populations, neither home nor arrived, not able to legally become refugees or asylum seekers because of their location at a distance from sovereign territory. Whether open or closed, publicly or privately managed, officially or unofficially sanctioned, facilities on islands serve the purpose of isolating migrants from communities of advocacy and legal representation, and in some cases from asylum claim processes that can only be accessed by landing on sovereign territory.

As noted in the introductory chapter, asylum claimant processes differ from programs designed to resettle refugees selected from abroad by governments ("government-assisted refugee resettlement programs"). Often, the processing of asylum claims can also be distinct on islands from that on mainland territories, precisely because of geographical distance (as in Australia's two-tier system). Recent scholarship has sought to detail struggles over migration transpiring on islands (e.g., Mainwaring 2012a; Bernardie-Tahier and Schmoll 2014). This collective research enhances knowledge of migration activities offshore, alongside contemporary debates about sovereignty (e.g., Steinberg 2005; Baldacchino and Milne 2006).

Asylum seekers often employ human smugglers and cross multiple borders to reach sovereign territory of nation-states with asylum claimant systems (Nadig 2002). Because they proceed in clandestine fashion to elude authorities en route, research on hidden routes, people, and enforcement activities proves challenging. Further complicating the picture, those detected en route become associated not with asylum but with criminality. Although limited, data on asylum seekers in temporal, spatial, and legal limbo between nation-states prompt conceptualization of enforcement practices as the haunting of sovereign and biopolitical powers and the recursive relationship between offshore and onshore detention practices.

Those countries with historically the largest per capita refugee re-settlement programs—Australia, Canada, and the United States—also exercise the most advanced "front-end" border enforcement strategies to inhibit what policy makers refer to as spontaneous arrivals, those who arrive to make a claim for protection without having been selected or assisted by governments. These wealthy resettlement states of the Global North prefer to exercise choice in the resettlement of refugees and posit the managed process of refugee selection to be—alongside border enforcement—"the right to sovereign assertion," as one Austra-lian immigration official explained to me (interview, Canberra, April 2006). The displacement that causes asylum seeking thus involves struggles over the respective agency, resources, and resourcefulness of migrants and authorities. These struggles transpire in the context of asymmetrical geopolitical fields where authorities and asylum seekers find themselves intertwined spatially, legally, and materially. States fulfill competing mandates to enforce borders and provide protection for those displaced, and migrants face these contradictions during their transnational journeys. These encounters and negotiations are acutely visible in enforcement practices in the peripheral yet strategic zones of sovereignty where migrants are detained on islands. These exclusions of noncitizens prove central to exercises in sovereign power (Arendt 1958; Agamben 1998; Perera 2009).

In addition to establishing islands as sites where nation-states exploit isolation to control migration, this chapter analyzes why and how island detentions have taken shape within the broader archipelago. As the pace of human migration intensified and public opinion turned against asylum seekers throughout the 1990s and into the new millennium, states displaced border enforcement internally and externally (Bigo 2000; Coleman 2007). In both cases, policing entered the mundane, intimate spaces of daily life.

Detention offshore exemplifies one manifestation of this process, where the bodies and subjectivities of asylum seekers are contained and regulated in the name of border enforcement, national security, and geopolitical imperatives. Through these processes, people on the move are haunted and haunt. Sociologists have primarily applied the concept of haunting where the sociological imagination demarcates oppressive practices carried out in daily life (e.g., Gordon 2008; Cho 2009). Here haunting does geographical work that reveals dimensions of sovereign power enacted offshore, well beyond mainland territory. As a concept, then, haunting serves an important analytical purpose in capturing the mobility of sovereign power as borders are relocated amid the residue of militarized, colonial landscapes. Past haunts present, and detention practices offshore, in turn, haunt detainees onshore. Haunting thus offers one way of mapping state violence. Detention facilities are built on histories of colonial occupation and disposession. In this sense, contemporary violence operates in the wake of earlier grounds of state violence (Sharpe 2016).

In this chapter, I explore not only the role of islands within the archipelago but the platform they provide for haunting of the past in the present. Haunting is appropriate because the silences of the present are broken by eruptions from the past. I proceed by framing understandings of power operating on islands with discussion of legality, securitization, and enforcement. The subsequent section elaborates on the concept of haunting, building on scholarship by Avery Gordon (2008), Grace Cho (2009), and other scholars. The rest of the chapter maps the geopolitical spread of offshore detention funded by Australia on islands in the Indian Ocean region and its embodied effects.

ISLANDS WITHIN THE ENFORCEMENT ARCHIPELAGO

From Robbin to Rikers, islands have historically been used as prisons. The processing of new migrant arrivals and detention of noncitizens have also long transpired on islands, with Ellis and Angel Islands on the U.S. East and West Coasts as examples. Longer-term detention of migrants on islands signals a new round of this phenomenon. This placement has much to do with the spatial relationships between flight, interception, and physical geography. Many transnational journeys to asylum involve water, making the sites where water meets land important thresholds for research on migration (Walters 2008). En route, migrants face possible deterrence through measures that rely increasingly on front-end security, applying the U.S. policy rationale of prevention-through-deterrence with the movement of enforcement offshore to stop people positioned as potential security risks from reaching sovereign territory. The proximity of islands to interceptions, combined with the presence of military bases with facilities that can be converted for processing, often leads to detention on islands. Because they arrive on territory where access to asylum is mediated by geographical distance, those who land do not necessarily become asylum seekers or refugee claimants but remain instead in interstitial legal categories without citizenship status in the territories traversed en route.

There are, of course, more capricious reasons why island detentions emerge. The distance of islands from mainland territory exacerbates the isolation of detainees, limiting access to advocates and asylum. State and nonstate institutions exert more control over detainees, information, and people moving into and out of facilities. Because people are held remotely and difficult to reach, they remain largely hidden from view of media and human rights monitors (Briskman et al. 2008). Like those held in facilities internal to sovereign territory, they are dispersed (Welch 2002; Bloch and Schuster 2005), their access to judicial processes mediated by distance. This dispersal also causes detachment from community and resources more readily available on mainland territory and in large cities such as Sydney, New York, or Vancouver.

Island detentions are not coincidental, though, like U.S. detentions in Guantánamo Bay (Kaplan 2005; Reid-Henry 2007); they are too readily explained as "exceptional." Like the search for asylum and asylum seekers themselves, islands are frequently shrouded in discourses and practices of exceptionalism (e.g., Nicolson 2007). Viewed in isolation, these detentions appear ad hoc, circumstantial matters of convenience, physical geography, and proximity. But when connected, significant factors include location, political status, and post/colonial history. Some, such as Guam, have colonial histories of invasion that have led to militarized landscapes and large bases. In several cases, detention becomes a form of economic development, a residual material haunting through neocolonial control (Teaiwa 2015).

While I map broad spatial and conceptual patterns, I do not want to do so at the risk of erasing particularities and histories. Indeed, the islands discussed differ in important ways, including regional location, proximity to mainland territory, political status, size, and colonial history. Analysis must illuminate in more depth the distinct colonial and neocolonial histories of islands (e.g., Lipman 2012), in the spirit of

FIGURE 9. Boat interception off of Christmas Island, 2010. Photograph by Kate Coddington.

"Where Is Guantánamo?" (Kaplan 2005), which traces the history of Guantánamo Bay, linking historical periods to contemporary biopolitical incarceration. Before 9/11 and the invention of foreign enemy combatants, detainees on Guantánamo included asylum seekers from Haiti and Cuba as early as 1991 (Koh 1994; McBride 1999). Through historical analysis, Kaplan foregrounds the continuities of sovereign power as histories of colonization, imperialism, migration, and militarization. Similarly, Reid-Henry (2007, 628) argues that the "grey area" prompted by Guantánamo's "(extra)territoriality" "has not been conjured out of nowhere: it too is closely indexed to the territory's imperial past." Similar examination of sites where potential asylees are detained will link contemporary detentions to historical trajectories.

Islands become sites of arrival, processing, and detention when migrants arrive or are intercepted as they approach by boat (as in Figure 9).

Similar to Reid-Henry's categorization of Guantánamo as "grey area," individual legal status and territorial political status complicate legality around asylum that arises from the intersection of partial sovereignty. The political status of the territory is determined by its sovereign power and post/colonial histories and, in turn, influences the legal status of

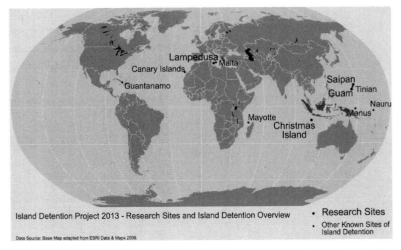

FIGURE 10. Map of islands where people seeking asylum are detained globally.

detainees and whether they will be able to seek asylum. This intersection of territorial status and individual legal status brings political geography and the spatial struggles for rights and sovereignty into relief. On these islands, struggles for legal status overlay complex histories of collective struggles for political autonomy and full citizenship and lay the foundation for further legal and political struggles to ensue.

Figure 10 maps islands where migrants and asylum seekers have been detained in recent years.

This mapping is contemporary and necessarily incomplete. A historical mapping of island detentions would be much longer. Access to asylum on these islands is uncertain, with many ways in which distance mediates claimants' access. The ability to seek asylum on each island is mediated by political status of the island, distance, technology, infrastructure, excision, and degrees of access to asylum and legal representation. One cannot, for example, seek asylum from Indonesia because Indonesia does not observe the 1951 Convention. One may, however, request that a claim be heard by the UNHCR. Other recent migration hot spots, such as Libya and Turkey, have similar political and legal dynamics and become places where people amass and are contained amid their efforts to enter. Further ambiguity ensues in island territories of Italy and Australia, where one can legally make a claim, but where the process is expedited and influenced by location in other ways. In the case of Australia, a two-tier system was developed with differential access for those held offshore. This eventually was extended to a three-tier system, with no access provided to those detained on Australia's behalf on islands belonging to other states (Indonesia, Nauru, and Papua New Guinea). Subsequently, excision was applied to the whole of Australian mainland territory, extending an ambiguous legal regime across broader swaths of territory, a move that resonates with Canada's recent and retroactive extension of its Safe Third Country Agreement to cover more geographical territory.

HAUNTING STATE MOBILITIES ON ISLANDS

Avery Gordon (2008) conceptualizes haunting as the effects of systems of power as they manifest in daily life, especially where they seem to have disappeared and, therefore, been silenced. Her analysis of haunting brings into relief the absent presence: that which is present but silent, not seen, spoken, or known. In the second edition of her book, she revisits the concept, explaining earlier usage and continued relevance:

> Haunting is one way in which abusive systems of power make themselves known and their impacts felt in everyday life, especially when they are supposedly over and done with, or when their oppressive nature is denied. . . . Haunting is not the same as being exploited, traumatized, or oppressed, although it usually involves these experiences or is produced by them. I used the term haunting to describe those singular yet repetitive instances when home becomes unfamiliar, when your bearings on the world lose direction, when the over-and-done-with comes alive, when what's been in your blind spot comes into view. (xvi)

Gordon's analysis implicates the state, calling attention to state violence. I draw on her ideas to conceptualize haunting as the work done on behalf of (though not always directly by) states on islands where sovereign and biopolitical powers envelop asylum seekers. As I show in chapter 4 in the case of Guam, colonial past haunts neocolonial present, often in ways not uttered, but emerging through affective eruptions of past histories of control in the present. These actions and affectual relations also involve complicity, coercion, financial entanglements, and contractual relations between states and nonstate third parties, such as the IOM, that capitalize on the physical geography of islands and colonial histories (Ashutosh and Mountz 2011; Camacho 2012; Teaiwa 2015).

I draw on Gordon to signal the residual effects of oppression and its connection to the state, even where the state appears absent in everyday life. Sometimes states appear absent because the island has entered into a postcolonial period. The colonial past nonetheless positions island populations as partial citizens or citizens who remain financially intertwined with earlier colonizers (e.g., Guam, Nauru, and Christmas Island), and therefore with limited self-governance, resulting in asymmetrical economies ripe for development through detention (akin to rural communities analyzed by Bonds 2009) and other forms of ruination (Stoler 2013). There colonial past haunts what Gregory (2004) and Kaplan (2005) would identify as colonial present. These islands depend on development projects from Australia or on military bases from the United States (Nethery et al. 2013). At other times, states appear absent because those on whose behalf detentions are carried out are obscured, and detainees do not necessarily know who has organized or funded their confinement. Yet, no matter how lost at sea, how complex the legality of liminal geographies, there is the state, present in some form—if concealed in another—to enforce the border, to contain by investing extraordinary resources offshore.

Exclusion requires silence and concealment of certain moves along the peripheral zones of sovereign territory. Through the displacement of the physical border and the reconstitution of virtual, smart, biometric borders elsewhere, sovereign and biopolitical practices increasingly haunt migrants through transnational enforcement, explained earlier. These practices follow migrants across jurisdictions, capture and detain in ambiguous interstitial sites, exclude them from landing on sovereign territory to make a claim for protection, hide them from view, distance them from advocates, and invest tremendous resources, privatizing along the way. These are performative actions, components of haunting that portray state movements offshore and practices of control in locales where migrants enter varying degrees of legal ambiguity. The partial forms of sovereignty, citizenship, and protection on islands (e.g., Baldacchino 2004; Steinberg 2005; Baldacchino and Milne 2006) provide conditions for exploitation and the undermining of responsibilities of signatory states. Island communities become exploited, caught up in the political economy of detention.

Cresswell (2006, 49) posits the state as "the metaphorical enemy of the nomad." He argues, "It is not that the state opposes mobility, but that it wishes to control flows—to make them run through conduits." For Taussig (2004, 294), islands prove one such conduit:

> Like the puppet theatre or the play within the play, miniaturization in the form of an island allows one to hold the world in one's hands, play with it, observe it from different angles, and provide it with different fates. . . . Time is framed in a spatial image. Surrounded by sea.

Offshore detention centers offer opportunities to map state mobilities and power with examination of how and where states are themselves moving to shape others' mobilities. Baldacchino and Milne (2006) locate islands as sites where sovereign power and governance might be understood:

> Islands provide bounded space for the emergence of ingenious new species of asymmetrical economies and governance. The pattern repeats itself again and again where typically large states make creative use of their small, far-flung and remote island jurisdictions to facilitate activities that would be simply anathema on home ground. (488)

Far from anathema, however, internal detentions show characteristics of island facilities, as in the "Gitmos across America" (*New York Times* 2007), to connect onshore and offshore detention of foreign nationals in isolated locations without rights. Taussig (2004), too, sees islands as central to understanding sovereign power and creates lists of islands with prisons, enticing readers to "think of some to add" (283). Whether offshore bank activity or incarceration, Taussig argues that activities occur on islands "not despite but because of the existence of the modern state" (287). John Urry (2014) also explores offshoring and its buffering of "the rich class" from the rest of the world.

Haunting of migrants transpires strategically at the nexus between political status of the island and legal status of the migrant or detainee.

Political status and limited autonomy that emerge from colonial grounds provide a backdrop for struggles over legality: potential asylum seekers enter territory that renders citizenship status ambiguous, thus mediating access to sovereign territory and asylum claimant processes.

Each island visited in this book demonstrates limbo, isolation, and struggles over access between migrants and authorities. Asylum seekers are haunted at the intersection of sovereign and biopolitical power on islands. Sovereignty plays out in these far-flung vanishing points, once theaters of war, now stages where those escaping conflict struggle. The states under discussion have all processed migrants intercepted at sea on islands and entered into legal negotiations over access in recent years. The islands are connected not only to one another but to the detention of migrants internal to sovereign territory as well. As such, the "carceral archipelago" (Gregory 2004) illuminates the biopolitical reconstitution of borders around bodies of asylum seekers where remote detention figures centrally and is itself a mobile practice in processes of securitization.

DETENTION ON ISLANDS: AUSTRALIA'S MANY SOLUTIONS

Islands seem inescapable, not only within the geographical form of the archipelago, but as an isolating form of exclusion. They are an extreme of sorts, exposing the extension of onshore regimes offshore, exploiting geographical distance to deny or restrict access to asylum and economic livelihoods. Australia serves as an exemplary, if extreme, case.

Perera (2009) details uses and meanings of islands in her book on the insular imagination of Australia as colonial settler state and island nation, reconfiguring Glissant's formulation of archipelago, colonialism, and island identities. Perera develops the thesis that the *topos* of the island, distinguished by the relationship between land and sea, proves "central to the geopolitical order of western modernity" (3). She historicizes aggressive, contemporary border enforcement strategies carried out by Australia, placing them in the context of long-standing imaginaries, institutions, and technologies that have produced the "logic of insularity" (5). In so doing, she links the historical containment of aboriginal Australians onshore to the contemporary containment of asylum seekers on islands offshore, thus effectively tracing movement between islands as material stage and spatial concept reproduced on-shore and offshore. Similarly, Bashford and Strange (2002) and Coddington (2014) trace parallel histories of detention and confinement of aboriginal and asylum-seeking populations.

Parallel and interlocking geographies of detention can also be traced between Australia's onshore and offshore enforcement regimes. Australia runs facilities on its sparsely populated northern coast, in the outback, and on islands that are difficult to reach. Indeed, Australia specializes in the design, renovation, and repurposing of its own and other states' territories in order to curtail access to asylum, having extended the reach of its enforcement across the Indian Ocean region through creative contortions of legal geographies. Beginning with John Howard's Pacific Solution, a two-tier system restricts and expedites access among those intercepted offshore. Not only do detainees find their access and mobility restricted, but so too do advocates and activists, including legal representatives and interpreters in sparse supply in remote communities. Although Prime Minister Kevin Rudd announced an end to the Pacific Solution in 2008, various policies and political campaigns prompted the frenetic closing and reopening of island facilities on Christmas Island, the Indonesian archipelago, Nauru, and Papua New Guinea's Manus Island. As if to prove Perera's point, in September 2013, Australia expanded marine interceptions (Operation Sovereign Borders) to stop potential asylum seekers traveling by boat and detain them in reopened facilities on the island state of Nauru and on Papua New Guinea's Manus Island (Hodge 2015).

Australia has had an especially pronounced, shrill relationship with islands in the region, cyclically moving asylum seekers here and there, opening facilities only to close them a few years later, and then reopen them a few years after that—at great expense. Unlike the United States, Australia is an island state that prides itself on control of cross-border flows. In 1992, the government implemented a policy of mandatory detention of anyone who arrived without a visa (Department of Immigration and Multicultural Affairs 2006). Despite this effort at deterrence, in the late 1990s, arrivals by sea increased with smugglers operating through Southeast Asia. Asylum seekers who arrived without visas were placed in detention in remote locations internal to sovereign territory in the outback and along the western and northern coasts (Hugo 2001). Geographic isolation resulted in more restricted access to asylum because detainees remained distant from advocates, information, interpreters, and legal counsel (Mares 2001).

In 2001, a Norwegian merchant vessel, the MV *Tampa*, rescued 433 Afghan asylum seekers from an Indonesian ship off the northern coast of Australia. The ship was prohibited from landing on Australian soil, however, so the captain tried to defy orders. He was told he would only be assisted if the ship remained beyond the twelve-mile zone delineating territorial waters. Prime Minister John Howard was up for reelection and facing low chances in the polls. He drew his line in the sand with the *Tampa* incident, and his reelection was largely credited to this maneuver (Mares 2001). Of course, political maneuvers that capitalize on xenophobia have lasting effects. This moment signaled the introduction of the Pacific Solution to extend remote detention practices offshore (Magner 2004). Australia would not land migrants arriving by sea. Instead, detention was outsourced to islands north of Australia, including the island of Manus in Papua New Guinea, and Nauru. The Solution was an attempt to deter smugglers and illustrates the use of islands to manage migration. The Pacific Solution led to offshore detention on Nauru, Manus, Christmas, and Indonesian islands. These islands have differing political statuses, economies, and geographies (prompting identification of the "Indonesian solution" and the "Indian Ocean solution") yet were all drawn into the geopolitical sphere of Australian border enforcement.

Following the *Tampa* incident, the Australian Parliament met and retroactively declared parts of its sovereign territory no longer to be included in Australia for the purposes of migration. This was called the "power of excision," depicted in Figure 11 and showing overlapping legal regimes: maritime law, which dictates that the captain rescue people imperiled on a ship in distress; international refugee law, which grants them a right to seek protection; and national migration law, from which this territory has been excised.

As a result, those detained offshore now continue to face more expedited hearing processes and fewer rights to appeal. Taylor (2005) argues that migrants carry the legal effects of excision on their bodies, such that even if they later make it from island to mainland territory, they are still excluded from legal channels to asylum by virtue of the location of interception and the corporeal islands that result. By 2012, Australia had extended the excision literally to the bodies of all

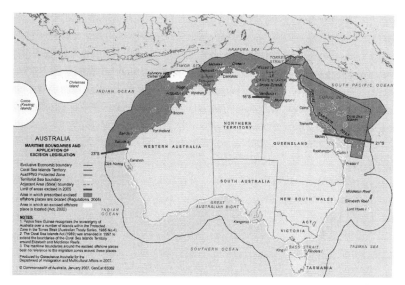

FIGURE 11. Map from Australian Parliamentary report showing "Maritime Boundaries and Application of Excision Legislation," and demonstrating contradictory legal regimes of domestic migration law, international refugee law, and maritime law.

"irregular maritime arrivals," no matter where they entered "Australia." As I explain in chapter 5, Canada would adopt this policy.

The Pacific Solution also corresponded with creative legal solutions to deterrence in the form of detention on Australian sovereign territory. Although the numbers of asylum seekers in detention decreased significantly with policy changes in 2005 and 2006, and a number of large-capacity facilities on mainland Australian territory were "mothballed" and available for reopening with short notice (Department of Immigration and Multicultural Affairs 2006), the immigration department nonetheless granted a lucrative contract for the construction of a controversial facility in the most remote corner of the most remote Australian overseas territory: Christmas Island. The new AU$398 million Australian detention facility that some refer to as the "Gitmo of Australia" opened in 2008 and offers another example of the creative use of geography to mediate access (Hawke and Williams 2011).

In 2008, new Labor leader Prime Minister Kevin Rudd shut down the facilities on Nauru and Manus but increased capacity on Christmas Island and across the Indonesian archipelago (Marr 2009; Taylor 2009).

Unlike other island detentions of the Pacific Solution, Christmas Island is Overseas Territory of Australia. It lies 2,590 kilometers northwest from Perth, the nearest large Australian city and the only current source of flights to the island, but only 350 kilometers south of the Indonesian island of Java (Schalansky 2009, 64). Like Guam, it is governed remotely by federal powers in the capital city, Canberra. The island has a complex governance structure. Its services are provided by the state of Western Australia, and island residents are subjected to all laws of the state of Western Australia, except where the federal government vetoes their implementation. There is a local government consisting of a shire council with limited autonomy. The federal government holds significant power through its ownership and management of the detention centers, the national park that covers much of the island, and, historically, phosphate mining, the main economic enterprise for which the island was originally developed (by the British Phosphate Mining Company).

Numbering approximately twenty-six hundred in July 2010, detainees nearly doubled the nonincarcerated resident population of approximately fourteen hundred. The number of people in detention on the island exceeded three thousand in 2012.

The island detentions of the Pacific Solution mirror the strategies and effects of dispersed detentions internal to sovereign Australian territory in that detainees were removed geographically from communities of advocacy located in larger urban centers. The Solution extended this isolation and invoked creative uses of geography to undermine refugee law, exercising sovereign and biopolitical powers by excising islands through aggressive interceptions at sea and bilateral arrangements to detain and repatriate, or cast migrants to "third countries" in between source and destination. The Australian government relied on third parties to accomplish these tactics, including poorer countries to whom it transferred aid in the source of development and organizations, such as the IOM, to whom the work was contracted. Detainees were successfully removed not only from communities of advocacy but from view altogether, with limited information on how to access the asylum claims process.

DETENTION AS STRATEGY FOR DETACHMENT AND DEVELOPMENT: NEIGHBORLY CONTROL

Australia continues to extend offshore control well beyond its own sovereign territory with a restless search for new islands on which to detain. Under John Howard's Pacific Solution, populations of small island states were put to work in the contracting out of Australia's processing and detention of asylum seekers. Part of the Solution involved heavy investment in interception of smuggling rings in Indonesia (Kevin 2004). As a result, through transfers in the name (literally, the budget line) of international development, the Australian government quietly constructed an extensive landscape for detention across the Indonesian archipelago as part of its own powerful enforcement archipelago spreading out across the region. In its strategy to move enforcement farther offshore, Australia funded detention in twelve to fourteen facilities across the Indonesian archipelago over the last several years.[1]

Nauru is a small, recently independent nation-state that was, from 2001 until 2008, part of Australia's Pacific Solution. Having been mined of phosphate and depleted as part of Australian colonial histories in the region (Teaiwa 2015), some predict the impoverished state may disappear as sea levels rise (Hussein et al. 2011). Migrants intercepted at sea during the Tampa incident and during subsequent interceptions were detained on Nauru. At the time that detentions began in 2001, civil servants on Nauru had not been paid for months due to a budget crisis (Mares 2001). Australia contracted the IOM to run the detention center. Conditions in the center were poor, and resulting illnesses have been well documented (Mares 2001; Gordon 2006). The Australian government would not allow human rights monitors, journalists, refugee lawyers, or priests to visit the island and even revoked visas in cases where they had initially been granted (interview, Canberra, April 2006). This shows significant and creative investments of resources to keep asylum seekers away from sovereign territory and legal advocates and information away from detainees.

People seeking asylum and isolated on Nauru had little information about their cases. Like Taussig's "play within the play," the statement by Monawir Al-Saber, detained on Nauru, with which this chapter opened about the jail within the jail, island within the island, was written during a letter-writing campaign between activists in Australia and detainees on Nauru that illuminated the presence and isolation of migrants intercepted by the Australian Navy and placed in detention (Burnside 2003). The statement highlights the compounding effects of detention on remote and impoverished islands. Although people were allowed at times to come and go from the detention center, they were not allowed to work or leave the island, nor were attorneys and human rights monitors allowed to visit Nauru. Through connections with activists in Australian cities, migrants were able to contract one lawyer in Canberra. She represented her clients for more than two years without ever being able to meet them (interview, Canberra, April 2006). Ultimately, the UNHCR arranged for many detainees on Nauru to be resettled in third countries, including Canada and New Zealand. Still others remained until Nauru's role in the Solution ended (for a time) in 2008.

In 2008, newly elected prime minister Kevin Rudd announced an end to the Pacific Solution. Eventually, some island detention centers, such as Nauru, were shut down, while the large, high-security facility was built to centralize all offshore detention on Christmas Island. By 2010, nearly three thousand detainees were detained on the small island. While mandatory detention ended in 2008 and the Pacific Solution looked like it would become a thing of the past, remnants of the Solution continued to haunt potential asylum seekers en route to Australia through the residual institutional infrastructure of state violence. The facility on Christmas Island opened, and those intercepted at sea continue to be detained there. They face nonstatutory determination processes, detention without administrative review for time limitations, and few rights to appeal (Australian Human Rights Commission 2010). Australia also pushed enforcement offshore with the quiet and hidden funding of the facilities in Indonesia.

In July 2010, newly elected prime minister Julia Gillard announced that all asylum seekers would be processed on East Timor (*West Australian* 2010). News emerged quickly, however, that East Timorese officials had not been consulted; East Timorese civilians protested, and this never came to pass.

In 2012 and 2013, amid continued boat arrivals and intensified political turmoil, offshore strategies were extended under three prime ministers, first under Labor leaders Julia Gillard and Kevin Rudd, and then under Conservative Party leader Tony Abbott. In July 2013, during his brief return to office, Kevin Rudd announced the Regional

FIGURE 12. *West Australian* front-page headline announces Prime Minister Julia Gillard's plans to process people seeking asylum in Australia on East Timor, July 7, 2010. Photograph by Kate Coddington.

Resettlement Arrangement with Papua New Guinea (Department of Foreign Affairs and Trade 2015): all asylum seekers arriving by boat on any part of its territory would be processed on Manus Island and Nauru and resettled in Papua New Guinea (Doherty 2015b), with no chance of resettlement in Australia. This involved the transfer of people detained on Christmas Island to Manus Island, forty-eight hundred kilometers away, beginning in November 2012 (Amnesty International 2013, 3). These transfers happened in the middle of the night, often with little to no warning in advance.

Amnesty International (2013, 3–4) found a host of human rights violations in the detention of asylum seekers on Manus Island, including risk of refoulement, discrimination against asylum seekers based on time and means of arrival, failure to provide procedural protections required under international law, and failure to treat all people in detention humanely. After his election in September 2013, Tony Abbott extended this offshore regime with an aggressive marine interception campaign called Operation Sovereign Borders and the continued detention of all asylum seekers on Nauru and Manus (Hodge 2015). According to statements by Scott Morrison, minister for immigration and citizenship, when the operation was launched, it relied heavily on the premise of deterrence:

> Our resolve to implement what we have promised the Australian people, to stop the boats, is absolute. Those seeking to come on boats will not be getting what they have come for. They will be met by a broad chain of measures end to end that are designed to deter, to disrupt, to prevent their entry from Australia and certainly to ensure that they are not settled in Australia. (cited by Tang and Hammond 2014, 3)

Once Operation Sovereign Borders was implemented, the number of people detained on the islands increased fivefold (Amnesty International 2013, 12). While men traveling alone and male unaccompanied minors were sent to Manus Island, women and families traveling together were sent to Nauru. There Amnesty also found poor conditions, including inadequate access to personal space, natural light, fresh air, or water for those detained. Those held had "little or no access to phones or internet" (6) and were blocked from accessing the UNHCR by telephone (the organization's website was also blocked). Amnesty also found support for medical and mental health to be inadequate (7). Amnesty International found that one year after the reopening of the facilities on Nauru, only 160 people had succeeded in submitting asylum claims, and none had yet received a refugee status determination (8). Even if successful in these claims, no claimants would be eligible for resettlement in Australia.

By September 2014, two years later, the population of people in detention on Australian territory, including Christmas Island, had dropped to 3,314 total, with 920 on Christmas Island and 2,394 in mainland facilities (Department of Immigration and Border Protection 2014). Approximately twenty-five hundred were being held in facilities on Nauru and Manus. Alarming reports of violence committed by local authorities against detainees emerged in 2013 (Hall and Gordon 2013) and continued into 2015. In protest of their detention and their resettlement on Manus and Nauru, people in detention carried out hunger strikes, riots, self-harm, suicide, and suicide attempts.

By October 2014, the number of people detained on the two islands climbed to 4,135. In January 2015, approximately seven hundred men detained on Nauru embarked on a two-week hunger strike, with some undertaking further self-harm by swallowing razor blades and washing detergent. The protest ended with local police breaking down barricades set up by detainees and placing dozens either in solitary confinement within the facility or under arrest in a local prison (Doherty 2015b). Similarly, in March 2015, two hundred adults and children were arrested during peaceful demonstrations on Nauru as managing authorities transitioned to a more open facility that allowed asylum seekers to come and go during the day (Doherty 2015a).

In the restless search for other island solutions in the region, in September 2014, Australia committed AU$40 million in aid to Cambodia over a four-year period to resettle an unspecified number of these asylees (Carmichael 2014). In this progression, exclusionary discourses made space for more exclusionary practices, and the enforcement archipelago extended outward into the region. Like Gillard's East Timor plan, this one went nowhere. Fewer than five people were resettled in Cambodia, and in 2016, a Cambodian official declared the agreement a failure.

The Australian government has thus contributed significantly to the death of asylum by steadily shutting down its asylum processing onshore, with the interception and detention of most asylum seekers now happening offshore. The securitization of migration in Australia's regional enforcement archipelago has been repurposed time and again by successive prime ministers. Each national political campaign rolled out a new strategy for interception and detention offshore, accompanied by xenophobic narratives that preyed on fear of outsiders (Tsiolkas 2013). Remaining invisible was the plight of detainees shuttled quietly and endlessly through the system, their lives devalued through their very invisibility to national and transnational publics.

A FOURTH TIER OF ASYLUM SEEKING IN THE REGION: INDONESIA

Following the creation of two tiers of asylum seekers with the Pacific Solution, Australia quietly also created additional tiers of asylum seekers farther offshore with the use of excision. The first tier includes those with the most rights who are "in" Australia for purposes of detention and asylum law. The second tier includes those who are in Australia (on Australian soil, such as Christmas Island) and in detention, but not in Australia for the purposes of migration, as they are in excised zones. The third tier includes those who are held under Australian control but not in Australia (e.g., people on Manus Island and Nauru). The fourth tier includes those who are not in Australian control—but directly influenced by Australian asylum policies and resources to contain offshore, but not in Australia (e.g., Indonesia).

Persons in this fourth tier are estimated to be in the hundreds. They were intercepted at sea and remained housed on islands for several years in Indonesia (Taylor 2009). The precariousness of those on their way to Australia to make refugee claims is linked to the neocolonial relations between Australia and the islands where it contracts out detention. In December 2007, I visited twenty-one Hazara men, women, and children who had fled Afghanistan in 2001 and were ensnared at sea and subjected to regional management. They were intercepted with a larger group of some 240 Afghans by the Australian Navy at Ashmore Reef and towed to the Indonesian island of Lombok. They had been living in limbo in an open detention facility—an inexpensive motel—in Lombok's capital city of Mataram for several years (Refugee Action Collective 2005).

Lombok offers an example of the ambiguity that asylum seekers confront in detention between states. Asylum seekers detained at the time were from Afghanistan, Iraq, Vietnam, and Sri Lanka (interview, Mataram, December 2007). They were held in Indonesia in facilities managed by the IOM, hired contractually by the Australian federal government to do "custodial care" with the cooperation of a complicit Indonesian government. With few avenues to resettlement in third countries, people stay in limbo for years in Indonesia. When I visited, Australian activists were still working to ascertain who was building and running the detention centers cropping up on Indonesian islands. Detainees received stipends to buy food from the IOM. They were allowed to come and go from the detention facilities but could not work or leave the island. They were visited regularly by Indonesian immigration authorities and encouraged to return home in exchange for AU$2,000 offered as a return package from the IOM. In mid-December, the men were removed suddenly from the women and children and sent to isolation detention on Sulawesi Island as a tactic to pressure them to hasten their departure from Lombok (personal correspondence, December 2007).

This island detention prompts a number of questions, including the amount of development offered to Indonesia by Australia in exchange for services. In interviews, immigration authorities mentioned "informal" development projects, such as a new airport computer system, in exchange for Indonesian contributions to Australia's offshore enforcement programs (interview, Canberra, April 2006). As with detainees on Nauru, activists and advocates in Australia found ways to communicate with and advocate on behalf of detainees on Lombok, particularly successful when pressing the Australian government with the change of leadership in December 2007. Australian refugee lawyers for the migrants on Lombok struggled to establish their legal status in relation to sovereign territory and to ascertain who was accountable for the conditions or the very fact of their detention. Under other circumstances, their country of origin—in this case, Afghanistan—would negotiate on their behalf, but the country struggled as the detention continued. Through behind-the-scenes negotiations with the new government, the small group was resettled in Australia in 2008. Hundreds of others from Afghanistan and elsewhere remained in limbo on Lombok and on a growing list of other Indonesian islands. Their presence signals the geopolitical relations among states in the region and the power to "contract out" asylum responsibilities through detention offshore. Although Prime Minister Kevin Rudd supported changes in detention practices onshore, interceptions and detentions offshore continued quietly until coming to light with the publicity surrounding the interception of Sri Lankan Tamils in 2009 (Refugee Action Collective 2010). Efforts to silence offshore detentions failed repeatedly at the hands of activists and asylum seekers themselves, who communicated their plight via mobile phone, internet, and mainstream media to global publics. Migrants on boats pursued new strategies, with one group of Sri Lankan Tamils refusing to disembark when intercepted by Indonesian authorities off the port of Merak, a refusal to enter island detention facilities onshore. They remained on the ship for a few months before authorities finally stormed the ship and placed them in detention.

By the time we returned to Indonesia to conduct research in 2011, there were twelve to fourteen detention centers funded by Australia in operation (Taylor 2009), shown in Figure 13. This map was remarkably difficult to assemble due to the difficulty of finding and verifying information, statistics, and locations. These facilities are managed with a high degree of secrecy, or people are held there with a degree of secrecy. In 2008, Australia's minister for immigration, Chris Evans, publicly denied their existence in a radio interview with the Australian Broadcasting Corporation.[2] The facilities varied greatly in terms of security, location, management, and the possibility of visits by outsiders. In the last few years, some of these facilities were no longer used to detain asylum seekers en route to Australia, and Indonesia began to contest Australia's marine interception practices in its territorial waters more publicly with Operation Sovereign Borders (Hodge 2015). Over the last few years, Indonesia shifted to "alternatives to detention," strategic alternatives to spatial confinement (see Missbach 2017).

As nation-states study one another for best practices, Australia played a key role in setting the stage for subsequent exclusions of asylum seekers arriving by boat globally. It has become popular in the new field referred to as global governance of migration (Betts 2010; Koser 2010) to connect migration and development. Few, however, have explored the more sinister side of regulating migration with detention as development strategy, as in the Australian case. Here the most economically and geopolitically powerful country in the region is able to exercise control over its neighbors to extend the enforcement archipelago through its substantial sphere of influence (shown in the map of detention in the region, Figure 14). This dynamic is not isolated to Australia in the Pacific but equally at work in what EU authorities refer to as their "neighborhood" (Geiger and Pécoud 2010) and by the United States in the Americas (Noble 2011).

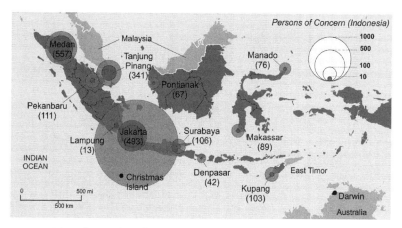

FIGURE 13. Map of Australian-funded detention of noncitizens on their way to Australia to make asylum claims and detained in facilities across Indonesia in 2012.

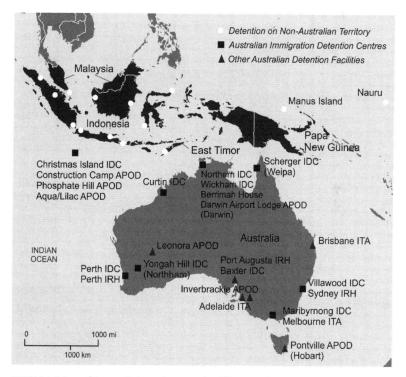

FIGURE 14. Map of Australia's onshore and offshore enforcement archipelago.

EMBODIED EFFECTS OF DETENTION

As important as mapping the material infrastructure of exclusionary state practices in the archipelago is documenting the experiences of people detained there, while they are in detention and after they are released. One former detainee from Palestine whom I interviewed in Sydney, Australia, in March 2006 had been held for several years, first in Port Hedland and then in the Villawood Immigration Detention Centre on the outskirts of Sydney. At Villawood, in the suburbs of Australia's largest city, he had more contact with the outside world. Prior to that, in Port Hedland, he was more isolated on the coast of northern Australia and had little access to information. He described what it was like not to know even basic world news until months later:

> Six months they kept us in small buildings. Twenty-four inside. Just we have one hour [outdoors] in the morning. One hour in the morning we get outside, and then back inside. . . . Six months inside there not knowing anything about what is happening in the world. After six months, I heard the news that George W. Bush was elected president six months ago.

As the global growth in detention and offshoring of border enforcement converge, migrants encounter proliferating spatial forms of the island along their transnational journeys. They end up crossing multiple borders and often spend time in different spaces of confinement in different countries over a period of years. The following journey of Aarif offers a case in point. We met Aarif when he was in detention in the western city of Perth. Prior to our interview, he had spent several years and invested many resources attempting to land. He made four journeys from his home country of Afghanistan, depicted in solid lines in Figure 15. Aarif was also deported twice, depicted by the dotted lines. On his first journey, Aarif traveled through Pakistan to Indonesia but was detained on Christmas Island and Nauru and then flown back home. His second and third attempts also went through Pakistan but ended in Iran. His fourth attempt was similar to the first but traversed Malaysia and involved several years in detention in Indonesia, before the journey resumed and he was subsequently detained on Christmas

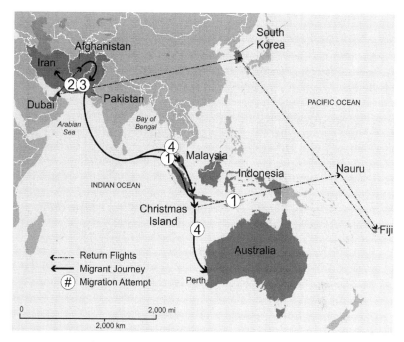

FIGURE 15. Map of one Afghan man's four journeys from Afghanistan to reach Australia over a period of seven years, which included detention, deportation, and movement through ten countries.

Island and in Perth. Aarif's journeys demonstrate the temporal and spatial limbo in multiple spaces of confinement along the way.

For the several thousand detainees held on islands farther offshore, the effects of isolation prove even more pronounced. Migrants carry the highly embodied burden of excision and offshore detention and the significant resources invested in keeping them in remote locations. Among their experiences of isolation is separation from family, whether those who remained behind at home, those lost during the journey, or those taken to other detention facilities. This situation becomes especially difficult for families with children, particularly when men are held separately from women and children.

Many children have been born into detention on Christmas Island, and pregnant women detained there experience a particularly acute situation. Because adequate medical facilities do not exist on the island, pregnant women are flown to the mainland for medical services. In 2006,

I interviewed an advocate based in Perth who was tracking the situation of one pregnant woman detained on Christmas Island. Every time the woman needed to see a doctor, she was flown on a charter flight with guards to Perth and then returned back to the island. Rather than transferring her to existing facilities in and around Perth, they continued this pattern of investment to maintain distance. As the advocate observed, "this pregnant woman was flown in excess of 50,000 kilometers during her pregnancy. This is the length that Australia will go to keep these people off Australian soil" (interview, Perth, March 2006).

After the opening of North West Point Detention Centre in 2008, the number of people detained on Christmas Island increased significantly. The practice was then to move pregnant women to Darwin to very large detention facilities with more access to medical services. The government was again criticized by refugee advocacy groups, this time for moving only women and not their male partners, resulting in separation of thousands of kilometers between pregnant women and partners. In late 2014, women with children held in detention on Christmas Island complained about environmental effects on their children's respiratory conditions, and the Australian government decided to transfer them to Nauru, then faced criticism from human rights groups, such as the Australian Rights Commission (2014) and Amnesty International, for rendering this group even more precarious with the shift to foreign soil. These moves of pregnant women and children and the separation of families are a form of Pratt and Rosner's (2006) global intimate, with intimate relations between physical distance, the body, and the emotional turmoil of remote detention carried by families and individuals. Nauru, furthermore, has a poor human rights record, with little accountability for issues directly affecting asylum seekers held there in the last few years. Issues such as sexual and physical abuse led to rioting and hunger strikes, and in May 2015, the authorities banned Facebook as a way to restrict the flow of information to or from the island. Critics linked this move directly to the efforts of activists and asylum seekers to share information about their plight (*Oceania* 2015).

In Indonesia, conditions were worse, with fewer guidelines issued by the UNHCR pertaining to detention of asylum seekers followed because the country is not a signatory. Key among these guidelines is that wherever possible, children should not be detained and families should not be separated. Take, for example, this excerpt from field notes recorded by research assistant Kate Coddington during fieldwork in Jakarta in December 2011:

> SURABAYA detention center: one man has three children . . . all under 6 years. All are in cell with 18 men. The baby, 14-month-old, was taken by guards. Sometimes they bring the baby to visit, at first through the fence but now father can hold baby. For 4 months the family was not let out of the cell but now they are able to get out occasionally. [Activists] alerted UNHCR, Canberra, Geneva. All claim that they are aware and can do nothing.

Too many people in prolonged periods of uncertainty in remote detention experience psychological and physical manifestations of stress brought on by uncertain status and prolonged separation from family: sleeplessness, depression, anxiety, stomach pain, and self-harm among these (see Steel et al. 2006; Coffey et al. 2010). Trauma is a widespread reaction to detention (Robjant et al. 2009). Research findings in Australia show correlations between the length of stay in detention and incidents of self-harm, suicide attempts, and mental illness (Green and Eager 2010; Neave 2013). Remoteness exacerbates these expressions of uncertainty, isolation, stress, and trauma and also reduces access to mental health care professionals, a finding of the Australian Human Rights Commission (2011). Within the national system of detention on Australian (mainland and island) territory, rates of self-harm are higher in more remote facilities (Neave 2013, 2).

As Savitri Taylor (2005) has argued from a legal perspective, even when detainees are moved to mainland detention centers or released from detention on mainland soil, they carry the lasting effects and legal ramifications of detention in one of Australia's zones of excision like legal and psychological bubbles on their bodies. The effects of offshore detention carried across time and space are not only legal but disciplinary and psychological as well.

For those who remain in detention for prolonged periods of time, the situation deteriorates. Consider the story of a Sri Lankan Tamil man after two and a half years in detention, first on Christmas Island, where we met him, and then in Melbourne, where Kate visited him a year later:

> Said that he'd had such destructive thoughts the past couple weeks—
> heard voices telling him to hang himself from the fan, from the
> fence, decided that a hunger strike was the least destructive thing
> he could do. First in 2.5 years of detention. He was so depressed that
> he didn't see other options. (field notes, Melbourne, October 2011)

We visited Dinesh on Christmas Island and Kate again one year later in
an onshore detention facility in Melbourne. After he was moved and had
experienced two and a half years in detention, he was losing his grip on
reality. Small objects in his environment were speaking to him, telling
him to harm himself and end his life. For Dinesh, the movement from
offshore to onshore detention and the relative "freedom" of detention
in Melbourne mattered less than the continuous suspension of time in
the confined life of the enforcement archipelago. Without losing his
life, Dinesh expressed his time in detention *in relation to his end of life*:
as a form of deathly living and living death.

Shortly after Australian prime minister Gillard announced her plan
to process all asylum seekers on East Timor, Canadian authorities intercepted a boat carrying asylum seekers from Sri Lanka and began public
debate of the Australian "solution" of interception offshore. Globally,
when protests erupted and media attention was garnered, migrants
were moved elsewhere: from Guam to Tinian, Lombok to Sulawesi,
and Lampedusa to Sicily. Amid intensified policing at sea and implementation of Italy's pushback policy to prevent arrivals with increased
interception and return to Libya, smuggling routes shifted and migrant
arrivals grew on nearby Greece and Malta (Lutterbeck 2009).

After having declared a dramatic end to the Pacific Solution when
elected to power in 2008, reelected prime minister Kevin Rudd not only
supported its revival by reopening the facility on Nauru but extended
the use of islands with his announcement in July 2013—when he was
campaigning against Gillard—that all asylum seekers intercepted by
boat en route to Australia would be processed on Manus in Papua New
Guinea (Department of Foreign Affairs and Trade 2013). The Pacific
Solution was thus reborn, but in more extreme fashion, with those detained beyond Australian territory no longer securing the right to seek
asylum. After all offshore asylum seeking was consolidated on Christmas
Island, people intercepted were brought once again to Nauru and Manus, where protests ensued and the facilities were burned down. Still,

detention there continued amid outcries regarding conditions and minimal access to protection (from Amnesty International and other human rights organizations). Amnesty International released a report in late 2013, several months after detention had been reopened on Nauru, that only one claim for asylum had been processed there. Eventually, those who were able to secure status through the UNHCR were resettled in third countries, including a people trade with the United States wherein refugees from Manus were flown there for resettlement in exchange for U.S. asylees flown to Australia. When this book went to press, over seven hundred had been quietly resettled in the United States, despite Donald Trump's insistence that this had been Barack Obama's "dumb deal" with Australia. Still others remained in limbo on Manus, including journalist Behrouz Boochani, who clandestinely created a film and award-winning literary memoir documenting human rights abuses on the island using WhatsApp. He was finally resettled in New Zealand in 2019.

Amid the hypervisible and shrill public discourse accompanying each of these vertiginous offshore shifts in the archipelago, what must not be forgotten are the lives of those experiencing prolonged detention and sometimes slow deaths as they languish in offshore detention. Dinesh continued behind bars five years after his arrival on Christmas Island. Even though he had been granted refugee status in Australia based on his claim, he was not granted a security certificate and therefore could not leave detention. Decisions surrounding security certificates are secret, with no reason given for the decision to turn someone down.

I have provided here but a few examples of the embodied effects of spatial, temporal, and legal limbo in the archipelago and return to further discussion of these experiences in chapter 5. The period of uncertainty and precariousness in detention is traumatic. For those who have fled trauma, it prolongs experiences of posttraumatic stress disorder and causes what has been called *retraumatization* (Sinnerbrink et al. 1997; Coffey et al. 2010). Many we interviewed expressed the despair and depression that come with not knowing when their situation will be resolved. As time goes on, people lose hope, and mental health issues become more pronounced. Deeper isolation exacerbates this problem (Neave 2013), and Christmas Island had the highest rate of suicide in facilities across the country. When it housed about one-third of detainees in Australia, more than 50 percent of the suicides and instances of self-harm recorded in the system transpired on the island (Bastians 2011).

CONCLUSIONS

Like the United States and the EU, Australia has shown a deep ambivalence toward migrants and migration, facilitating the arrival of
some while taking extreme measures to repel and punish others. This
ambivalence takes expression through vertiginous movements of border enforcement and detention capacity that proliferate onshore, then
move populations offshore, and then on and off again. No sooner is one
offshore detention regime, such as the Pacific Solution, declared unjust
than another begins, with new infrastructure to detain across Indonesia
and older infrastructure reopened on Nauru and Manus in Papua New
Guinea. These repeated offshore moves capitalize on multiple forms of
distancing. Island and archipelago are repurposed at a frenetic pace, a
mechanism through which the Australian government dehumanizes,
invisibilizes, and moves migrants offshore.

As borders move offshore to create carceral spaces, detainees are
haunted by the nexus of sovereign powers, subnational jurisdiction,
and biopolitical surveillance. Although remote from mainland territory, islands prove central to understanding sovereign power offshore,
detention practices onshore, and the death of asylum. The dislocation
of those detained remains intimately linked to the displacement of the
border and its reconstitution in detention centers on islands. At the
same time that islands proliferate within islands in the enforcement
archipelago, so too are islands mobilized beyond islands to isolate
people with precarious status on mainland territories (which I explore
in detail with regard to Canada in chapter 5).

Migration scholars increasingly study liminality of status and jurisdiction (Maillet 2017; Maillet et al. 2018). Baldacchino and Milne
(2006, 490) argue that binaries between sovereign and nonsovereign
territory no longer serve as helpful tools for understanding sovereign
territoriality and the international state system. But exclusion feeds on
the blurring of work done by sovereign and nonsovereign actors and
with the mobility of enforcement practices between offshore and onshore
locations. The blurring of inside and out, onshore and off, becomes a
highly productive ambiguity for sovereign power. Just as strategies of
war abroad are used at home (as in the securing of American cities after
9/11), so too are islands prototypes for detention practices enacted on
mainland territory.

Taussig (1997) argues that states grow more powerful through dis-embodiment. The dizzying array of institutional actors who carry out detention and processing embody this power and the intimate econo-mies in which they are embroiled (Conlon and Hiemstra 2016). It be-comes unclear who is detained on islands, and by whom. Geopolitical arrangements among state and nonstate institutions, whether entrepre-neurial with third parties or bilateral with other states, carry out the complicated work of processing, deterrence, and detention, replacing sovereign arrangements in the management of displacement. The mobile border is perpetually reconstituted around the body of the asylum seeker in a proliferation of sites between states, national and international legal and security regimes, and state and nonstate actors. The political geography of islands thus entails the study of paradoxical locations (the fluid port of entry, the island within the island), with sustained attention to interstitial sites. Haunting is one tool to understand state oppression through the complex geographical arrangements designed to control mobility.

In this chapter, I mapped the enforcement archipelago as it ensnared potential asylum seekers en route to sovereign territory to make a claim for protection. The practices discussed in this chapter require researchers to move to peripheral zones of sovereign territory from the margins to the center of their analyses. There liminality is lived in the global intimacy of remote detention and the intimate economies of waiting. Here I explored islands as sites of territorial struggle in the archipelago and locations where states manage migration and shrink spaces of asylum through strategic use of islands to govern migration. A global constellation of European, Australian, and North American islands function as strategic sites of migration management where disputes over legality, access, and sovereignty erupt.

Asylum-seeking trends provide insight into geopolitical fields where authorities and migrants negotiate displacement. Island detentions are one containment strategy that reflects broader geopolitical relations between states and prompts questions about what kinds of power op-erate in "exceptional" sites. Geopolitically paradoxical, islands occupy marginal zones far from administrative centers of power, visibility, and public scrutiny. Some become backdoor entrances to work and asylum. Simultaneously, states utilize islands for processing and detention, with people held simultaneously hypervisible to island populations yet invis-ible to international communities and national publics on mainland territories. This analysis thus prompts attention to the dialectical spatial relations between administrative centers and geographical margins of sovereignty, the registers of exclusion and visibility operationalized there, and the urgency of analytical attention to such sites by political geographers.

Most knowledge in the state-centric field of immigration is arranged around a desire to document the experiences of particular categories of people moving from or to particular countries: source country, nationality, ethnicity, legal status, religion, or occupation in the "host" country. But data collected at national territorial scales often overlook exclusion at the border, whether onshore or offshore. I have organized analysis around an alternative geography: management of migration on islands. Global migration by definition crosses borders between states, but little attention is paid to such spaces in between (see, however, Das and Poole 2004; Nevins and Aizeki 2008).

This shift brings sites of struggle over asylum into conceptual models of sovereignty. Asylum seekers on islands are detained at the nexus between political status, which involves partial sovereignty (which means legal ambiguity for the asylum seeker), and biopolitical power, which captures the individual through everyday productions of legal status through surveillance. Intensified practices of exclusion thus require an ontology that accounts for silence and a methodology to document concealment offshore.

While studied in isolated fashion, analysis that conceptualizes islands not as isolated sites but rather as component parts of broader spatial patterns within the archipelago proves vital to understanding the relationship between remote detention and the securitization of migration. As introduced in the preface, the island is a proliferating spatial form that produces and intensifies precarity across the archipelago. Further microgeographies of isolation take place in situ: the separation of those seeking asylum from information, representation, and fellow asylum seekers. Christmas Island has been repurposed as one such punitive space within the larger system, with the design of additional solitary confinement cells. Detainees held elsewhere across the country are flown there and placed in solitary confinement when they are deemed a threat either to others (often due to participation in protests) or to themselves. There they are held—ironically or absurdly—in the most isolated part of the high-security facility on the most isolated part of the most remote bit of Australian territory.

The topological border is reproduced on the island, with islands replicating within themselves. What, after all, is a prison on an island but an island on an island? And what is a solitary confinement cell within that prison but an island within an island within an island? The person detained becomes an island within an island within an island within an island.

Given these conditions, the body becomes the only remaining political space from which to speak, and self-harm, hunger strikes, and suicide attempts and successes increase in number. In their strategic reclamations of their own visibility, such as those that opened this chapter—migrants sending missives to mainland audiences by writing letters about islands as jails and digging their own graves in detention compounds—migrants continue to haunt the international state system as ghostly figures that are out of place, not belonging, but nevertheless not going away.

The body too becomes an island in an environment that bestows much value on the isolating effects of bits of territory. The island affixes itself to the body, following migrants and asylum seekers with legal bubbles, suspended time, and retraumatization. One need not travel to remote islands to see the form and features of islands; they are everywhere.

Subsequent research must historicize islands in colonial, postcolonial, and militarized landscapes. Next steps thus include close readings of individual islands through historical, geopolitical, and geoeconomic lenses to further understand their role in the intersecting processes of migrant displacement and relocation. Part of the way that the past haunts the present is through the repurposing of previous military sites for migration management. Through this infrastructure, and through forces unseen and unheard but ever present, the past assembles the present, with histories of occupation and colonization an absent presence. Not only are asylum seekers made invisible on a heavily militarized island foreclosed upon but so too are the colonial grounds on which this happens. Forces of control affect everyone on the island, if not in the same way.

The Australian example shows the extreme desire of states to isolate and the extraordinary resources they are willing to invest to carry out the spectacular and performative spatial fetish on islands. Yet the spatial fetish of the island is not confined to the island; it is a form reproduced and reverberating across facilities in mainland territories as well.

4

Remote Detention: Proliferating Patterns of Isolation and Confinement

In this chapter, I locate and detail emergent spatial patterns and practices in detention, drawing primarily on discussion of the U.S. detention system. Whereas Giorgio Agamben (1998) theorizes the historical trajectory of the modern camp as one that is perpetually reconstituted everywhere and threatens everyone, this chapter posits contemporary detention practices as strategically located in particular times and places to position particular racialized groups in marginalized, isolated, and exploitable locations. As the genealogy of externalization showed, the United States has played a leading role in developing and implementing exclusionary enforcement practices over the last four decades (Mountz and Loyd 2014; Loyd and Mountz 2018). Chapter 1's genealogy located the United States as the first country to externalize asylum and develop offshore detention. While neither alone nor hegemonic, the country is particular for the size and scope of its detention regime. It is also revealing of patterns of detention and capricious legal geographies that resonate in other national settings.

The United States today holds the largest population of detainees and the most expansive landscape of detention onshore with the greatest reach offshore. Numbers of detainees and deportees have reached historic highs in recent years, with the largest number of people ever deported from the United States in one year (under President Barack Obama during fiscal year 2013). From October to December 2015, the United States detained an average of 29,784 on any given day in 209 facilities (ICE 2015). After President Trump took office in 2017, immigration-related enforcement intensified again (McElwee 2018).

Within the U.S. system, detainees are hidden, invisibilized in a variety of ways. Remote forms of detention proliferate. This system traffics in isolation and invisibility with spatial forms detailed throughout this chapter. The United States detains on mainland territory and on islands (in its own territory and others'). The same forms of isolation found on islands can also be found onshore. This chapter and chapter 3 discuss both, juxtaposing them to disrupt the binary that artificially divides enforcement practices happening onshore and off.

Sometimes detention facilities are themselves geographically remote—distanced from powerful urban centers and legal representation, rendering people confined there dispersed, detached, hidden. Through dispersal, a degree of geographical and legal *ambiguity* accompanies the many disparate locations of detention. In other cases, people may be held in urban centers and mainstream facilities, essentially hidden in plain sight and in close proximity to more populated urban settings. In addition to drawing on empirical research, this chapter introduces efforts to map detention being undertaken at national and transnational scales. These efforts include activist campaigns to locate detainees and to map detention in Europe, the United States, and Australia, a topic to which I return in chapter 6. Activists—detainees and former detainees among them—design campaigns to counter the isolation of detention. In effect, they create countertopographies (Katz 2001) built on a politics of location: projects that aim to locate and reveal, embody and recover, in the wake of concealment and loss (Tolia-Kelly 2006). These efforts offer political potential because locating and mapping operate as tools to reconnect migrants to families, networks of advocates, and broader communities by challenging exclusionary spatial orders.

HOW REMOTE DETENTION DIFFERS FROM THE "CAMP"

As a result of the global growth in and geographic sprawl of detention and border enforcement, spaces and periods of confinement that migrants experience during their journeys across borders have increased. These are highly varied spaces of confinement, ranging from the formal high-security, purpose-built facilities to more informal and ad hoc detention spaces where authorities intercept people.

The growth of remote detention—geographical locations designed to inhibit access and paths to asylum—capitalizes on ontological insecurity, prioritizing the precarity of legal limbo and the violence of detention over refuge and contributing to the ontological death of asylum. Ontological death differs from ontological insecurity (Giddens 1991; Katz 2007; Hyndman and Giles 2016). Whereas ontological insecurity introduces precarity and threatens social identity, ontological death means the end of the possibility of that identity existing. For example, when asylum seekers are prevented from landing on sovereign territory where they become asylum seekers by virtue of the legal recognition of a claim to asylum, they will never actually become asylum seekers; this category of people ceases to exist for those relegated to and confined on offshore sites. This growth in detention offshore mirrors the dynamics of enforcement across the archipelago where, as their landing is prevented, people are prevented from becoming asylum seekers. They are often not referred to as asylum seekers but rather as migrants.

Remote detention therefore proves fundamental to the ontological death of asylum; when people are removed from view, they become paradoxically hidden and securitized by the spectacular nature of this security industry. The search for asylum is lost in this double move, the journey disappearing alongside asylum seekers themselves. As a result, scholars have shifted focus to these journeys (e.g., Collyer 2007, 2010; Khosravi 2010; Vogt 2013; Mainwaring and Bridgen 2016; Crawley et al. 2018).

Migration and border studies scholars have also been drawing on Agamben's (1998) conceptualization of the "camp" as paradigmatic of contemporary forms of sovereignty and political violence. For Agamben, the camp always looms as a threat that can be mobilized in any time and place deemed exceptional as a mechanism to exclude. Claudio Minca (2007, 78, 90) extends this work on the camp into a new spatial ontology of power, with the camp and permanent state of exception "a new *nomos* on global politics." Agamben's theory of the camp is well rehearsed and critiqued in existing literature on detention and refugee camps. Adam Ramadan (2012), for example, argues that the camp can be understood as a space where refugees forge solidarity and identity and exercise human agency. Here I build on existing critiques of Agamben by Ramadan (2012) and others seeking to understand refugee camps by looking at spatial patterns of detention, confinement, and isolation not as ubiquitous, universal, or totalizing but as historically and spatially patterned. For Ramadan, the refugee camp is a place where sovereign power is spatially configured in particular ways; I extend his analysis to remote detention and ask whether the island is the new camp.

Remote detention diverges from Agamben's camp in three important ways. First, these are not universal or ubiquitous geographical spaces but historically and spatially patterned. As Agamben (2005, 55) notes, "the precise scope and location of sovereignty and its jurisdiction is never final, but always fleeting." Yet these fleeting and fluid understandings of sovereignty do not always feature their historicization, their important colonial geographies and ligatures, or what Ann Stoler (2013) calls "imperial debris." Geographies of exclusion and confinement must be located spatially and historically to be more deeply understood as continuities between past and present (e.g., Kaplan 2005; Vine 2009).

While remote detention sites may appear ad hoc, understanding them as spatial patterns shows how geographies of exclusion operate beyond local and regional scales, connecting national contexts to global trends, onshore to offshore strategies (Loyd and Mountz 2018). This chapter reviews a range of ways in which this isolation occurs on mainland sovereign territory and calls attention to the ways that states have entered into the intimacies of the daily lives of migrant workers on a security continuum.

Scholars also show how nation-states operate across borders to capture migrants through arrest, detention, and—for some—deportation. For example, Nancy Hiemstra (2012, 2013) shows how detention and deportation function as entwined systems; these entwined systems work together to suppress access to asylum. In so doing, states extend fields of security and sovereignty (Collyer and King 2015), linking internal and external security measures and "converging on the figure of the migrant, as the key point inside a continuum of threats" (Bigo 2000, 174). Sometimes detainees move through this continuum rapidly, and other times—and more recently—they are in a painstakingly prolonged limbo, languishing behind bars in remote locales (Conlon 2011; Turnbull 2015). Detention facilities onshore and offshore become vanishing points (Gregory 2007) where geography and the law conspire to obscure and exclude.

Second, remote detention differs from Agamben's camp in looking not at how spaces of exclusion will affect a universal figure (as in *homo sacer*, or bare life) but instead at how they target specific, racialized groups in historically and spatially specific ways (Mitchell 2006; Mountz 2011c). Like camps, detention facilities involve exercises in sovereign power wherein more powerful people confine and contain less powerful people in less powerful places. These are racialized practices and histories that advance what Cacho (2012) calls "racialized rightlessness" (see also Sudbury 2005; Gilmore 2007; Paik 2016).

In a third, related critique, Agamben's analysis leaves little room for resistance to the exclusionary and exceptional spaces he imagines. Feminist scholars have noted a lack of agency and space for resistance within Agamben's totalizing theories (e.g., Sanchez 2004; Pratt 2005; Ramadan 2012). Remote detention houses people in a global political economy of incarceration that closes in. Yet, amid landscapes of emotion, trauma and other forces affectively traverse the boundaries of detention, continually finding their way in and out (Conlon and Hiemstra 2014; Coddington 2017). People detained are not mere pawns, nor are they "bare life." As shown in previous chapters and by other scholars (e.g., Collyer 2012), even people detained or stuck in limbo exercise agency and act politically.

Detention is punitive, relying on geographical isolation and assuming the logic of deterrence: that time confined and deported will prevent further or subsequent migration by those detained or future migrants. The stories of what happens to people who are detained in remote locations reflect both the power of isolation and the simultaneous failure of deterrence. Detention removes people from the places where they were living and working prior to their arrest. Once spatially entrapped within national systems of detention, they are funneled quickly to detention in ever more remote locations. As a result, they find themselves far from family members, friends, coworkers, resources, and potential advocates. Yet even as detention isolates, it fails to deter. Governments seem willing to invest without limits in deterrence; migrants similarly invest, often risking their own lives, in their attempts to land through unauthorized entry.

Remote detention contributes significantly to the death of asylum, advancing its physical, ontological, and political death. The geographical arrangement of institutions reduces access to asylum and the resources needed to actually get asylum. Those that are institutionalized experience confinement, trauma, and physical harm; they are removed from society as workers, as family members, as people, their social identities increasingly tied to spaces of confinement. This disappearance removes them from public awareness and discourse and further serves to criminalize. As those held in detention are deemed security threats, their political chances for asylum disappear.

Whereas the enforcement archipelagoes discussed in chapters 1, 2, and 3 developed primarily through offshore border enforcement, parallel moves to exclude were happening simultaneously onshore, connecting offshore and onshore enforcement regimes through the mobilization of islands as spatial tools of isolation beyond islands themselves. Within the archipelago, remote detention emerges as a pronounced form of isolation. But "remote" can be defined in many ways (Mountz and Loyd 2014). For some, remote detention happens far away from cities and the resources they tend to house for migrants and asylum seekers. For others, remoteness can be defined more narrowly according to accessibility of legal services. These all contribute to the exclusionary geographies and patterns of isolation that propel forward practices of remote detention.

GEOGRAPHIES OF EXCLUSION: PROLIFERATING PATTERNS OF ISOLATION

Detention, obviously, isolates individuals. But beyond isolation, its manner and location matter. Detainee detachment is often taken to extreme measures through remote detention. Authorities and policy makers rehearse an array of strategies to explain the detention of immigrants, asylum seekers, and noncitizens.[1] Some authorities call detention *suppression* or *disruption,* signaling an effort to curb human-smuggling industries and unauthorized entry. Still others use the term *deterrence,* which is the idea that detention will discourage future migration when word gets out that detention is among the punishments migrants will suffer for crossing borders without papers. But few will readily discuss the ways that enforcement practices pull (im)migrant workers into detention via increased policing in the intimate and mundane spaces of daily life, such as homes, workplaces, shops, and churches. Detention is one stage of a series of state security strategies that are increasingly dispersed and pervasive (Coleman 2009). Under the Trump administration in the United States, interior enforcement intensified, once again calling attention to the mundane, intimate spaces where immigration policing funnels people into detention.

In this chapter, I discuss six of the many ways that detention isolates individuals, populations, and communities: through *dispersal, separation, concealment, control, death,* and the *creation and creative use of islands* (with islands expanded on in chapter 4). The extreme landscape of detention in the United States serves as an example. It is important to note, however, that these patterns are common, in use across a range of national contexts and not only those addressed here.

DISPERSAL

Dispersal involves the intentional use of distance to remove people from access to resources and communities. First, dispersal is a form of isolation that occurs in many countries (Bloch and Schuster 2005). In Ireland, asylum seekers are detained in facilities in deindustrialized, low-income, urban areas (Conlon 2007). In Australia, under former prime minister John Howard, most asylum seekers were held indiscriminately in remote locations in the outback or on the sparsely populated northern coast. Additional Australian detention centers were built offshore, in remote, isolated locations such as Christmas Island, Nauru, and Manus Island. Whether onshore or offshore, mainland or island jurisdiction, sovereign or foreign territory, these locations remove detainees from their families and communities and from infrastructure for advocacy—interpreters, legal representation, and advocacy groups—more commonly located in large cities, such as Sydney and Melbourne.

Within the United States, dispersal and dislocation materialize in distinct spatial patterns determined, in part, by the agglomeration of different kinds of facilities used to detain, as well as historical patterns of migration, interception, legal geographies, and political negotiations around detention siting (Loyd and Mountz 2018). Federal detention facilities exclusively designated for holding those with foreign citizenship only detain a minority of people; some 67 percent are instead incarcerated in county and city prisons, which are not dedicated to migrant detention (Detention Watch Network 2015). In fact, ICE owned only 5 of the 209 facilities where noncitizens were detained in 2016 (ICE 2015). Approximately 58 percent of those detained in 2016 were in facilities owned by city and county governments. While some of these facilities are located in cities, many are in more remote, rural locations. There the federal government contracts space for detainees in local prisons, paying per bed. The average per diem cost was $162.76 per person. Aggregated, the federal government spends some $4.85 million on detention per day, with a total cost of about $1.77 billion in 2016 (ICE 2015).

Not only are people often detained in locations distant from where they live and work but they are transferred quickly among centers (Human Rights Watch 2009). This removes them from resources that they may have amassed in a location where they were detained, in the form of advocacy, friendship, and legal representation, for example. About half of detainees were quickly funneled south in the United States (Schriro 2009), and many of the largest detention facilities in the country were constructed recently in the U.S. South, in Georgia, New Mexico, and Texas. Arrests are high in dense urban areas in the Northeast and on the West Coast, but large detention facilities are built and filled quickly in the South. In 2014, the United States experienced a surge of asylum claims from Central America with the arrival of approximately 68,541 unaccompanied minors from El Salvador, Guatemala, and Honduras and an equal number of minors traveling with a guardian (Planas 2015). In response, the federal government constructed the largest detention facility in the country in Dilley, Texas. Designed to hold mothers and children in response to the arrivals, the center had a planned capacity of twenty-four hundred beds (Planas 2015). This remote location inhibited access to asylum and advocates (Pskowski 2016). Subsequent arrangements were made by the Trump administration to hold asylum seekers in Mexico ("Remain in Mexico," formally the "Migrant Protection Protocols"), the subject of a Supreme Court challenge in 2020.

Moving people through the system to remote sites (whether large, dedicated federal facilities or small county jails) makes the initial location of and communication with detainees difficult and obscures the statistical accounting of the numbers of foreigners being held by authorities at any given time. Legal counsel and family members frequently report that clients are moved quickly, overnight, without warning to detainees, families, or lawyers.[2] Not only is it difficult to then find them but advocacy networks must be restored or created anew. Although legal advocates have fought to reduce these transfers among centers because they inhibit and complicate legal representation, the practice continues.

In Syracuse, the small, Rust Belt city in upstate New York where I lived for eight years, the U.S. Border Patrol heavily polices the Regional Transportation Center, the local bus and train station where Amtrak, Greyhound, and Trailways operate (Kim and Loyd 2008; New York Civil Liberties Union 2011). Because the station falls within one hundred miles of the U.S. border with Canada, it has been designated a port of entry where people are questioned as though they are entering the country. In choosing whom they question, federal authorities rely on racial profiling, routinely approaching people of color and people with accents in the station and on trains and buses to ask them for identification. I witnessed these encounters myself, as did many fellow colleagues, students, and activists using the bus and train station who found themselves not only witnessing but harassed.

A scathing report released by the New York Civil Liberties Union (2011) showed that Department of Homeland Security (DHS) employees working border patrol along this upstate corridor were offered financial incentives, such as extra vacation days and shopping credits at popular retail outlets, in exchange for arrests of foreign workers without documents. As a result, hundreds of arrests were made of people picked up on buses or trains, in the process of boarding, or in the small stations of upstate New York. Because they were often en route from Chicago to Boston or from New York City to Buffalo when people disappeared in upstate New York, family and friends had a difficult time locating their loved ones. This dislocation was exacerbated by the rapid transfer of detainees from the Public Security Building in Syracuse to county jails in Cayuga, Onondaga, Oneida, Oswego, and Wayne counties or to the large federal detention facility for men in the small town of Batavia, more than a hundred miles west of Syracuse, near Buffalo.[3]

The local Task Force on Detention at the Workers' Center of Central New York formed in 2007 in response to raids upstate, where what are called "collateral arrests" were taking place: the arrest of those present in a home or workplace where another person might have been the target of an enforcement operation. The very nature of these local raids reflects the ways that enforcement authorities capitalize on the vulnerability of undocumented workers by isolating them. They surround worksites, homes, churches, and local stores in their raids, and those under siege are often not aware of their rights to refuse search or entry. Activists in Syracuse, Rochester, Buffalo, and much smaller rural towns in between—such as Sodus, where the harshest enforcement campaigns unfolded in the early 2000s—referred to this as a "campaign of fear and intimidation."[4]

It was challenging for these groups to respond to enforcement strategies because they happened in small communities and targeted people at greater risk if they spoke out because of their precarious legal status. A class action lawsuit, for example, requires extensive documentation of systematic violations of rights, which is challenging to gather in a landscape of fear where the intimate spaces of home, the community spaces of church, and mundane yet essential places such as grocery stores, buses, and health clinics are targeted for enforcement.

Law students and faculty at the New York University–affiliated Immigration Rights Clinic worked with anonymous plaintiffs to file a lawsuit contesting the racial profiling and harassment happening upstate and its deleterious impact, namely, the placement in custody and subsequent deportation hearings of people following their removal from trains and buses in upstate New York (New York University Law 2015).

SEPARATION

Detention and dispersal lead to separation from family and community networks, often by sudden disappearance. In countries like Australia and the United States, where rapid transfers carry detainees across the country to other facilities (Schriro 2009), families affected by detention may spend weeks or months looking for relatives arrested in workplace raids or on public transit. Much of the work to support detainees is the labor of location: families and organizations try to locate loved ones who disappear into the system. These separations became more extreme during the Trump administration, with overtly stated policies to separate families.

As Leigh Barrick (2018) notes, U.S. border enforcement has always separated families. Separation exacerbates the trauma of detention, which often follows other traumatic experiences of displacement and border crossing, prompting health scholars to characterize time in detention as a period of "retraumatization" (Coffey et al. 2010). More prolonged experiences of detention often lead to more acute trauma during periods of confinement (Green and Eager 2010), often a continuation of the violence of conflict, displacement, flight, and life underground. Remoteness exacerbates separation and the stress caused by detention, ideations of suicide, and rates of self-harm in detention (Neave 2013).[5]

Beyond disruption, disorientation, and dislocation of the individual, raids, arrests, and detentions of individuals have serious effects for households. While the individual is detained, families often lose a source of financial support for the household. Advocates in Syracuse witnessed this form of isolation time and again. At worksite raids, for example, often the person providing the main income for a household is arrested. Separation from home and detention leaves families without money to buy food or clothing or pay rent. Detention thus disrupts not only the life of the individual but the family and its social, economic, and community networks maintained prior to arrest. These socioeconomic ruptures extend beyond the fabric of local communities, reverberating transnationally where migrants are often a source of financial support for households, such as in Mexico, Guatemala, El Salvador, and Ecuador (Hiemstra 2012).

CONCEALMENT

Third, remote detention becomes a strategy of detaining people through the insidious process of concealing identities of those detained. This concealment proves even more onerous for family members searching for people from locations inside and outside the country. For example, Nancy Hiemstra (2012, 2013) found that remittances sent to Ecuador from the United States decreased as deportations to Ecuador grew due to increased enforcement in the United States. She worked with La Casa del Migrante, a government-funded organization in Cuenca dedicated to supporting migrants and their families. When people contacted the organization about the disappearance of a friend or family member in the United States, employees and volunteers embarked on an intricate process to locate the person—often detained in the United States—by calling county jails, federal facilities, and workers inside the detention system. The process was so complicated that when Hiemstra volunteered with the organization in 2009, she created a sixteen-page guide— distributed in Spanish and English—detailing how to find people in the U.S. detention system (Hiemstra 2012).

Government methods to suppress identities differ across national contexts. In Australia and the United States, only people whose full names were provided could be visited or telephoned. Australian officials have been accused of dehumanizing detainees by only referring to them by numbers (Australian Human Rights Commission 2010). In the United States, an "alien number," or "A number," was assigned to every detainee from the time of detention to release or eventual deportation. All visits, information, telephone calls (which are centralized), and mail delivery require knowledge of this A number, making it key to identification, location, and communication. Yet this number is neither publicly available nor readily released by detention center staff. Such control measures add to the invisibility and isolation of those held inside by making them more difficult to find and reach by telephone, by mail, or in person.

In Syracuse, the task force worked to build alliances with workers and visitation ministries at local jails to find out these numbers. Often, however, by the time a volunteer learned identification details, the person would have been transferred to another facility. Across Australia, activists pursued similar strategies by befriending local guards and prison clergy to reveal names and make first contact. They then would find out the names of others through detainee networks of friends and compatriots.

In response to the concealment of identities, activist nuns in Australia and the United States are often sent into jails because they are the least likely to be searched or challenged by guards and can hide identity documents in their clothing to assist migrants and asylum seekers with legal cases. A group of sisters in Chicago who were denied access to an ICE staging facility held weekly prayer vigils outside (since they were not allowed inside the facility) for several years. When they threatened civil disobedience to block an entrance to the facility, they were granted permission to board the buses carrying detainees to longer-term facilities (personal communication, September 2009). These vigils went on for years and continue as I write.

Dispersal fosters concealment: migrants are hidden from view in multiple ways—not only locked behind bars but omitted from or hidden within records and statistics.

CONTROL

A fourth form of isolation involves the control of information. Authorities have the power to control information moving in two directions: information about detainees released to the public (including their families) and information provided to detainees about their rights, resources for legal representation, and other details about their cases. This control of information further isolates people in detention, some of whom do not even know where they are being detained, much less when they may have a chance to see a lawyer or judge or where they might find resources or paths to freedom. Whereas detainees are often denied information, authorities exercise their right to information connected to detainees by intercepting their mail and monitoring telephone calls and visits.

Additional microgeographies of information control take place within and immediately surrounding detention centers. In Australia, newly arrived asylum seekers were commonly held separately from those who have been detained for longer periods of time and have learned how to make asylum claims and contact lawyers. In the United States, detainees held in mainstream facilities find themselves remote in other ways, without shared information or resources to contact friends, family, or lawyers or to make telephone calls at all.

Whereas a lack of knowledge about world affairs makes people on the inside feel isolated and forgotten by the world, the control of information about their case status and detention and deportation processes inhibits the resolution of their detention, prolongs uncertainty, and restricts access to outside support, including legal representation (National Immigrant Justice Center 2010; Hiemstra 2012). As authorities hide information about the world from people inside detention facilities, they simultaneously hide information about people detained from the outside world. This said, people are never detained in total isolation. In fact, despite prohibition of mobile phone use and restricted access to the internet, people on the inside sometimes remain well informed and transnationally connected (Coddington and Mountz 2014), once again challenging Agamben's characterization of "bare life."

DEATH

Fifth, medical neglect (which sometimes leads to death) in detention facilities is common and has been well documented by activists, researchers, former detainees, and journalists. As Figure 19 maps, there have been many deaths of people held in detention facilities in Australia, the United States, Canada, and elsewhere. At least 152 detainees died in U.S. detention between October 2003 and July 2015, according to ICE (2015). One notorious case involved a thirty-four-year-old computer engineer, Hiu Lui Ng, who died while detained in a Rhode Island facility in 2007. The autopsy revealed that Ng was riddled with cancer and suffering from a broken spine. For months he was refused a wheelchair and denied visits for medical appointments (Bernstein 2008). His is one of many deaths that have occurred in U.S. facilities (Bernstein 2010). Mr. Ng's death resulted in the removal of all detainees held for ICE from the facility.

At other times, death is self-inflicted: suicide as protest, suicide in despair when there seems no way out and no safe way home. Suicides have taken place commonly in countries where asylum seekers are held in detention for long periods of time, including in Canada and in greater numbers in Australia and the United States (where there are significantly higher numbers of people detained). Suicide in detention centers happens not only quietly among those facing extreme isolation but in highly publicized episodes staged to call attention to poor treatment. At the infamous Woomera facility in the Australian outback and on Christmas Island, Nauru, Manus, and across the Indonesian archipelago, groups of detainees sewed their lips shut in protest, while others killed themselves on the barbed-wire fences that enclosed them (Perera 2002).[6]

Along the security continuum, deaths also happen long before migrants become detainees. Several researchers have documented the relationship between intensified border enforcement and more harrowing risk taking on the part of human smugglers and their clients (Nadig 2002; Hiemstra 2013). Intensified border enforcement measures have translated into increased deaths among those desperate to cross borders (Nevins and Aizeki 2008; Weber and Pickering 2011). No More Deaths counted 206 fatalities along the Mexico–United States border in Arizona between October 2008 and October 2009.[7] The U.S. Border Patrol (2017) reported 2,827 fatalities along the Mexico–United States border between 2010 and 2017. African migrants traveling the Sahara Desert in Libya en route to the Mediterranean pass clusters of bodies, the skeletons of those who died of hunger and dehydration en route. Bodies washed ashore regularly at times onto the coasts of Morocco and Spain's Canary Islands. The IOM (2014) estimated that some thirty-seven hundred people went missing, presumed deceased, while crossing the Mediterranean Sea in 2014. The first half of 2015 saw a sharp rise as the number of losses at sea in the region reached historical highs (Williams and Mountz 2016). Combined with the deaths that happen in detention centers, these deaths en route paint perhaps the most powerful evidence of the geographical isolation experienced by migrants globally and its contribution to the physical, ontological, and political death of asylum.

ISLANDS

Sixth, islands are used as spatial control strategies. In 2007, the *New York Times* published an editorial called "Gitmos across America," referencing yet another geographic strategy used to isolate detainees: the construction of detention centers on islands and the mobilization of these forms of isolation beyond the island itself. The title of the editorial signaled both the importance of the use of islands and the relationship between detention offshore and detention onshore. The Bush administration placed people labeled "foreign enemy combatants" on the U.S. Guantánamo Bay naval base precisely because of the legal ambiguity that accompanies its location. President Obama's administration failed in its attempt to close the facilities and did not remove all detainees from Guantánamo. Where this has happened, former detainees have not been freed but have been sent to other islands willing to accept them, including the independent Micronesian island state of Palau and the United Kingdom Overseas Territory of Bermuda. There, too, the extreme isolation and trauma of prolonged limbo have meant that the body becomes the only remaining space of political struggle and space of resistance. In 2013, a hunger strike spread quickly among foreign nationals detained on the base in Guantánamo, intensifying public debate about the ethics of forced tube feeding through which they were kept alive (*New York Times* 2013).

There are many islands where asylum seekers have been detained in spatial and legal limbo for years. As chapter 3 established, Australia leads in the exploitation of remote island locations, first under Prime Minister John Howard's Pacific Solution, whereby asylum seekers' access to the asylum process and legal representation was restricted due to their detention offshore on Australian territory (e.g., Christmas Island) and not-Australian territory (e.g., Nauru, Indonesian islands). Australian detention is contracted out to third parties, such as the IOM, and private companies or to third states, such as Indonesia and Nauru. U.S. offshore detentions occur not only in Cuba and historically throughout the Caribbean but on Guam and Saipan, its westernmost territories. A degree of geographical and legal ambiguity accompanies the many disparate locations of detention, particularly those offshore. Recent attention has been paid to France's remote control practices to try to curb asylum seeking with processing on Mayotte and in Niger (Nossiter 2018).

Geography is used to deny migrants and asylum seekers access to rights with the creation of islands. These islands are created through remote detention onshore and the use of actual islands to detain offshore, as discussed in chapter 3. The growth of detention centers on islands is a global trend that reflects the characteristics and patterns of isolation outlined earlier. The harms of isolation are exacerbated by remote physical geography. Islands offer extreme forms of dispersal that capitalize on geographical distance, holding potential asylum seekers far from sovereign territory, where they could make an asylum claim. It is easier for authorities to control information entering and exiting island detention facilities, and the infrastructure there to support asylum claims and other migrant services is often thin. On Guam, for example, where many foreign national migrants work on visas and many others make asylum claims on a regular basis, there were few migrant advocacy organizations and no immigration judges posted on the island to hear claims. On islands, migrants and entire detention facilities can be better hidden from the view of publics, journalists, and human rights monitors. This was the case on Lampedusa, the Italian island close to Tunisia mentioned in the introduction to this book, where human rights monitors were denied entry for several years (Andrijasevic 2006).

On one hand, these are actual, material islands where people are detained. At the same time, the spatial form of the island is reproduced across domestic or mainland territory. Those held internally within sovereign territory also find themselves isolated in legal and geographical limbo. Thus islands onshore and offshore make migrants difficult to locate, and it is challenging for them to learn information about their cases or to access legal representation. Whereas islands where asylum seekers are held were discussed more fully in chapter 3, here I discuss in more depth the archipelago in the Pacific, distant from U.S. mainland territory: colonized Pacific territories.

STATUS IN MICRONESIA, "WHERE AMERICA'S DAY BEGINS"

Of course, remote islands can also be overseas territories, as is the case with Christmas Island. The forms of isolation happening through remote detention onshore appear more geographically pronounced in offshore sites because of the exploitation of geographical and psychic distance between mainland and island. In his tracing of the origins of the island mentality that informed U.S. military strategy around forward-reaching bases established to exercise control in decolonizing regions, David Vine (2009) located a historical concept called the "strategic island concept." As his reproduction of the list of islands that could potentially become the location of bases shows (Vine 2009, 62), many of these same islands, which were once used to mobilize U.S. power abroad, are now also sites used to exercise power over human mobility moving toward the United States.

While many Americans may not know about detention in their own communities happening in close proximity, far fewer know about migration struggles happening far offshore. Immigration from Mexico occupies daily headlines and topics of conversation in the United States, yet crossings offshore on U.S. territory are more distant and out of sight. This invisibility means that they are less seen and less talked about. Farther away from the mainland, there are important negotiations over migration, interception, displacement, and resettlement happening in U.S. territories in the Pacific.

For example, the Marianas archipelago is some six thousand miles from the western coast of North America (see Figures 16 and 17). Guam is the largest island in the archipelago and the westernmost U.S. territory, located in the Mariana Trench. Guam is "Where America's day begins," as its slogan suggests, some fourteen hours before the day begins in Washington, D.C. Guam's location places the island closer to China, Japan, and the Philippines than to California, and its history has involved colonial struggle (Rogers 1995), geostrategic military buildup, and associated displacement and dispossession. On Guam, contemporary and historical landscapes of migration, complex jurisdiction, and partial forms of citizenship intersect with racialized histories of colonization and occupation to create a gray landscape of entry, exclusion, access to asylum, and rights to belonging (see Camacho 2012).

Guam is unincorporated territory of the United States. Guam was a Spanish colony handed over to the United States in 1898 after the Spanish–American War, as part of the Treaty of Paris that also ceded Puerto Rico and Cuba to the United States. During World War II, Guam was occupied by Japanese forces and then "liberated" by American forces, who, in 1944, established one large naval base and one large air force base on the island (Rogers 1995; Lipman 2012).

The UN Special Committee on Decolonization counts Guam among the last remaining colonies in the world (UN Special Committee on Decolonization 2009). Guamanians—many of whom identify ethnically as Indigenous Chamorro, a hybrid mix of heritage from Spanish and Filipino predecessors—are U.S. citizens with full rights to mobility within the United States but with forms of citizenship that are partial in other ways. Chamorros can vote in national primaries, for example, but not in national elections, because they do not have full participation through representation in Congress. These are among the contradictions in subnational island jurisdictions identified by Baldacchino and Milne (2006). There are growing movements on the island and beyond to contest militarization and fight for greater self-governance.

A recent estimate places Guam's population at 167,358 (Index Mundi 2018). With two large bases, Guam's economy and population rise and fall in close correlation with U.S. military expansion and contraction. In 2006, Japan and the United States planned to move several thousand marines and their families from the Okinawa base to Guam. Though resistant to militarization in myriad ways, and to this plan in particular owing to its potential deleterious environmental impact, Guamanians have also grown economically dependent on the bases and benefit

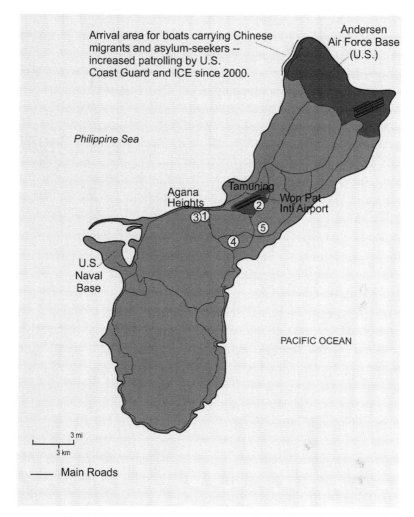

FIGURE 16. Map of Guam showing the extent to which military bases and other government-funded infrastructure structures the landscape.

economically from U.S. military expansion. Most families have at least one person who is military personnel, granting them access to bases and the services, education, health care, and shopping opportunities offered there. Increases in military personnel and families have significant economic, social, political, and environmental consequences on the island (Owen 2010).

Guam is a place where people seek asylum on soil distant from mainland territory but more proximate to countries of origin. During the Vietnam War, some one hundred thousand Vietnamese were resettled there and inhabited temporary camps en route to resettlement elsewhere (Lipman 2012). During the first Gulf War, sixty-six hundred Kurdish refugees were resettled through Guam and spent time on the bases en route to new homes on the mainland (Lipman 2012).

Whereas the arrival and departure of military personnel and migrant workers on Guam are visible aspects of daily life, few island residents know of the continuous, if numerically small, presence of asylum seekers in prison and the ongoing reconfiguration of the carceral landscape. This group is hidden from view of the mainland population due to distance but hidden from view of the local population because of the nature and location of their imprisonment. Until recently, most asylum seekers intercepted across the archipelago were held in the Hagatna facility on Guam (depicted in Figure 17). They have come into view, however, during times of crisis and heightened visibility associated with particular arrivals.

The United States has long housed asylum seekers intercepted at sea on islands, including Cuba and other parts of the Caribbean, as discussed in chapter 2 (Koh 1994; McBride 1999; Van Selm and Cooper 2006). But less known are more contemporary interception practices by the U.S. Coast Guard surrounding the Mariana Trench (Mason 1999). In the late 1990s, when large boats carrying migrants from China were arriving on Guam, Hagatna prison operated beyond capacity. When it seemed the ships would continue to come directly from China, the government created a "tent city" outside of the local jail to house the excess population. Civilian residents joined the efforts of the Coast Guard to locate and intercept ships by telephoning in ship sightings (interview, Guam, July 2008). An air of crisis prevailed, and the U.S. Coast Guard began to divert boats headed for Guam to Tinian (Mason 1999).

Guam and Tinian hold distinct political statuses in relation to the United States, and therefore people have different access to asylum on each island. Although people can file asylum claims on Guam, an unincorporated territory of the United States, they may not travel to the mainland until and unless they are accepted as asylum applicants. Once beds at tent city filled, the coast guard began to tow intercepted boats to Tinian for processing. Tinian is part of the Commonwealth

FIGURE 17. Hagatna Detention Facility, where noncitizens are detained and visited weekly by ICE officials on Guam. Photograph by Emily Mitchell-Eaton.

of the Northern Mariana Islands. Until late in 2008, U.S. immigration laws did not apply there, and therefore migrants could not seek asylum.

Although asylum claims can be filed from Guam, immigration and refugee advocates on the mainland have expressed concern about the lack of knowledge and oversight of the asylum process on Guam (Mason 1999; National Immigrant Justice Center 2010). In 2010, the National Immigrant Justice Center declared Guam the most isolated place to be detained in the United States, with its main measure of isolation being the availability of legal representation for detainees (14). Few lawyers were available to represent people detained on Guam in the late 1990s, when ships carrying large groups arrived. When we conducted research years later, there were fewer. One small firm on the island handled all immigration matters, including asylum cases. Although a sizable number of people await processing of applications sent from Guam to California, the federal government had not posted anyone on Guam permanently to adjudicate claims. Instead, most hearings were heard via televideo conference by a federal judge in Honolulu, Hawai'i, some thirty-eight hundred miles away. Although Chamorros have a history of volunteering with displaced groups on the island (notably, Vietnamese, Kurds, and Burmese; Smith et al. 2010), no community organizations were dedicated to immigrant services or asylum advocacy during research conducted on the island between 2008 and 2012.

While doing research on Guam in 2008, I observed some of these cases by accompanying an attorney representing claimants. Asylum applicants and their lawyers visit the DHS office on Guam for the hearing. The immigration judge and DHS lawyers are broadcast live from where they sit in a similar room in Honolulu. The judge telephones a disembodied interpretation service, whereby a live person located in a third, undisclosed location interprets proceedings by conference call. Participants questioned the quality of access, given the distance between Guam and the mainland. One lawyer I interviewed described hearings as a "circus." He suggested that largely inexperienced interpreters would grow distracted by the televised proceedings and sit as though watching a film, forgetting their roles as interpreters. He argued that the confusion of sociospatial distance across time zones was not transcended by technology, including difficulty with interpretation and the restricted ability of the judge to read the body language and affect of claimants (interview, Guam, July 2008). Research on Guam in 2010 and 2011 confirmed that little had changed.

Passed by the U.S. Congress in spring 2008 as an Omnibus bill, the Consolidated Natural Resources Act pulled governance of migration on the other islands of the Commonwealth of the Northern Mariana Islands under control of the DHS, extending U.S. immigration law. By summer 2008, immigration attorneys were anticipating an "onslaught" of asylum claims among people traveling by boat from other islands, where immigration attorneys estimated that more than half of the migrant population has no documentation and would be returned home by the DHS as a result of the National Resources Defense Act (interview, Guam, July 2008). Most attorneys I interviewed on Guam in 2008 identified the island as "exceptional" in many ways, including the processing and adjudication of asylum claims. Referred to as *federalization,* the ensuing process began in 2009 and brought nearly 515,000 people on Saipan and Rota into legal immigration status by April 2011 (U.S. Government Accountability Office 2011). This set the border in motion again, opening the possibility of institutionalizing use

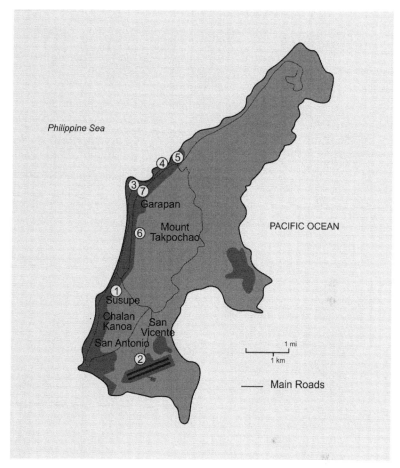

FIGURE 18. Map of Saipan in the Marianas Trench.

of islands to isolate and restrict access to asylum. In June 2011, the U.S. government opened a new detention center on the island of Saipan. Like Tinian, Saipan has distinct political status from Guam, and asylum claims are generally not yet accepted from Saipan, though I met one lawyer on Guam in July 2008 who claimed to have submitted the first asylum claim ever made from Saipan.

When we did research on Guam and Saipan in 2010 and 2011, ICE had been transferring detainees from Guam to Saipan (Figure 18). Although the Consolidated Natural Resources Act included provisions for asylum seeking among transported detainees, it had been decided that no access to asylum would be allowed until the five-year transition period ended in 2014, thus shifting the borders of sovereign power once again and creating barriers to access with punitive carceral space on Saipan. Interviews conducted by research assistant Emily Mitchell-Eaton on Guam and Saipan in 2010 and 2011 found that authorities were exploiting the punitive movement of populations between islands. Detainees were transferred from Guam to Saipan as a way to restrict access to asylum, effectively shifting the border from island to island across the region. Thus the islands seemed to provide endless capacity for the movement of borders, people, and their invisibilization to broader publics. In late 2013, it was announced that the period of transition would be extended to 2019, effectively extending the legal limbo of those held in detention on Saipan (Eugenio 2013). In 2014, the new detention center on Saipan was closed.

Across the archipelago, claimants were haunted by distance and decisions that accompany colonial control over remote territory. They contended with a general silencing of their presence among the public on mainland territory and the population on the island too, most of whom were not aware of the presence of asylum seekers in the local jail, despite local histories of volunteer work with refugees en route to resettlement (Smith et al. 2010).

Whereas state authorities utilize islands as distant posts in the periphery from which to govern migration, those who live, work, and are confined there experience the unbearable, paradoxical proximity of crowding and isolation in small spaces. Put another way, this enforcement work of distancing others through remoteness requires a certain kind of proximity, namely, intimacy. Interviews with staff at the prison on Guam showed a lack of knowledge about foreign nationals held on federal contract, a sense of powerlessness, and correspondingly intense emotions about the work. I draw here at length from an interview with a supervisor at the Hagatna Detention Facility on Guam. The first excerpt relates the experience of detaining approximately seven hundred asylum seekers intercepted by boat from China in 1999 and placed in detention on Guam, exceeding local capacity and leading to construction of a tent city and other provisional arrangements outside of the facility. One supervisor reported the following:

> So yeah, I was involved in, you know, watching them.... It was very nerve-wracking because, again, we don't know who they

are. We have no background on these people. Of course they said they were immigration, you know. They're here for immigration, but they could be fleeing their country for committing a crime of murder, and we don't know. And we could—there's like a big, big barrier, English barrier—language barrier, of course. And there was a lot of them. There's a lot of them. And some of them didn't get along with each other anyway. So there was fights. There were little groups and cliques and things. And then, you know. And they're talking, you don't—at first you're like, "What the hell?" Because they talk loud. When they talk, "Mrrrmr!" That's how they talk. You know, we're all panicking, you know, because when they speak, they're verbally aggressive. And there was a lot of fights. There was fights. And when it broke out, it got pretty bad. Usually it was over food. Oh, my God, feeding time was crazy. Some supervisors get all stressed out. Like all the phone calls I just got, you know, other supervisors might be all panicky and already have trouble. Power went out, they'll be screaming and yelling. Jesus Christ, just got to relax. Take your aspirin, you know. (interview, Guam, July 2012)

In this first excerpt of the interview, the supervisor, someone with institutional authority and power over others, expresses fear, panic, stress, nervousness, and anxiety regarding these encounters of his own and his employees with unknown others. He narrates these others in terms that turn them to less-than-human subjects to be feared at "feeding time."

The interview continued:

And like I told one officer before, I said, "We're the court's bitch." Just take it when they give it to us, and that's it. We have no power over anything else. We're the bitch. . . . Yeah, we have no control over our budget. I mean, like I said, as long as there's a document that says hold them, we have a job to do it. You know, we can't pick and choose who we're going to confine or when we're going to confine or what. Just we got to do it, you know. Like that's what I told the officer one time . . . I said, "But we are. I mean, what are we going to do? What are you going to do? Tell the judge no? Go ahead. I dare you." . . . Who's going to do that? (interview, Guam, July 2012)

As this narrative shows, authorities managing the facilities had little training or preparation for work with people in immigration custody.

Ironically, while charged with detaining others, authorities themselves expressed powerlessness in their assignment by the federal government to detain noncitizens.

Gordon (2011) suggests that haunting is an "animated state in which a repressed or unresolved violence is making itself known." It is the repressed and unresolved violence of dispossession, occupation, militarization, and colonialism that haunts the manager who erupts in this interview. In this exchange, the colonial past erupts into the colonial present, collapsing past and present, with Guam's history of militarization and occupation—a continuation in its present use as site of militarization and incarceration. The repressed and unresolved violence of dispossession, occupation, militarization, and colonialism haunts, trauma transmitted through affective eruption. As Coddington and Micieli-Voutsinas (2017, 53) note, "as past memories of trauma are triggered by present-day events, or present-day events are recalled in relation to past traumas, the blending of past and present occurs in jarring, unexpected ways."

The manager here, although in a position of power, articulates the feeling of helplessness involved in the detention of ICE detainees, the place where one takes orders or carries out contracts. This feeling of helplessness was articulated in the context of a long history of federal control over island economies and governance. Following histories of colonization, occupation, and "liberation," Chamorros experienced decades and generations of militarization as the United States established large military bases on the island, dispossessing locals of their land and dedicating that land to geostrategic location of bases that would serve as platforms from which to operate in the region. The island's economic livelihood remained dependent on the bust and boom of the U.S. military. Current social movements are fighting continued militarization and dispossession and seeking self-governance.

In this context, the despair and feeling of powerlessness of a manager with power over others signal the historical and imperial grounds on which detention facilities are built and civil servants are required to work as the "bitch" of the federal government in its latest project to contain human mobility on the island. This affective eruption in the middle of an interview—affect jumping from the page of the transcript—exposes a wrinkle in time when past erupts into present (Mountz 2017).

The hidden nature and isolation of foreign nationals, migrant workers, and asylum seekers in the region is a part of U.S. carceral society that is little known but highly representative of the ways that migrants find themselves isolated and invisibilized in detention on the mainland. Islands may occupy geographically marginal locations, but they prove prominent in the geographical imaginations of authorities and their strategies to exercise sovereign power. Detention on islands links individual legal status to collective histories about power, control, governance, and belonging. Islands can be sites of remote detention where more extreme forms of isolation take place. As such, they prove central to understanding forms of isolation on nonisland locations in mainland territory.

RADICAL MAPPING AND OTHER PROJECTS DESIGNED TO LOCATE AND REVEAL

A growing number of activist groups have been working to expose, document, and counter remote detention, building on a politics of location. I introduce some of their work here and return to it in more detail in chapter 6. By mapping detainee locations and providing statistical information of the numbers of people in detention, activists locate and call attention to those who have been dislocated, isolated, and hidden from the public. In Australia, for example, a tightly networked coalition movement emerged in the late 1990s and early 2000s in response to the extreme isolation experienced by asylum seekers held in remote detention facilities. Similarly, in the United States, the Detention Watch Network (DWN) is a national coalition that formed in 1997 to respond to the substantial growth in detention following the restrictive immigration legislation implemented in 1996. The DWN became a member-driven organization in 2005 with—at that time—eighty-four organizational members (and many more individual members) across the country. The network launched an interactive mapping project that used a combination of geographic information systems and community participation to map detention sites across the country. Network members and members of the public were asked to add information to the map when they discovered additional sites of detention.[8] A research endeavor that embarked on mapping at a more global scale is the Global Detention Project.[9] Like the DWN, the Global Detention Project created a dynamic interface where developments in detention can be readily updated. In addition to maps, the site provides detailed information gathered primarily through access to information requests on detention policies and statistics in as many countries as possible. Creative migrant and migration mapping projects unfolded in the EU, such as the Atlas of Migration in Europe authored by Migreurop (2013a). As stated in its introduction, this was "a committed Atlas that underlines the inconsistencies and the consequences of migration management in the European Union" (Migreurop 2013b). Migreurop's atlas renders legible the intersections of geopolitical conflict, economic asymmetry, and enforcement landscapes that drive migration and simultaneously make it more precarious. These eloquent maps make visible the dehumanizing, psychic distance achieved by offshoring racialized others.

These groups succeeded in documenting hidden geographies by creatively mapping data gleaned through research, access to information requests, and analysis of publicly available data. These mapping projects are as dynamic as migration and enforcement patterns themselves, always changing and therefore well distributed online as a dynamic interface that provides a platform for continuous change and topographical renderings of power, mobility, and immobility.

Some of the challenges these groups face involve the transitional, dynamic, and sometimes fleeting nature of detention and the concealment of people detained. In the EU, for example, detention takes place at more than two hundred sites, some near or within airports, some very small. Additional detentions are happening along and beyond EU borders, but they are not all known or documented. Indeed, some are highly provisional, as illustrated in the history narrated by the young Afghan man in Sicily that opened chapter 1. In the United States, immigrants were detained in 209 facilities (DHS 2016). Australia has attempted to conceal some of its offshore detentions in other countries, particularly Indonesia, where it funded some twelve to fourteen facilities through Australian development funds (Marr 2009; Taylor 2009; Nethery et al. 2013). Australia refused to resettle people detained on Nauru and Manus who were found to be refugees, instead "trading" them with the United States (Karp and Farrell 2016; Cave 2018).

Mapping projects are also often bound by national borders. Maps may not include offshore detentions undertaken by the country where the maps are made. In other words, detention offshore is so removed from large population centers and seats of political power that these locations are more challenging to map. Both the DWN and the Global Detention Project have struggled to map those more interstitial sites along borders and on islands where sovereign jurisdiction grows more ambiguous, including sites on the outer edges of the EU where detention has increased.

In addition to projects that are national and global in scope, local mapping initiatives also exist. Where states remove detainees from urban loci of support, advocates respond by forming groups in more rural locations to visit and support detainees and connect them to local communities and national networks. One such group in Australia was Rural Australians for Refugees. This group successfully visited detainees, hosted those who were released, and convinced rural small towns to become "welcoming centers" for refugees (Coombs 2004; interview, Mudgee, March 2006). Similar groups have organized visitation programs in urban and rural locations across the United States, notably in New York, New Jersey, Arizona, and Georgia.[10] Networks of former detainees also organize more informal visits to friends still being held in detention. These networks and visits are easier when detainees are not transferred to remote sites.

People in detention exercise resistance by working together to counter isolation in other ways that build on a politics of location, befriending each other and the friendlier guards to share information and working with legal counsel and local visitors who smuggle in documents, cameras, and other tools to build legal cases. They also provide support in the form of connection to sources of support on the outside. Former detainees work to stop their friends from sliding deeper into depression and despair as they languish on the inside. I had the opportunity to accompany one such group in Sydney, Australia, in 2006. We brought a picnic that included halal meat (which was not available at the center), chocolate, new underwear, cigarettes, mobile phones, and calling cards. Because the former detainees knew and befriended guards working there, they had more freedom in carrying these and other items into the detention center.

Alongside mapping, additional technologies have been utilized to transcend national borders and the vast geographical distances that isolate advocates and detainees from each other. Email lists have proven highly effective when people are moved suddenly from one location to another, because advocates located thousands of miles apart are able to inform each other when someone disappears and then reappears in another facility. Australians undertook letter-writing and telephoning campaigns to communicate with those far away, who were either unable or not allowed to visit islands such as Nauru because of the friction of distance, prohibitive costs, and passport and visa requirements (Burnside 2003). Increasingly, detainees use social media, such as Twitter and Facebook, to connect with advocates on the outside, detainees in other facilities, and families and communities at home in countries of origin.

Central to all of these efforts—mapping, visits, letter writing, advocacy, and resistance—are the simple and not-so-simple projects of identification and location, the contesting of distance and isolation through connection, close networks, and shared circuits of information. Mapping detention centers globally is a crucial project of representation: figuring out who is detained, and where, and how that information can be publicized to garner public attention, to advocate, to change policies and practices, and to support detainees in the immediate challenges they face, survival key among them. These strategies have been designed to fight the modes of isolation discussed earlier.

While states conceal, these maps reveal, and the revelations are ripe with political potential for national lobbying efforts and more localized resistance on the ground. Locating people in detention offers political possibilities for reconnection: bringing migrants back into families and communities, and into contact with networks of advocates and legal avenues to emancipation. Mapping patterns of detention and isolation also may prove to be a crucial step in holding states accountable for their policies: documenting and publicizing detention practices with the goal of eventually changing them.

CONCLUSIONS: WHERE DOES MAPPING LEAVE US?

Mapping detention facilities holds potential to counter the politics of erasure and invisibility, to counter the racialized distancing and dehumanization of remote detention with a politics of location. Many social movements are mapping to locate, call attention to violence, and call national and international communities to hold states accountable. In January 2010, Nina Bernstein published an article in the *New*

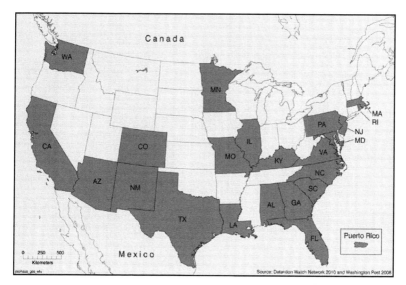

FIGURE 19. Map of deaths in the U.S. detention system by state.

York Times detailing the ways that immigration authorities had hidden immigrant deaths in detention facilities across the United States. Figure 19 maps the locations of these deaths by state, a visual illustration of the depth of isolation discussed in this chapter. Those who died were dispersed across the country in a range of facilities, separated from family and community. State authorities had concealed their identities and controlled information about their deaths, treating detainees as though they lived and died on islands, isolated from other detainees, families, journalists, and basic protections of their human rights. This documentation gave rise to statements by the DWN and other groups calling attention to neglect and abuse on the part of authorities.

The intimate, localized forms of isolation are shared globally. Detention facilities are built strategically in proximity to borders, as projects with the promise of providing jobs to local communities and in places where they are less likely to be opposed. Using geography, law, and psychology, states hide, isolate, and dehumanize detainees, manipulating their location to deny access to information and rights. As a result, dehumanization and "racialized rightlessness" (Cacho 2012) through incarceration have intensified. As important as it is to highlight the ways in which detention isolates, it is equally important to contextualize detention as one piece of the broader strategies of immigration enforcement that isolate individuals and communities. These processes of isolation and dehumanization contribute to the death of asylum, with people removed from society, hidden from view, and criminalized as threats to security—racialized foreigners held at a distance. The construction of detention facilities in remote locations also proves part of the larger picture: the death of asylum. Here colonial ligatures serve states in their continued projects to control territory and human mobility, as in the continued state projects of control against which the supervisor of the prison on Guam erupted in the interview. These historical contexts must also be mapped, as they serve as the colonial foundations on which contemporary practices of enforcement, such as detention, unfold. Like the historical research undertaken to understand contemporary detention in Guantánamo Bay (Kaplan 2005), so too must the colonial continuities of the contemporary immigration and asylum detention landscapes be brought to bear on the ontological death of asylum.

Maps, too, have colonial histories linked to the control of space, but they can also be tools of liberation in the most elemental sense of the term. To be identified and located is to exist. Having an A number and a released name means that one can be visited, receive mail and telephone calls, and be accounted for in the most basic of ways. To be located, even as a dot on the map or as a participant in mapmaking where detention is hidden, is to call out the secrets barely whispered by state authorities. Once revealed, this information offers political potential if it is taken up, publicized, and used as a catalyst for change.

Although isolating and destructive, detention happens within local and transnational contexts and communities. There remains hope for social justice in the remarkable, creative, and broadly based coalitions that have formed in response to these strategies, countering isolation with revelation. Some researcher–activists have embarked on "countermapping," using alternative modes of documenting the journey through everyday migrant lives and perspectives (Tazzioli 2015). I will turn in chapter 6 to the countertopographical forces of activism introduced here. These forms of documentation, resistance, and protest have—at times—given rise to significant changes in policy. At other times, time and space fold in; history repeats itself.

Upon his arrival in office in January 2017, President Trump signed a series of executive orders. Some provided greater resources, a stronger enforcement mandate, greater discretion, and a larger workforce for U.S. Border Patrol. Specifically, one early executive order signed by Trump during his first week in office increased border patrol and facilitated the expansion of deportations. These orders, accompanied by Trump's pro-border enforcement discourse, fueled speculation about growth in the detention and deportation regimes with campaign promises and plans to use existing detention and deportation criteria and infrastructure to their fullest capacity. These enforcement moves instilled fear in people with precarious status and unleashed—again—the full force of remote detention by separating people who had lived for years as family and local community members from the ties that sustained them and which they, in turn, sustained. At the same time that President Trump fortified boundaries on mainland territory, he also turned his geographical gaze offshore, with the rehearsal of preparatory military exercises on Guantánamo Bay (Rosenberg 2017) and suggestions to Congress that safe spaces for refugees must be made at home (Peterson 2017). Trump worked what the *New York Times* (2017) editorial board identified as his "island mentality" onshore and offshore, on islands both figurative and material. This was not the first time that refugee resettling countries of the Global North behaved like large islands, able to isolate themselves from displacement by devising creative ways to restrict access to asylum (e.g., *New York Times* 2017).

PART III

POLITICAL DEATH
Hidden Geographies

5

Mobilizing Islands to Restrict Asylum Onshore in Canada (or the Death of Asylum, Even in Canada)

Asylum seeking and procedures have undergone important transformations in Canada in recent years. Like the islands discussed in chapter 3, Canada shifted over the last ten years from a space of refuge to a place where asylum is treated as exceptional and criminalized rather than a norm. This piece of the story is essential to understanding the death of asylum and why its obituary begins and ends in Canada. This chapter outlines recent changes and shows the effective mobilization of the specter of boat arrivals as crises to create islands through legislation within a country with very few boat arrivals. Although Canada has few boat arrivals and does not detain on islands, authorities succeed in mobilizing many of the spatial strategies and discourses surrounding detention on islands. Legislative changes to asylum seeking in Canada over the last fifteen years illustrate how the discourse of exceptionalism that surrounds and criminalizes asylum seeking actually works its way into legislation.

Canada enjoys geographical isolation. It is buffered from human migration by sea, long and rugged coastlines, and its wealthy, border-policing neighbor. Canada's wealth and refugee reception place it in league with other countries where asylum seekers are disappearing, discussed thus far. While a global leader in refugee resettlement, Canada also has an underbelly that is better known in enforcement circles than by Canadian and international publics, namely, offshore enforcement (Mountz 2010) and its preclusion of asylum seekers (Hyndman and Mountz 2008). Canada developed this leadership over the last three decades, culminating in successful reduction in asylum seeking over the last fifteen years. The two roles of resettlement and policing seem contradictory but are consistent insofar as the states that invest heavily in offshore enforcement also tend to resettle refugees from abroad, demonstrating a clear preference to manage refugee resettlement—which involves the opportunity to choose those resettled—rather than receive "spontaneous arrivals" unknown to authorities until their arrival on Canadian soil.

Recent legislative changes to asylum seeking in Canada serve as a case to illustrate how the discourse of exceptionalism that surrounds and criminalizes asylum seeking actually works its way into legislation and shrinks paths to asylum. A fierce discourse of exceptionalism accompanies talk of asylum, explicitly through criminalization of asylum seekers and implicitly through the general silence surrounding asylum seeking—as I will explain. This chapter offers insights into recent processes and spatial dimensions of securitization that shut down paths to asylum in Canada.

Securitization is paramount to the death of asylum. Canada is an important example because of the place it occupies as a global leader in refugee resettlement practices. Recent legislation was introduced following the interception of only six migrant ships in 1999, 2009, and 2010. These arrivals had a disproportionately large effect on Canadian enforcement, targeting asylum seekers who now face greater deterrence, criminalization, and punitive measures. These included intensified enforcement offshore and onshore, including mandatory detention, designated safe countries whose nationals face expedited access to asylum, designated dangerous countries whose nationals face lengthier security checks upon making claims, and greater concentration of discretionary power with the minister to intervene and adjudicate cases. By detailing *how* spaces of asylum disappeared offshore and onshore in Canada, I show not only that Canada itself functions as an island but that kinds of islands have been mobilized in a country that does not detain on remote islands.

Canada was celebrated as a leader in refugee resettlement and integration until the decade of Conservative governance led by Prime Minister Stephen Harper that failed, among other things, to resettle Syrian refugees and that put in place many restrictions on asylum seeking. In 2015, the new Liberal government led by Prime Minister Justin Trudeau improved that reputation with innovations in refugee resettlement. Yet many enforcement-oriented policy and legal changes had already been enacted and remain in place. These include, for example, mandatory detention for people designated "irregular maritime arrivals" (Gros and van Groll 2015; Kronick et al. 2015).

The situation has become especially dire for those seeking to make refugee claims (the equivalent of seeking asylum) in Canada. In my research in other parts of the world, I found that even seasoned activists and advocates in other countries still respect Canada as a paragon of progress and a world leader in refugee resettlement and refugee determination processes; they are slow to realize that much of the robust legal architecture has, of late, been undone. A recent publication serves as an example. In their paper on the externalization of migration controls and their impact on asylum seekers, Bill Frelick et al. (2016) take on what they see as the countries carrying out this work, detailing externalization policies and the authors' policy recommendations for intended audiences in the United States, Australia, and the EU. Not only is Canada mentioned only once in the article (in relation to U.S. border policy), but it does not register for the authors as leader or peer in externalization of migration control. This is because the death of asylum has happened quietly, under the radar of otherwise well-informed international audiences and the Canadian public.

Canadian law and enforcement practice (such as detention) increasingly treat people *as* islands, with borders affixed to the asylum-seeking body. While Canada does not detain strategically on remote islands, federal law, policy, and enforcement practice increasingly, quietly, treats noncitizens *as* islands, mobilizing some of the same legal geographical tactics of exclusion to advance the political death of asylum. I detail how in this chapter with the objective of locating Canada within the global trends in asylum seeking and enforcement infrastructure discussed thus far. By revisiting Canada's place on the world stage in the responses of wealthy countries to displacement, my goal is to locate the country geographically and legally in relation to enforcement archipelagoes at work in the world and detailed in this book.

Given my placement of Canada as a key contributor to the death of asylum, I return here briefly to revisit the three kinds of death outlined in my introductory chapter. In terms of physical death, Canada has intensified border enforcement in ways that make it more difficult for people to enter. Although the Canadian public rarely hears about them, there are border deaths along the Niagara River dividing upstate New York from southern Ontario (Helleiner 2016). The death is also ontological, with the reduction of ways to enter and increase in reasons for blocking entry. As a result, there exist fewer routes to actually becoming a person who files a claim for protection in Canada, resulting in a statistical drop in claims in recent years (UNHCR 2014b)—followed by a subsequent rise—as well as a silence surrounding asylum seeking in public discourse. Finally, the death of asylum has been political, in part through the absence of public discourse about the 2012 legislation— Protecting Canada's Immigration System Act—and the ways that it quietly and effectively stripped rights from refugee claimants, refugees, permanent residents, and Canadian citizens alike.

The resulting violence enacted on asylum seekers beyond the national frame is hidden from view and too rarely discussed among members of the Canadian public. Instead, struggles against these measures have been left to specialized groups acting in the interest of Canadian refugees and refugee claimants: advocacy groups such as attorneys and doctors who sued the Canadian government with the hope of restoring health insurance and legal protections. They fought to sustain small allowances for refugees and asylum seekers in a country once known for its robust social safety net. The political death is also made possible by existing discourses about refugee claimants. Discourses about legislative changes criminalize and dehumanize by scripting bogus refugees as security threats who are not deserving of protection (Atak and Crépeau 2013). Like the paradoxical hypervisibility and invisibility of asylum seekers offshore, the simultaneous silence and criminalizing noise work in tandem to advance what Audrey Macklin (2005) identified as the discursive disappearance of refugees.

LEADING THE WORLD IN OFFSHORE ENFORCEMENT

Canada's role in border enforcement is paradoxical and worthy of investigation. On one hand, Canada does not detain asylum seekers on islands. Nor does the country experience ample migrant boat arrivals to justify a basis for comparison to Australia or southern member states of the EU, in terms of its responses to geographically proximate boat arrivals as humanitarian crises. And yet, over the last twenty-five years, Canada placed itself voluntarily in this league, importing and exporting policies from and to regions facing far greater numbers of asylum seekers by boat. Canada leads in the archipelagic development of border enforcement, in part through a strategic leveraging of those few boats that did arrive—working boat arrivals at the anxious spot where land meets sea to alter existing policies and laws. In this pattern, which I will detail shortly, Canada mobilizes islands as a spatial form of confinement to detain and isolate asylum seekers, using geography and law to curb access.

Like other countries with higher numbers of resettled refugees, Canada also leads the world in the securitization of migration. While infused with exceptional resources and taken to new measures under recent conservative leadership, the process of securitization is by no means new. The development of securitization in Canada corresponds generally with the trends and turns identified in the genealogy mapped in chapter 1. As discussed there, early seeds for stopping potential arrivals offshore were planted in the 1980s with the development of offshore policing in the form of the network of ICOs introduced in the genealogy. This network was largely designed to foster informal collaboration and information sharing among authorities working abroad to police human smuggling, unauthorized entry, and false documentation. Canadian immigration enforcement authorities consider themselves early developers of interdiction (Mountz 2010), practices for which they have been criticized (Kernerman 2008; Human Rights Watch 2011). The Canadian Border Service Agency boasts its own success rate in this arena, noting that 79 percent of people moving without proper documents were intercepted before reaching Canadian territory (Canadian Border Services Agency [CBSA] 2014; Public Safety Canada 2018). According to Sandy Irvine (2011, 103–4, 120), Canadian officials actually cite their ability to enforce offshore without "traditional forms of oversight" as the advantage of interdiction. In this case, "traditional oversight" includes compliance with Canadian immigration and refugee law, the Canadian Charter of Rights and Freedoms, and international refugee law (specifically, the 1951 Convention and 1967 Protocol, and the principle of non-refoulement). As Irvine (2011) observes, few formal structures exist to govern offshore enforcement.

In 2011, Canadian and American leadership cemented cooperation and coordination with the Declaration on a Shared Vision for Perimeter Security and Economic Competitiveness and its accompanying action plan, Beyond the Border (Public Safety Canada 2018). Much of this plan involved the transformation of border enforcement with implementation of systems—such as the Beyond the Border entry/exit system—to share information that would allow Canada to conduct risk assessment of travelers and cargo prior to arrival on Canadian sovereign territory. The CBSA (2014, 9) identified "irregular migration" as among the top three risks. The agency's Risk Assessment Program "'pushes the border out' by seeking to identify high-risk people, goods, and conveyances as early as possible in the travel and trade continuum to prevent inadmissible people and goods from entering Canada" (CBSA 2014, 20).

Whereas the United States led the way in exceptionalism surrounding offshore migration enforcement at sea in the early periods of externalization traced in chapter 1, Canada today leads the way in the geo/politics of exceptionalism surrounding asylum and asylum seeking. What began as interdiction offshore in the 1980s blossomed into remote detention internally to sovereign territory in British Columbia in the late 1990s and 2000s. These policies intensified and were codified in legislation under conservative prime minister Stephen Harper to become legalized forms of exclusion that mirrored the politicization of asylum in other places. Although Canada intercepts very few asylum seekers by boat, the xenophobic hysteria surrounding responses to the six boats that were intercepted over a twenty-five-year period planted seeds that furthered rounds of securitization onshore and offshore, through a panoply of measures categorized broadly as "front-end security."

SECURITIZATION ECLIPSES SAFE HAVEN

With the unprecedented move in the late 1970s and 1980s to resettle more than sixty thousand Indochinese displaced during the Vietnam War (Molloy and Simeon 2016), followed by the establishment of its refugee determination program in 1989, Canada began to enjoy a global reputation for its refugee protection and refugee resettlement programs. This reputation was consistent with other values that residents often identify as Canadian, such as the protection of human rights enshrined in the Canadian Charter for Human Rights and practices of international diplomacy that once characterized the country's role on the world stage. In recent years, however, those protections have been chipped away with the erosion of refugee claimant and determination processes, protections and services, and the offshoring of borders. This began with development of the first Immigration Control Network of civil servants working abroad in 1989 and was extended with Canada's Multiple Borders Strategy. In the 1990s, these agreements advanced collaboration in the form of the Multiple Borders Strategy (Arbel and Brenner 2013, 24), built on the notion of a North American Perimeter, popular in the 1990s and advanced by then U.S. ambassador to Canada Paul Celluci. The idea drew on the notion of the EU's Schengen Area that would erase internal borders and collaborate on a thickening of the external border. The strategy was designed to "'push the border out' so that people posing a risk to Canada's security and prosperity are identified as far away from the actual border as possible, ideally before a person departs their country of origin" (CBSA, cited in Hyndman et al. 2014, 10). The September 11, 2001, terrorist attacks on U.S. soil ended political will to police the perimeter and erase the interior border to enhance mobility within North America (amid false perceptions that some of the perpetrators of the attacks had entered across the Canadian border). Perimeter theory fell out of favor, but the agreements remained in place, with the ideas renewed and institutionalized in the 2011 Beyond the Border Declaration.

The transformation from leadership in resettlement in the 1980s to multiple borders that drove agreements between Canada and the United States in the 1990s and 2000s and their securitization of those seeking safe haven was rapid, when placed in historical perspective. This makes Canada remarkable, with its leadership held as a paragon around the world, and then its securitization placing it in a league with other comparable immigrant-receiving and refugee-resettling states that have also been offshoring borders.

Much securitization of human mobility in Canada involves cross-border agreements with the United States that endeavor to balance trade and security (Gilbert 2005). In the 2000s, following 9/11, Canadian immigration and refugee policy underwent two major legislative transformations. The first was new legislation: the Immigration and Refugee Protection Act (IRPA) in 2002. The second placed a major brick in the wall of securitization (Hyndman and Mountz 2008) that dramatically shifted the material landscape of access to asylum, foreclosing on safe haven in Canada: the Safe Third Country Agreement (STCA), part of the 2001 Smart Border Accord. The STCA drew on a practice implemented in and imported from the EU in the 1990s, with the introduction of the Schengen Area. Like EU member states, Canadians sought to foreclose on the possibility of what policy makers call "asylum shopping," instead requiring that all asylum seekers make a claim in the first country where they land that has an asylum system. Confronting the perimeter talk and the possibility of the STCA in the 1990s, refugee advocates and activists in Canada were successful in fighting this move toward border harmonization. Their arguments succeeded on the grounds that the U.S. asylum system discriminated against those making claims from noncommunist countries of origin (Bon Tempo 2008).

The implementation of the STCA in December 2004 significantly altered the landscape of asylum in North America but especially in Canada, where—previously—approximately one-third of refugee claimants once traveled through the United States en route to Canada. The agreement ended this possibility (with some exemptions for Haitians and people with family members in Canada). Those who attempted to make a claim along the land border would be turned back and required to make the claim in the United States (or, in the case of U.S. citizens, such as war resisters, they would be barred from making a claim in North America). The STCA is shot through with geographical contradictions and exceptions, however. For example, it bars entry from the United States for those crossing land borders at ports of entry but not for those entering by air or boat or making inland claims. This is why Canada saw a rise in the entry of asylum seekers on foot across land borders of Manitoba and Quebec after Donald Trump took office in January 2017 (Harris 2017).

The anticipated results of the STCA were significant (Macklin 2003). In the immediate lead-up to its implementation, there was a rush to the border from the United States. Organizations working along the border, such as Casa del Migrante in Buffalo, New York, were overwhelmed by the rise in numbers of people seeking assistance as they approached the border. Immediately following the implementation of the STCA, the number of people seeking asylum in Canada dropped by the expected 50 percent. Within a couple of years, however, it had risen back to previous levels. Those working along the border heard accounts of increases in human smuggling and clandestine entries from the United States (interview, Buffalo, 2010). Legal scholars analyzed what NGO workers affirmed: speculation that this border restriction fueled the smuggling industry. When U.S. president Trump issued an executive order to impose a travel ban on visitors from seven majority Muslim nations and barred all refugee resettlement for four months in 2017, Canada once again saw a significant rise in unauthorized crossings from the United States into Manitoba and Quebec (Harris 2017).

In the wake of 9/11, there were also overhauls of border governance and immigration departments on both sides of the border. In 2002, the Immigration and Naturalization Service was renamed and subsumed by the DHS, the largest reorganization of federal government since FDR's New Deal (Nemeth 2010). In Canada, border enforcement was detached from Citizenship and Immigration Canada with the creation of the Canadian Border Services Agency (CBSA) in 2003. Canada also increased its investment in its most popular form of externalization, increasing the number of ICOs working abroad.

Early exclusion increased in the 1990s and 2000s with the intensification of front-end security: greater visa requirements, such as transit visas and the imposition of visas on countries of origin that have relatively high numbers of claims (Kernerman 2008; Gilbert 2013a, 2013b). Securitization and criminalization were advanced in concert in public discourse and policy.

The securitization of human mobility and the border taking hold in Canadian policy in the 2000s were accompanied by securitizing discourses in Canadian media (Razack 1999; Ibrahim 2005; Gilbert 2007; Bradimore and Bauder 2011; Krishnamurti 2013). Scholars analyzing Canadian newspapers identified the repetition of themes of crisis, risk, race, and criminality during immigration events in Canada that parallel the "big events" identified in the genealogy as those that propel externalization agendas forward (Hier and Greenberg 2002). Though sparse, the six boats intercepted off of Canada's west coast in 1999, 2009, and 2010 constituted these big events and crises that advanced legislation on securitization.

BOATS AND THE BOGUS REFUGEES WHO NEVER ARRIVED

This section discusses the most significant boat arrivals in Canada over the last thirty years and the responses to them. Processes of securitization and criminalization can be mapped at the thresholds where land meets sea. Although Canada does not detain on geographically remote islands, Canadian responses to refugee claimants arriving by boat show the mobilization of island logic onshore. Recent Canadian history features very few boat arrivals, and yet the Canadian government succeeded in mobilizing the *fear* of more boat arrivals to advance exclusionary agendas and reduce asylum seeking. The two largest groups to arrive by boat were the four intercepted boats in 1999 carrying people smuggled from Fujian, China, and, in 2009 and 2010, two boats carrying refugee claimants from Sri Lanka, also intercepted off the coast of British Columbia.

The 1990s development of offshore enforcement strategies in Canada corresponded with the criminalization of asylum seekers globally. In Canada, the new millennium arrived in the turbulent wake of boat interceptions in 1999 that stoked the fears and imaginations of Canadian authorities and residents. When authorities sequentially intercepted four boats carrying people smuggled from Fujian on rusty cargo ships over a period of a few months, the west coast drama played out at sea, on land, in detention and courts, and on the front pages of Canadian newspapers. The 1999 arrivals raised the specter of asylum seekers traveling by boat as criminal or security threats, and exclusionary measures ensued (Mountz 2004). Securitization followed a steady progression, with offshore and onshore enforcement measures, from increasing the capacity of multiple agencies to intercept at sea to expanding mechanisms and resources to more aggressively criminalize, arrest, deport, and detain onshore.

These changes happened not only in the wake of 9/11 but after the highly dramatized, racialized, and publicized interception of four boats from China in 1999 off the west coast of British Columbia. While many attribute changes in border governance to post-9/11 context, significant changes to immigration and refugee policy changed through legislation in Canada that followed boat arrivals (Ibrahim 2005). As one of the Five Eyes, Canada shares these initiatives. Canada has imported and exported the measures detailed in this chapter, adopting some from Australia and exporting others to New Zealand. Although small in number, it is important to consider the significance of boat interceptions in Canada in contributing to the context in which significant rounds of securitization follow through legislation. As the boat arrivals fueled the political will to remove protections, the effects of these politics were seen quickly in the legal infrastructure of asylum seeking and refugee determination processes in Canada, architecture that was designed not long ago.

Like other countries built through settler colonialism, Canada's history is replete with boat arrivals—from explorers and colonists to the mass migration that characterized population growth in North America in the 1800s and 1900s. Of course, in the racialized history of Canadian boat arrivals, some arrivals were facilitated, while others were excluded—as in the arrival of British Indian colonial subjects on the *Komagata Maru* (Kazimi 2012). Over the course of the last five decades, however, the number of people arriving by boat per year, on average, is extremely small compared to other national settings—just over one boat per decade. Given this low average, the numbers increased dramatically with the arrivals in 1999, 2009, and 2010 but remained insignificant when compared to the number of people traveling by boat to the EU or even Australia during this same time period. Thus, Canada is "a bit player" on the international stage of marine arrivals when placed in the context of southern EU member states, Australia, or the United States. Canada remains relatively protected by geography from large numbers of people arriving by direct route. There were 599 people on the four boats intercepted in 1999 and 568 on the two boats intercepted in 2009 and 2010 (76 on the MV *Ocean Lady* in 2009 and 492 on the MV *Sun Sea* in 2010).

When they were intercepted in 1999, nearly six hundred migrants were believed to be transiting Canada with the goal of entering the United States. Once intercepted, they made refugee claims and were brought by CIC to Esquimalt Naval Base (in a suburb of Victoria, British Columbia). A legal struggle ensued when refugee lawyers requested permission to represent clients. The response to this request involved an informal policy called the *long tunnel thesis,* explained by bureaucrats interviewed the following year (Mountz 2010). Officials in CIC and the Department of Justice altered the designation of the base to a port of entry to legally defend the decision not to allow access. The thesis likened the base to an international airport where travelers land but must walk through a long tunnel to customs and immigration before entering the country. With this microgeography, states curtail their access to asylum or legal representation.

This isolation did not last long but affected the outcomes of refugee claims in the tribunals where information gathered during initial interviews at Esquimalt was used against them (Mountz 2010). The altered legal designation of the base as a port of entry demonstrates the state's ability to control legal geographies and the extension of this territorial control to influence access to legal representation and claimant processing. Biopolitical data collected during the information-gathering process were linked to the sovereign control of territory and border enforcement. Though located in close geographical proximity to advocates and legal representation, access was mediated with manipulation of the space and time of detention. Thus authorities worked creatively at the intersection of law and geography toward outcomes that favored exclusion and deportation.

This struggle over access occurred on Vancouver Island, which is not nearly as remote as other islands discussed in this book. Yet the example illustrates that even in Canada, where access to the refugee determination process is protected by the Charter on Canadian sovereign territory, decisions in the daily work of enforcement and processing influence the quality of access to the claimant process. The Fujianese claimants faced low acceptance rates compared with other claimants from the People's Republic of China in 1999. Advocates argued that low acceptance rates reflected remote carceral geographies that distanced detainees from lawyers, interpreters, advocates, and the Immigration and Refugee Board and therefore affected the quality of their access to the claimant system.

Ten years later, this process repeated itself when authorities intercepted Tamil men, women, and children from Sri Lanka. The migrants made claims once they were intercepted, but the process of legal representation was delayed, and they were held in detention en masse, this time in Surrey (a suburb of Vancouver). While they traveled through distinct geopolitical fields, traces of previous interceptions remained as history repeated itself in muted fashion. The effects of detention on outcomes of the process are yet to be discovered, but the sites of interception and long-term detention corresponded between events. Here colonial past haunted the present as migrants sought shelter in commonwealth states of Australia and Canada with long histories of holding migrants at bay (Kazimi 2012). The process of criminalization intensified with the second round of arrivals. In many ways, the response to the 2009 and 2010 boats mirrored the 1999 arrivals: detention en masse in British Columbia, limited access to legal representation, or restricted resources so that refugee claimants were represented en masse.

One of the key differences in the federal response to the second set of arrivals involved their handling by federal ministers—indicative of the process of securitization (Canadian Council for Refugees 2015). The 1999 Fujianese arrivals were addressed by then minister of citizenship and immigration Elinor Caplan. Caplan framed the tightening of Canadian border enforcement and legislation as "closing the back door" on unauthorized migration to "open the front door" (CIC 2001). In 2009 and 2010, in contrast, the main government representative who responded publicly to the boat arrivals was then minister of public safety Vic Toews rather than the minister of citizenship and immigration. At the time, Toews frequently invoked fear by linking Sri Lankan Tamil refugee claimants with the separatist nationalist Tamil Tigers. Other law enforcement agencies also participated in criminalization of asylum seekers. In October 2009, for example, Royal Canadian Mounted Police commissioner William Elliott was quoted in the *National Post*: "While it was too soon to conclude whether any of those who arrived aboard the ship posed a threat to Canada, 'the fact of their arrival, and the potential for others to follow, does raise security concerns.'" Although out of proportion to the size of boat arrivals, authorities effectively used the specter of illegality and criminality to securitize migration in the wake of the highly visible boat arrivals in 2009 and 2010 (Canadian Council for Refugees 2015).

While the discourse of "bogus refugees" was pronounced and fueled public perceptions of generous Canadian social welfare policies somehow being taken advantage of, the facts diverge from this common belief. Most who arrived on the 2009 and 2010 boats were Tamils fleeing the height of violence in the drawn-out Sri Lankan civil conflict that had plagued the country since 1983 (Bhandari and Amarasingam 2014). Subsequent reports by human rights organizations found and continue to find extensive violations of the human rights of Tamil citizens. Particularly cited was the rounding up and isolation of civilians in the northern Wanni region in 2009, when the violence peaked and led to declaration of the end of conflict.

When they reached Canada, as well as Australia and other countries, these were not so-called bogus refugees. Many Tamils from Sri Lanka in fact were determined to be Convention refugees and received asylum in Canada (including those on the *Ocean Lady* and *Sun Sea*), Australia, and elsewhere (Canadian Council for Refugees 2015). And yet memos obtained via the Access to Information Act from CBSA showed that the agency was anticipating the arrival of the second boat and preparing to use detention as a deterrent as aggressively as possible (CBSA 2012). The politics surrounding the boat arrivals in Canada advanced momentum set in motion years before with the boats from Fujian Province and the rounds of securitization and enhanced border enforcement that followed 9/11. These changes are detailed in the following pages; they are part of Canada's movement away from being a safe haven for asylum seekers (Kaushal and Dauvergne 2011).

MOBILIZING BOAT ARRIVALS TO CRIMINALIZE AND CHANGE LEGISLATION

This section explains how the boat arrivals, though small in number, were mobilized effectively to criminalize asylum seekers in Canadian legislation and policy. Processes of criminalization and securitization were readily on display in the public discourse, public statements, and legislative response to these arrivals. Important rounds of legislation followed each round of boat interceptions. IRPA was drafted and read by parliament after the 1999 boat arrivals and eventually implemented in June 2002 (Ibrahim 2005). Additional legislation followed the 2009 and 2010 interception of two boats carrying Tamils from Sri Lanka to the west coast of British Columbia. Each case involved changes to the refugee claimant system, including greater punitive measures for un-authorized entry, criminalization of human smugglers and those they transport, increased capacity for exclusion and detention, and targeting and punishment of people traveling by boat as irregular arrivals.

Despite the relatively small number of people who arrived by boat in Canada in recent years and decades, new legislation implemented in late 2002 and again in late 2012 capitalized on rounds of securitiza-tion following on the heels of the aforementioned boat arrivals. In both cases, criminalizing discourses *about* people who had recently arrived by boat from China in 1999 and Sri Lanka in 2009 and 2010 influenced legislation, a process that scholars identify as the securitization of migra-tion (Huysmans 2000; Ibrahim 2005). As Maggie Ibrahim (2005, 164) writes in her Foucauldian analysis of the securitization of migration to Canada, "government laws and policies are an outcome of discourse, and reaffirm discourse," with her objective "to bring together the differ-ent dispositions, different tools and methods that form the dominant discourse which has securitized migrants." Ibrahim (2005) examines the racialization of this discourse and its direct movement into legislation, specifically examining the 2002 IRPA. Following the manufactured crisis of the 1999 boat arrivals (Hier and Greenberg 2002), the IRPA criminalized and penalized human smuggling with more legal tools for legislation and greater likelihood of imprisonment. Ibrahim analyzes the movement of boat arrivals as "migration event" into government policy vis-à-vis racism premised on cultural differences that threaten the social body (164–65). Ibrahim shows racism at work in the securitization of migration in Canada. She accomplishes this with analysis of six mainstream Canadian newspapers (both national and regional in terms of headquarters and circulation) and the perceived threats to Canadian security contained therein (174).

People who arrived on the boats from Fujian in 1999 quickly saw the integrity of their asylum claims undermined in the mainstream media, where they were scripted as "illegal" and "bogus refugees," although they had not committed crimes and had a right to make refugee claims. In my book, I traced how this criminalizing discourse made its way into the refugee determination process, remote detention, and claimant outcomes. Ibrahim (2005, 180) maps the movement of this securitization through criminalization into legislation. Bill C-11, which became the IRPA, was framed as opening the door to legal, skilled migrants by closing the door to those deemed security threats and less desirable, drawing on a classic trope in policy-related narratives about immigrants as good or bad, desired or not (Razack 1999). IRPA brought in new measures to detain, prosecute, and fine human smugglers. The act expanded criminality, setting the stage to increase the scope of who could eventually be detained, and positioning migrants as "a danger to the security of Canada" (Ibrahim 2005, 181). IRPA also addressed organized crime and involvement with the organization of human smuggling and trafficking. Finally, IRPA "tightened the appeal process" (Ibrahim 2005, 182) by removing some of the infrastructure of protection by reducing the two-person panel of Immigration and Refugee Board (IRB) members to one person hearing claims. This thinning out of the infrastructure of protection is a measure that would be repeated again several years later, slowly chipping away at a once robust system.

In 2009 and 2010, seven years after IRPA came into effect, the boats were intercepted carrying Sri Lankan Tamils, who made asylum claims.

After the patterns of the response were repeated—detention en masse and spectacular media attention—the national environment was once again ripe for another legislative round of the securitization of migration and erosion of asylum in Canada. The specter of criminalization from detention and securitizing discourses about racialized refugee claimants made its way into new rounds of legislation once again. In 2010, parliament passed the Balanced Refugee Reform Act, designed to "accelerate the processing of refugee claims" and "help deter abuse of the system" (CIC 2012b). In 2012, in the wake of the two boats from Sri Lanka, Prime Minister Stephen Harper's government introduced Bill C-31, the Protecting Canada's Immigration System Act. This bill proposed another round of reforms that would accelerate these measures and result in a more restrictive refugee system. CIC's "Backgrounder" documents (2012a, 2012b) on the reforms promised "faster decisions" with an accelerated timeline for hearings and decisions that would be made by a new layer of civil servants rather than IRB members, "timely removals" of those determined not to be eligible to make claims or with failed claims, and introduction of the Assisted Voluntary Return and Reintegration pilot program, discussed in more detail subsequently. In addition to expediting processing and decisions, the bill brought in further measures to address human smuggling and introduced the collection of biometric data from temporary foreign workers and foreign nationals in Canada from twenty-nine designated countries and one territory (Palestine).

The policy of "irregular maritime arrivals" leveraged the spectacle of boats, their association with criminality, and codification in law. This policy essentially targets "groups" arriving together by boat, with a group numbering two or more. The policy granted discretionary power of designation as irregular arrivals to the minister of public safety. The policy amounted to the targeting of particular bodies through their modes of entry, a lesson learned from Australians. This designation triggers mandatory detention—as in Australia—and restricted access to permanent residence and family reunification (Hyndman et al. 2014).

Reilly and Davies (2013) tracked the movement of the language and policies of irregularity from Australia to Canada. In Australia, "asylum seekers have been broken into two categories since the Howard government introduced new policies targeting boat arrivals. Those categories are Irregular Maritime Arrivals (IMAs), meaning people arriving by boat, and Non-Irregular Maritime Arrivals (Non-IMAs), meaning people arriving by plane" (Reilly and Davies 2013). In the Canadian case, however, there was an even more disproportionate leveraging of a statistically small number of boats.

The 2012 legislation targeted asylum seekers, imposing increased deterrence, criminalization, and punishment. It denied refugee claimants access to health care, opened paths to mandatory detention for those designated "irregular arrivals," and removed chances for refugee status with what Hyndman and coauthors (2014) identify as preclusion and externalization, or stopping potential refugee claimants abroad or en route, before they reach Canadian sovereign territory. Other measures made people holding a range of legal statuses more precarious, including lists of safe countries whose nationals face expedited asylum processing with fewer chances for appeal, lists of dangerous countries whose nationals face lengthier security checks upon making claims for asylum, and greater concentration of discretionary power with the minister to intervene and adjudicate cases. As these measures were enacted, asylum itself became more exceptional. By positing asylum as something exceptional in Canada, I mean that it is something rarely discussed and silenced in public discourse (until February 2017, when refugees started entering Canada from Trump's more openly hostile version of the United States). I mean that asylum is not treated as something that is necessary or a status that people search for or offer due to necessity and with integrity. Instead, asylum processes are more typically treated as a magnet for fraudulent claims and asylum seekers as people acting with ill or criminal intentions.

The 2012 legislation provided the legal architecture for grounds of exclusion and greater discretion placed in the hands of the minister and civil servants who operationalize policy: greater powers to detain, to strip legal status from refugees and citizens, and the removal of rights to health care. Other significant changes to asylum seeking in Canada relate to the refugee determination process (RDP) itself. Although Canada was once heralded as having developed the most robust RDP in the world, the government removed much of the infrastructure that once made the system robust. Under former prime minister Stephen Harper's Conservative leadership from 2006 to 2015, this included dismantling legal means for appeal and leaving the very body that adjudicates claims—the IRB—anemic by replacing independent members with civil servants. So, while the number of claims was reduced significantly through prevention, such as offshore policing, and in Canadian law and policy, the chances for those who succeeded in arriving onshore to file a claim were also reduced (UNHCR 2014b; Keung 2019). Chances for an expedited process grew, while chances for appeals shrank.

The deterioration of the right to seek asylum (or refugee status) in Canada has been relatively quiet and piecemeal and therefore rather successful. No One Is Illegal, the Canadian Council for Refugees, and the Canadian Association of Refugee Lawyers all designed campaigns to fight these changes. Unfortunately, mainstream Canadian civil society remained largely unaware, unaffected, and uninvolved.

Another important component of the legislation was granting the minister of public safety the right to designate groups of people as "irregular arrivals," in the event that the minister suspects the group cannot be examined in a timely manner or that the group might have been smuggled into Canada for profit (Hyndman et al. 2014, 35). Just as Ibrahim traced the movement of racialized discourse about refugee claimants who arrived by boat in 1999 into restrictive legislation in 2002, Hyndman and coauthors (2014, 35) note *discursive slippage* from refugee claimant to "irregular arrivals."

This discursive slippage can be located in the 2012 legislation, with the assignment of ministerial administrative discretion to deem groups of people irregular. As Hyndman et al. note, those designated as "irregular arrivals" face mandatory detention and—should their claims be accepted—the delay of permanent residency and family reunification for five years. The legislation also expanded surveillance and investigative powers. This restriction of access with expedited processes and streamlined procedures offers an example of the creation of tiers of refugees and further criminalization of claimants with the introduction of punitive measures.

The act, working in concert with other enforcement measures discussed in this chapter, succeeded in significantly reducing the number of refugee claims to a historic low in 2014 (Wingrove 2014). Then immigration minister Chris Alexander boasted of this historic low as being a direct result of the deterrence of applicants from "safe" countries. Alexander stated, "We have achieved great results in making the refugee system work for refugees and for taxpaying Canadians" (Wingrove 2014).

Of course, these changes in Canada, placed in global context, were not unusual. Intensified criminalization of asylum seekers in Canada—and specific policies designed to target those traveling by boat—corresponded with global trends (Crock and Ghezelbash 2010). The discursive slippage is transnational in scope. Immigration minister Jason Kenny traveled all the way to New Zealand to encourage Kiwis to use the term *irregular*. Far from superficial or inconsequential, these discursive wars prove central to the social death of asylum seekers, with refugee claimants replaced in public discourse by "irregular maritime arrivals" and "bogus refugees." Of note is the significance of this shift in recent *Canadian* history, as well as the particular devices designed for these exclusions. For the latter, I turn to lists, algorithms, visas, and the geopolitics of asylum.

GEOPOLITICIZING CLAIMS: LISTS, ALGORITHMS, AND VISAS

While some potential refugee claimants are stopped from making claims once they land on sovereign territory, far more people are stopped offshore with what Robert Davidson (2003) calls *passive-preemptive* interdiction. As Gerald Kernerman (2008, 232) notes, the remote operation of these measures—such as visa requirements and carrier sanctions—makes such practices difficult to observe, know, study, or contest (see also Frelick et al. 2016; Marwah et al. 2016; Maillet et al. 2018). As quiet evidence of the importance of offshore interception to Canadian border enforcement practices, for several years the Canadian government has had an official based in the Privy Council Office whose role is to address interdiction.

Under the Harper administration, however, exclusionary practices came out into the open. This occurred in part with legislative moves by the government to severely restrict claims from any one country of origin. The 2010 Balanced Refugee Reform Act granted the Canadian government the authority to identify Designated Countries of Origin (DCO), implemented in 2012 and ended under the subsequent liberal administration in 2019 with the removal of all forty-two countries from the list. The Protecting Canada's Immigration Act further elaborated use of the DCOs as a policy tool. According to CIC's "Backgrounder" for media, DCOs are "countries that do not normally produce refugees, respect human rights and offer state protection" (CIC 2012a). "The aim of the DCO policy is to deter abuse of the refugee system by people who come from countries generally considered safe." Claimants from these countries have their claims processed faster, ensuring that "people in need get protection fast, while those with unfounded claims are sent home quickly through expedited processing" (CIC 2012a). This measure was presented as a policy tool designed to assist the government in its response to spikes in claims from particular countries.

The placement of countries on the DCO list is determined with quantitatively measured thresholds "or limits set out in a ministerial order" (CIC 2012a), with triggers for placement based on rejection, withdrawal, and abandonment rates from any one country. An algorithm was put into place, determining that a rejection rate of 75 percent or higher or an abandonment and withdrawal rate of 60 percent or higher triggers a review (CIC 2012a). Countries with a low number of claims would also have a qualitative checklist. The review would determine whether the country should be placed on the list. By October 2014, two years after the act was implemented, the forty-two countries in Figure 20 were on the DCO list, having been placed there between 2012 and 2014 (Immigration, Refugees, and Citizenship Canada 2019).

The Canadian Association of Refugee Lawyers (CARL) formed in response to the 2010 legislation and deemed the list "arbitrary, unfair, and unconstitutional" (Canadian Association of Refugee Lawyers 2012). An attorney associated with CARL criticized the list for creating "a two-tier refugee determination system which discriminates between refugee claimants based on their nationality (i.e. their country of origin)" (Berry 2012). The group also contributed to expert testimony on detention before parliament in 2014. Grant and Rehaag (2016) analyzed IRB data and found that from 2003 to 2012, "10,150 individuals obtained refugee protection in Canada from countries that were designated during the DCO regime's first two years of operation. In 2013–14, under the new refugee determination system, 337 more claimants from these countries obtained refugee protection." Furthermore, Canada accepted hundreds of refugee claims from Mexico and Hungary, both countries on the DCO list, for their safety (Hyndman et al. 2014, 34).

A second category of countries was assembled and labeled "High-Risk Countries" (Immigroup 2013), designed to target foreign nationals from these designated countries with greater security measures, including mandatory detention, a refugee hearing within forty-five

Country	
Andorra	Liechtenstein
Australia	Lithuania
Austria	Luxembourg
Belgium	Malta
Chile	Mexico
Croatia	Monaco
Cyprus	Netherlands
Czech Republic	New Zealand
Denmark	Norway
Estonia	Poland
Finland	Portugal
France	Romania
Germany	San Marino
Greece	Slovak Republic
Hungary	Slovenia
Iceland	South Korea
Ireland	Spain
Israel (excludes Gaza and the West Bank)	Sweden
Italy	Switzerland
Japan	United Kingdom
Latvia	United States of America

FIGURE 20. Table of Canada's Designated Countries of Origin as of July 2016 (CIC 2016).

rather than sixty days, and no right to appeal the decision. With this list developed in 2013, foreign nationals from these countries were automatically deemed to be higher security risks and were subjected to greater biometric surveillance, such as mandatory fingerprinting. Twenty-nine countries and one territory were placed on this list.

Significantly, the DCO introduces greater administrative discretion and makes greater space for the role of geopolitics in determination of refugee claims. Kernerman (2008) studied one such case that preceded the formalization of these geopolitics with the DCO list: Canada's response to Roma refugees from the Czech Republic from 1997 on. Following the 1997 airing of a documentary on Czech television that showed Czech Roma enjoying legal status and social welfare services in

Canada, some fifteen hundred Roma refugees came to Canada (Kerner-man 2008, 237). The Canadian government eventually responded to this influx by imposing a visa that essentially eliminated the arrivals. Another notable example was the controversial visa required of all Mexican nationals, causing diplomatic tension between Canada and Mexico. The visas required of Czech and Mexican nationals were both introduced in 2009, following a spike in refugee claims from the latter (Gilbert 2013a, 2013b). These were dropped in December 2016, under new leadership.

These geopoliticized interventions into country status hold power-ful ramifications for individual legal status and chances for mobility. Intensifying the politicized realm of ministerial discretion and geo-politics into the refugee claimant process reduces access to protection by group identity. The spirit of refugee law holds that claims are to be individualized in the adjudication process. The IRB has always con-sidered changing conditions in the country of origin as an important element of its research and context in making decisions about individual claims. Yet the blanket removal of some countries and securitization of others assigns more weight to the country of origin—and, by proxy, to geopolitics—and therefore increases chances of discrimination against claimants and their individual histories on the basis of country of origin (i.e., identity, ironically).

An additional securitizing measure that draws on the power of dis-cretion involves the introduction of security certificates. Certificates were operationalized through IRPA, "which allows the ministers of public safety and citizenship and immigration—acting on the basis of secret information—to cosign a document deeming a person without Cana-dian citizenship status to be 'inadmissible' to Canada and authorizing that person's indefinite detention pending expulsion from the country" (Larsen 2014, 78). This legal architecture contributed to expanded use of detention that followed in subsequent years. Shifts in temporality—specifically, the possibility of indefinite detention (Larsen 2014)—fueled the expansion and use of detention capacity in recent years.

In 2015, when the Liberal Party returned to power in Canada, the DOC list and other measures of securitization remained in place, al-though broad consultations were held about potential changes to im-migration and refugee policies.

THE EXPANSION OF INFRASTRUCTURE: DETENTION, DEPORTATION, AND THE IOM

The introduction of mandatory detention for "irregular arrivals" (as designated by the minister for public safety) and detention without limits meant increased legal and built infrastructure to detain. Fifteen years ago, some 455 people were detained in any given year (Gavreau and Williams 2003, 68). As Gavreau and Williams observed, "Canada's problem is that we often look good by comparison" (68). These numbers increased significantly in the 2000s (Chak 2014). In 2017, 6,251 people spent time in detention in Canada (Global Detention Project 2020). No One Is Illegal–Toronto and the End Immigration Detention Network were active in fighting these slides into precarity and hidden forms of limbo. Figures 21 and 22 offer two snapshots from the Global Detention Project, captured in 2014, that demonstrate this increased capacity and its spatial distribution. Activism focused in part on a detention facility in the small town of Lyndsay, Ontario, 134 kilometers from the immigration court in downtown Toronto. Several people there were experiencing detention without limits. The distance outside of Toronto meant that few lawyers or visitors were willing to travel to the facility, nor could people detained there receive telephone calls.

A confidential report involving monitoring by the Red Cross of Canada found poor conditions in Canadian detention facilities run by the CBSA, including inadequate support for children and people suffering from mental health issues and inadequate space for all (Bronskill 2014). In 2016, a death in detention called attention to the growing number of deaths and the lack of information available to the public about them (Perkel 2016). In 2017, a new study found a significant increase in the number of children detained in Canada (Fraser 2017).

Another quiet yet significant arrival in Canada was the IOM, which opened its first office in Toronto in 2013. The IOM worked in collaboration with CIC, CBSA, and the private security firm GS4. The IOM provides migration-related services for fees to governments, and Canada is one of its largest donors. Until recently, this funding went to support IOM projects offshore and the transport of refugees to Canada. Recent work of the IOM in Canada involved a controversial pilot testing of

FIGURE 21. Landscape of detention in Canada, 2009. Courtesy of the Global Detention Project.

FIGURE 22. Landscape of detention in Canada, 2020. Courtesy of the Global Detention Project. Map data: Google, INEGI, ORION-ME.

the Assisted Voluntary Return and Reintegration (AVRR) program in Toronto. A 2012 CIC document described the pilot program (CIC 2012b):

> The Assisted Voluntary Return and Reintegration (AVRR) pilot program will also help to remove low-risk failed refugee claimants more quickly. The AVRR pilot program will be launched in the Greater Toronto Area and would now include claimants from all countries when it begins, not just those from Mexico, the Caribbean, and Central and South America. In addition, the AVRR pilot program would be opened to those in the current system in order to expedite removals and further contribute to overall backlog reduction efforts.

By the end of 2014, 3,143 failed claimants had been returned home through the program (CBSA 2014, 10). At the end of its pilot phase in 2015, the IOM closed its offices (CBSA 2015).

Few Canadians were aware of the IOM's potential to facilitate the disappearance of refugee claimants and their families from Canadian society. The IOM is an intergovernmental agency created after World War II. This is a confusing organization to place. It is often thought to be part of the United Nations, though it was not until 2016. The IOM does not hold status as a not-for-profit organization. Analyses have shown the IOM able to operate where states cannot (Andrijasevic and Walters 2010).

Security officers accompanied individuals who agreed to deportation through the AVRR program to Toronto's Pearson International Airport, all the way to the gate. GS4 officers held travel documents until program participants boarded the plane. The highly controversial and critiqued AVRR program was run as a pilot program by the IOM in Toronto but had ended by 2015.

THE DUPLICITOUS STATE

I want to return here to Boltanski's notion of the "politics of pity" (engaging with Arendt 1958) and the distancing of humanitarianism and externalization. We can better understand these ideas and how invisible forms of violence operate onshore through dehumanization and the invisibility of asylum seekers, contrasted with the hypervisibility of their securitization (as "bogus refugees" and "irregular arrivals"). Since the election of the Liberal government in 2015, leadership has not emphasized these processes of securitization but rather its humanitarian rescue and resettlement of 40,723 Syrian refugees between November 2015 and November 2016 (CBSA 2015). One of Prime Minister Trudeau's early successes was fulfillment of the campaign promise to resettle twenty-five thousand Syrian refugees, after previous leadership failed to resettle more than a few hundred per year. This politicized and profiled their resettlement, placing Canada in stark contrast to the United States, where President Obama's efforts to resettle Syrians were blocked by state governments across the country. When President Trump subsequently banned their resettlement and the entry of people from majority Muslim countries in January 2017, Prime Minister Trudeau posted the following tweet: "To those fleeing persecution, terror & war, Canadians will welcome you, regardless of your faith. Diversity is our strength." The tweet was popular: it was "liked" more than 723,000 times.

Still, the uses of distance and remoteness and the intertwining of geography and legality can be observed unfolding and utilizing parallel logic. Obscured is the extensive offshore enforcement archipelago that Canada has quietly devised since its development of the Immigration Control Network in the 1980s. The use of geopolitics to thwart asylum seekers from particular countries in recent years extends the treatment of asylum as exceptional by quietly hiding from view in plain sight the violence of their exclusion.

Over the last ten years, Canada has increased its detention capacity onshore. In Canada, remote detention has a different meaning than in Australia or Italy. As in Italy, Australia, and the United States, the enforcement archipelago evolves simultaneously onshore and remotely offshore. Yet its form is notably different in the Canadian context. Remote border enforcement offshore has also intensified, but not in the form of detention facilities on islands.

Migrants' lives are at stake as sovereign power is reconfigured through the performative work of border enforcement that plays on what is hypervisible and what—or who—is left unseen (Mountz 2010). The politics of migration is often a duplicitous and paradoxical politics of crisis and in/visibility (Nyers 2005). But this duplicity and accompanying paradoxes take different forms in distinct national contexts. In Canada, the silence surrounding these changes represents the social death of asylum seekers. The form of the island is quietly mobilized as the legal space of precarity, liminal status, and isolation onshore.

The theme of hypervisibility and invisibility recurs in much contemporary scholarship on sovereignty. Diane Nelson (2009), for example, posits states as duplicitous and "two-faced": articulating one plan while hiding another. In the Canadian setting, the juxtaposition of helping and rescuing through resettlement operates in tandem with aggressive, hidden, offshore forms of exclusion. Like the humanitarian–enforcement nexus at work on the Mediterranean and along the Mexico–United States border, this onshore–offshore binary is a productive topology that fuels the social death of asylum seeking in Canada by lauding one kind of resettlement and obscuring a simultaneous exclusion.

Wealthier states labeled "immigrant receiving" remain duplicitous in their desire for and rejection of migrants. They hold the power to determine lives that are valuable and valued and those that are not, and this de/valuation is construed through discursive framings of visibility and invisibility. The enforcement archipelago is constructed on this devaluation. Butler's (2009) questions about civilian deaths can be asked of border zones where migrant deaths occur routinely (e.g., Nevins and Aizeki 2008). Whose deaths are grievable, and what exercises in political responsibility would "attend to the precariousness of life, checking the transmutation of life into non-life?" (Butler 2010, 177). The unmourned and uncontested dehumanization and disappearance of those excluded offshore in the shadow of mainland territory reproduce an inhumane political field. There migrants are homogenously scripted as security threats and blamed for the very security measures that intensify their precarity and in many cases cause their deaths. Violent state policies and practices of dehumanization are hidden by narratives of security. Within the enforcement archipelago, detention must be brought into view to shift from Gregory's vanishing point to grievable loss of life.

CONCLUSIONS

In this chapter, I have located Canada's role in the death of political asylum. The Canadian case shows that asylum seeking, while not illegal, has itself become a form of exceptionalism. Nation-states are increasingly behaving as islands. Silence and lack of knowledge about migration among general publics worsen the situation, advancing the social death of asylum seekers. The death of asylum in Canada involves the use of geopolitics and bilateral arrangements to prevent the arrival of refugee claimants, legal and geographical maneuvers to exclude onshore and offshore, criminalization, securitization, and the movement of borders to the body. Such bubbles of excision and isolation have recurred throughout this book, with the treatment of asylum seekers' bodies as islands—isolated geographically and socially. While many of the shifts outlined happened quietly and without much protest from those who reside in Canada, their impacts have been swift and devastating, altering chances for refuge not only in Canada but across North America. This chapter has shown the multitude of ways that asylum seeking is shrouded in discourses of exceptionalism, making access to asylum itself exceptional—the designation of countries of origin deemed safe or dangerous and the use of this designation to exclude asylum seekers.

In the absence of a visibly spectacular crisis of the magnitude of the MV *Tampa* incident, or an island like Lampedusa or Christmas Island appearing overwhelmed by boat arrivals, Canada still—in its own quiet way—managed to mobilize island logics and reproduce maritime policies in response to crises associated with migration events elsewhere. These nonislands have been leveraged into islands of another kind through their reproduction in Canada in the form of proliferating spaces of confinement and legal maneuvers that render people as islands, isolated by law and carceral geographies. These are emerging in institutional spaces—increased use of detention and legal scope for detention—but also in the isolation of individuals, treating people as islands with the assignment of greater legal precarity and less access to social welfare. As I have shown in this chapter, these have been leveraged most powerfully in Canadian legislation that has relatively quickly dismantled many of the protections once enshrined in the Canadian RDP.

The death of asylum in Canada shows that this death is not only happening on islands and in the borderlands but in the treatment of people as islands within law and geopolitical machinations between states. Canadian policy contains many expert moves to prevent asylum seeking, within the realms of law, policy, and geopolitics. These maneuvers are especially pronounced in the response to boat arrivals and the crises they engender.

I have focused on the ways that Canada has altered the landscape for refugee claimants *in and before arriving in* the country. Canada was failing migrants and asylum seekers not only at home but in its role abroad as well. This chapter has located Canada relationally in the death of political asylum with a dynamic story that continues to unfold. Canadian leadership changed in 2015. But, as has been shown in the transition from President Bush to President Obama in the United States, this does not necessarily mean that policy and legal changes can or will be easily or readily undone.

There has been much hope and some change in the time since Prime

Minister Justin Trudeau entered office in late 2015. The visa imposed on Mexican nationals was lifted, as one important example of the undoing of measures implemented by Stephen Harper's previous administration. However, the refugee law and advocacy communities were still waiting to see what changes the Liberal government would roll back. Meanwhile, in the opening years of the new Trudeau administration, public discourse and resources prioritized and celebrated the significant Syrian refugee resettlement while obscuring the plight of others seeking safe haven in Canada. As President Trump took office south of the border, these criminalizing discourses and accompanying enforcement actions took on a more shrill tone, leaving Canada in an interesting and contrasting—if geopolitically delicate—position.

While not widely known by Canadian or international publics, these changes in Canada did not go uncontested. They were challenged by refugee lawyers, Ontario doctors, and activists protesting new forms of detention and deportation. Stories of precarity and injustice have been told by the mainstream Canadian media. These stories of activism to fight the death of asylum are happening not only in Canada but around the world—the subject of my next chapter.

6

The Struggle: Countering Death with the Life of Activism

> If we stay with the sense of loss, are we left feeling only passive and powerless, as some might fear? Or are we, rather, returned a sense of human vulnerability, to our collective responsibility for the physical lives of one another?
>
> —JUDITH BUTLER, *Precarious Life*

While much discussion in this book so far has been about loss—the loss of migrants at sea, the loss of life worth living in detention, and the loss of asylum itself—there is hope yet and political futures to be found in the wreckage and in the life of activism. Amid unimaginable loss and adversity, life continues on. An important component of that life contends politically with the death of asylum—whether in the mundane, collective forms of getting by or the extraordinary moments where collective unrest erupts into political mobilization to call attention and demand change. Butler (2004) suggests relationality and accountability as essential components of the way forward. This last chapter is about how people around the globe are working together—often by forging connections across great distances and fortified walls—to confront devastating losses related to migration with the life of activism. In this chapter, I explore some of the resilience and creativity born of incarceration, activism, and the desire to confront state violence, including the oppressive forces of exclusion. To do so, I build on a politics of location, working with ideas about countertopography (Katz 2001, 2004) and the body as political terrain within antidetention activist campaigns (Hodge 2019) and understandings of asylum (Puumula and Kynsilehto 2016). People confined in remote locations have the political space of protest reduced to that of the body. Conversely, transnational activist campaigns traverse boundaries, enabling movements to traverse great distances to build the networked spaces of campaigns—to *expand* the political space of individual bodies. These campaigns are forged over different kinds of distances (geographical, emotional, political) precisely to contest the isolating and dehumanizing effects of distance and confinement in the archipelago. Through activism, people inside and outside of detention work together to extend the political spaces of confined bodies.

I am mindful, thanks to the work of Sarah Hughes (2016) in particular, of the tendency to romanticize and overemphasize the agency and actions of confined people as resistance. My goal is neither to emphasize nor to overlook but rather to heed and to find hope in the visions that antidetention movements present for alternative futures.

Several years ago, I met a senior nun at her home in the suburbs of Sydney. Like other nuns whom I had met and interviewed in Australia and the United States, she was involved in detention-related social justice campaigns and had spent years visiting people detained in the Villawood Detention Centre, located in the outer suburbs of Sydney. During our visit, she showed me images she had recorded on videotape from a televised documentary series in Australia called *Four Corners*. The documentary featured footage leaked from the Australasian Correctional Management Corporation. It showed people held at the Woomera Detention Centre wrapping themselves in the razor wire fencing that surrounded the infamous facility in the Australian outback (open from 1999 to 2003). In one of a series of protests captured by security cameras, a man slit his wrists with the barbed wire. As he carried out this act, he looked into the security camera and offered his body to the Department of Immigration and Multicultural Affairs[1] and to the Australasian Correctional Management System, a subsidiary of Wackenhut, now called GEO, the largest transnational corporation in the business of constructing and managing prisons and detention facilities in the world.

These and other acts of protest emerge from despair, depression, and limbo behind bars in remote detention—in the outback, in this case. In this instance of self-harm, direct eye contact traveled across time and space with the assistance of technology, becoming more rather than less urgent as the years and the knowledge of despair passed from security camera to corporate whistleblower, documentarian to televised broadcast, nun to researcher. Although Australia mothballed Woomera in 2003, the government has continued to open facilities in more remote locations offshore, repeating a cycle that capitalizes on and exacerbates despair. In 2011, additional mainland facilities were mothballed as detention rates increased offshore with the 2012 reopening of Manus and Nauru, detailed in chapter 3. People detained ever more remotely continued to protest with self-harm, riots, and hunger strikes as some of the few effective political tools available to them.

While I have witnessed and in this book characterized many authorities and also publics, such as the Canadian public, as largely complacent in the death of asylum, I also want to document important collective struggles that have gone on inside and outside of facilities—sometimes at the precise threshold between inside and out, testing the limits of life and the resilience of fencing and the body. These protests were designed to contest the disappearance of spaces of refuge. Largely designed to call attention to the mundane yet hidden violence of detention, they are countering the death of asylum with the life of activism. A broad coalition of people carries out this work. They organize at different scales, from highly localized actions to visit, support, and represent nearby detainees or declare welcoming communities to global coalitions, such as the International Detention Coalition, which is mounting worldwide campaigns to reduce the use of detention, get children released, pursue alternatives to detention, and improve conditions where detention exists (Sampson 2013). Some identify as activists, while others instead consider participation a part of their work as nuns and doctors or their duty as citizens' and workers' rights groups. These coalitions build on existing networks and forge new ones. They are built to share information and carry out projects premised on a politics of location and memorialization: the impulse to locate, show, reveal, and remember people detained remotely in faraway places that most people will never have the resources to witness firsthand.

Countless productive encounters are happening in these seemingly forgotten zones. There authorities, migrants, and activists exist in dialectical geographical relation to one another as they move between administrative, urban centers of power and more marginal zones where sovereignty is exercised, if not weakened. As states expand enforcement outward and pursue ever more creative geographies of detention using isolation and distance, activists respond with strategies designed to overcome distance and isolation. With examples from campaigns organized by activists in Australia, Italy, and the United States, this chapter examines the politics and resources mobilized in attempts

Category of action	Associated activities
Counting	Documenting data that are difficult to access on deaths, enforcement operations, and confinement
Mapping	Projects to locate and visualize, carried out by collectives
Remembering	Memorialization through events and material structures, such as sculptures
Organizing	Multiscalar networks, coalitions, organizations, campaigns, and movements; collectives forged to carry out media campaigns and visitors' groups, to lobby government and inform the public about particular issues
Visiting	Individuals and groups establishing relationships of trust through regular visits and visitor campaigns
Protesting	Inside and outside of facilities; in remote locations and in large cities to call attention to and contest hidden geographies of remote detention

FIGURE 23. Forms of antidetention activism.

to form countertopographies to state tactics of exclusion. They carry out the work of location through various methods listed in Figure 23: mapping, documenting, remembering, exposing, and protesting zones of exclusion.

Figure 23 offers a typology I constructed to understand the array of activist campaigns, such as detainee visits, bail posting, legal advocacy, project mapping, and other strategic political interventions. My ensuing discussion of these collective actions will also demonstrate the broad range of people involved in social movements designed to free people from detention. Looking especially at advocacy aimed to challenge extraterritorial enforcement practices, I argue in this chapter that activists engage the same transnational landscape as states with distinct political projects to create radical spaces of hope: spare rooms for refugees, countermapping projects, letter-writing campaigns, bus tours to detention centers, artistic renditions of spaces of detention, and investigative reports that expose human rights abuses. In addition to those resisting the use of borders and bases to exclude and dispossess (Vine 2009; Davis 2011; Jones 2012b), I also examine detainee involvement in these efforts. By accessing technology and social media, those who are confined work toward freedom collaboratively with people on the outside.

FIGURE 24. North West Point Immigration Detention Centre, Christmas Island.

I find inspiration in, learn from, and locate the social movements that have arisen to contest the global detention industry, its continuous mobilization of fear, and the cynical belief that "no one cares," to quote one manager at the North West Point Immigration Detention Centre on Christmas Island, shown in Figure 24, in explaining to Kate Coddington and me why there were very few visitors to people detained there. This dismissive statement that "no one cares" was simply not true. It erased and denied the activism happening across Australia and around the globe, not to mention frequent protests taking place inside of the detention facility and the existence of a visitors' group formed by island residents. This denial also overlooked the fact that Christmas Island is one of the most remote pieces of Australian territory. It is extremely difficult to visit due not only to the island's remote location (landing it on Schalansky's [2009] list of one hundred remote islands that she will never visit) but also to the prohibitive cost of arriving and staying there.

The chapter is organized around six kinds of activist campaigns, constructed with empirical data from fieldwork: counting, remembering, mapping, visiting, networking, and protesting. In my discussion of each category, I attend to the different roles of the body and meanings of countertopography. Contending with technologies *of* the body and the body *as* technology in this chapter enables me to explore spaces of political protest in relation to spaces of confinement. Those isolated through banishment to small spaces in remote locations might have experienced the shrinking of political space down to that of the body. On the other hand, many are highly connected through social media to global networks and engaged in transnational social movements (Coddington and Mountz 2014; Hodge 2019). Thus the body is at once a political space and a technology connecting the self to larger political spaces and movements, a theme to which I return most explicitly in the penultimate section of this chapter.

THE BODY AS POLITICAL SPACE

While much of this book thus far has documented the extensive nature and incredible resources invested in topological bordering projects designed to exclude, hide, and isolate, there are equally relentless projects fueled by energy, passion, and political commitments to locate, reveal, and challenge. Drawing on scholarship by Cindi Katz (2001, 2004), I position these as countertopographical forces (Mountz 2011b). In Katz's analysis, countertopography involves the geographical forging of connections between places around the globe to contest capitalism. Katz's countertopography is a form of transnational feminism that "bring[s] the politics of location and differentiation to bear on the dislocation experienced by asylum-seekers trapped between states of migration" (Mountz 2011b, 382). Her use of the concept is designed to link seemingly distant and disparate locations, the work of connection happening with the goal of challenging colonial and imperial relations. Whereas authorities move the topological border to confine others through exclusionary enforcement, countertopographical forces open up alternative kinds of connections and solidarities across groups and distances by mapping these exclusionary infrastructures and associated violence. Advocates and activists design antidetention and antideportation campaigns with the goal of freedom: pushing down fences, transcending isolation and distance, and connecting those experiencing confinement with others on boats, those in other detention facilities, and those enjoying the freedom of mobility on the outside.

Like the decision to dig one's own grave (discussed at the end of chapter 3), the self-harm with which I opened this chapter involved a spectacular display of violence, designed to call attention. Like the North West Point Immigration Detention Facility on Christmas Island, the Woomera facility was known for isolating asylum seekers in the outback and for poor conditions on the inside, including the restriction of access to views of the outside world. The effects of this isolation on physical and mental health on asylum seekers and refugees and the persistence of these effects years after release from detention are well documented by scholars in health and psychology (Sobhanian et al. 2006). This institutional design made life for those confined inside miserable: by design, the state contained bodies in ways that intensified suffering in order to deter asylum seeking. In this way and in others, the global detention industry profits from the biopolitical and bureaucratic management of contained life and isolated bodies, the result of which is the shrinking, the disappearing, and, as I argue, the death of asylum itself. But there are other forms of mundane violence, hidden yet unfolding daily.

These questions of life and death can be witnessed through exploration of the political spaces of the body and activism. The life of activism uses the body as a space of political struggle, in at least two ways addressed in this chapter. First, forced confinement endeavors to isolate people, reducing the space of politics to the physical body. Self-harm, hunger strikes, riots, and suicide attempts ensue, utilizing the body as technology. But—second—detainees, activists, activist detainees, and detained activists also embark on efforts to use technology and social media to expand the political space of the body through transnational networks and social movements. The activist campaigns discussed in this chapter endeavor to document, map, broadcast, and memorialize the location and confinement of bodies on the move—to expand corporeal political space with the kind of scalar stretching from intimate to global spaces and relations (Pain and Staeheli 2014).

While an exhaustive account of antidetention activism around the globe lies beyond the scope of this chapter (and indeed merits its own book; see Tyler 2013; Marciniak and Tyler 2014), I review important work being done here to find hope and not forget the importance of the fight against the death of asylum. This hope remembers violence that has occurred, bringing humanization of individuals back into the frame alongside a commitment to alternative futures. As Butler (2004, 30) suggests in the lines that opened this chapter, we all hold "collective responsibility for the physical lives of one another." The different strategies, tactics, campaigns, protests, and movements discussed in this chapter hold one thing in common: a desire to counter the hidden by bringing people and their exclusion into view as one step toward collective accountability. Sometimes this means bringing one's own self into view, as activist, as writer, as detainee. Sometimes this means the body is the last remaining space of political protest, itself a technology mobilized for social change. At other times, movements for social change have extended the social, political, and affective dimensions of the body.

COUNTING AND DOCUMENTING DEATHS

Too often, antidetention activism begins with the counting of and accounting for bodies of those who disappeared en route to safe haven. In 2014, Kira Williams and I embarked on such a project to document losses at sea. We had found little existing work analyzing the relationship between migrant ship losses and enforcement operations at sea. This was surprising, given how frequently social scientists and activists argue that greater enforcement intensifies precarity (e.g., Nevins and Aizeki 2008). The dearth of data was *not* surprising for other reasons: losses and enforcement operations are difficult to document due to their hidden nature and the racialized dehumanization and devaluation of migrant lives and losses of life. Methodological procedures of state enforcement agencies also lead to manipulation of *how* bodies count, which makes government data unreliable (including in European and Australian contexts). There have, however, been important, recent efforts to document and count migrant deaths in different regional contexts, including Central American and Mexican journeys to the United States (Burridge 2009; Brigden 2016), losses at sea among people from various countries of origin trying to reach Australia (Hutton 2015a), and in the Mediterranean Sea among those headed for the EU (Spijkerboer et al. 2015).

In the absence of an existing, centralized, global database, Kira and I began by searching internet and media sources for documentation of any known ship losses and enforcement operations by year and location. We were not the first to endeavor to document loss. Many of these efforts have centered a particular region—usually a politicized crossing where border enforcement and deaths are believed or known to be high. Activist groups such as No More Deaths have been working for many years along the border between Mexico and the United States. They assemble

FIGURE 25. SIEV X memorial on Christmas Island, built to remember people who died on a boat that sank on the way from Indonesia's Sumatra Island to Australia to seek asylum. Photograph by Kate Coddington.

statistics using death certificates issued by county morgues (Nevins and Aizeki 2008; Burridge 2009; Last et al. 2017). More informal efforts to memorialize deaths have also been happening throughout Mexico and in the northern border region (Brigden 2016).

In Australia, two efforts are well under way following the tragic sinking of the SIEV X (Suspected Illegal Entry Vehicle number 10), an unmarked ship en route from the Indonesian island of Sumatra to Christmas Island in October 2001. It is believed that more than four hundred people were on board and that 353 died when the ship sank in a storm in international waters south of Java. It took two days for the first authorities to arrive to rescue some forty-four survivors, leading to a government inquiry. Former MP Tony Kevin (2004) documented this loss and the efforts of authorities to cover up their role and excuse themselves from responsibility for this incident. Australians have memorialized this loss with monuments in Canberra and on Christmas Island (see Figure 25). Marg Hutton has also named a website that tracks losses in honor of SIEV X and those it carried (Hutton 2015a). SIEVX. com documents "confirmed and probable drownings" of migrants en route to Australia from 1998 to 2015, estimated to number 1,550–1,560 (Hutton 2015b).

Sharon Pickering and Leanne Weber are feminist criminologists based in Australia who designed a method to count border deaths. They estimated some forty thousand such deaths worldwide over a recent ten-year period (Weber and Pickering 2011). Pickering runs the Border Crossing Observatory at Monash University, a site that documents border deaths of those attempting to enter Australia through its Australian Border Deaths Database (Border Crossing Observatory 2015). By July 2015, four years after its launch, 1,970 deaths were recorded in the database (Border Crossing Observatory 2015).

In the European context, Thomas Spijkerboer ran the largest contemporary project to study migrant losses. His research team contacted morgues in several hundred municipalities in southern EU border regions to assemble data. UNITED for Intercultural Action (2014) also maintains and updates a list of documented refugee deaths throughout the EU since 1993, which it argued stood at 18,759 people as of September 12, 2013. Spijkerboer's main method was to employ research assistants who visit or consult with every morgue in more than seven hundred municipalities located along the southern border regions of the EU. In 2015, his project launched a website called Border Deaths, which estimated that "3,188 people trying to reach Europe were found dead between 1990 and 2013" (Border Deaths 2015). In 2014 and 2015, Spijkerboer and his team organized workshops of approximately ten people doing the work of documenting migrant losses in the EU (personal correspondence, 2015), broadening the scope to include a more global set of scholars over time.

This business of documentation can be understood as a direct political response to state efforts to deny, hide, or diminish the value of lives lost at sea. As Butler (2004) argued, these lives have been dehumanized and devalued. They are not memorialized in obituaries. They count less. Counting them, therefore, became political currency in the fight to reduce the harmful border enforcement that fuels precarious risk taking and abuse of desperate clients by those working in human-smuggling industries. The efforts to document border deaths resonate powerfully with efforts by antidetention activists to locate disappearances into and transfers across detention centers.

The politics of counting is also, in part, about the business of bodies and the politics of memorialization. In our own efforts, Kira and I worked to engage physical sites of memorialization in cyberspace. We discussed which politics of location would have greater political impact:

the affective experience of loss that accompanies a physical memorial or the dissemination of empirical evidence so crucial to public policy. Both, albeit in different ways, were premised on the role of remembering and rendering mappable these oft-invisibilized losses.

REMEMBERING

Subsequent to the work of counting and accounting for losses detailed in the previous section is the process of remembering. Remembering those who disappeared is one kind of "emotional recovery work." Perhaps as a result of the scale of losses at borders, scholars in migration studies are writing more about loss, death, grief, memorialization, and what many refer to as the "present absence" of people—often without status—who disappear from national and international systems of recognition (e.g., Delano and Nienass 2014). This work of memorialization embraces and embodies Butler's argument about dehumanization: that those not valued—and often not documented, in life or death—cannot be grieved. Some have conceptualized this remembering as a kind of haunting, in Avery Gordon's (2008) work, an oppression that lives on and has not been resolved (e.g., Cho 2008; Thiranagama 2011). Still others seek traces of those lost, whether through forensic architecture, genealogy, or the labor of collecting death certificates at municipal morgues. One notorious and highly publicized example is a loss that occurred in the Mediterranean in 2011, known as the Left to Die Boat. This ship is alleged to have been in distress for several days, during which time distress calls were made to various policing authorities associated with NATO. Scholars at Goldsmiths University in London used forensic architecture to undertake a detailed accounting of what happened to people on the ship, the journeys of migrants to the ship, and then the ship itself. They also researched who was contacted while the ship was in distress and adrift for fourteen days within a NATO Maritime Surveillance Area and why authorities failed to assist the sixty-three people who lost their lives (Forensic Architecture 2016). More recently, in 2016, a ship that sank months earlier in the Mediterranean was located underwater. Until that date, the number of people who died at the time of sinking had been unknown. The raising of the ship forced a kind of remembering and reckoning with the scope of loss.

Accounting for losses of migrants, or "border deaths" (Weber and

Pickering 2011; Spijkerboer et al. 2015), proves challenging due to the uncertainty surrounding the circumstances, whether through tragedy at sea or trauma on land. Delano and Nienass (2014), for example, discuss the recovery of those migrant workers forgotten in the memorialization of the 9/11 attacks in the United States. Because their work in the World Trade Center and its vicinity was not legally documented or formalized in life, migrant workers' deaths were more difficult to document—leaving their families without entitlements accorded to other "9/11 families." Delano and Nienass show how the Mexican embassy delicately addresses this silence surrounding unproven deaths with an annual remembrance ceremony that—unlike the larger remembrance in New York—includes everyone.

Still other memorials exist not in the pages of academic articles but in sites along the border where they transpired, as in the case of sixteen-year-old José Antonio Elena Rodriguez. According to eyewitness accounts, Rodriguez was not involved in the exchange between Mexican nationals and U.S. Border Patrol on the other side of the fence in the Nogales twin cities that resulted in his death. Yet Rodriguez was shot by Border Patrol through the border fence as he walked home from work (Binelli 2016). As for the Left to Die Boat, a documentary film was shot and posted online to document the affair, but Rodriguez's death was also memorialized at the physical site of his border death in Nogales.[2]

Other forms of memorialization unfold in places where the precise location and cause of death remain unknown. Instead, memorialization takes place across the vast geographical distances of journeys. Many such memorials can be found along the tracks of the cargo train known as La Bestia, the "Beast," which travels the dangerous routes that many Central American migrants take to cross Mexico en route to the United States. This train is notorious as a site where violence has been carried out against migrants attempting to ride the rails, many disappearing along the way, their bodies commodified (Vogt 2013) and lost as what Imogen Tyler (2013) identifies as the waste of neoliberalism (Brigden 2016).

Communities proximate to sea crossings also experience tragic losses in close proximity, sometimes witnessed by and subsequently haunting communities as primary and secondary trauma. Some of these communities have found ways to memorialize these losses to remember those who survived and those who did not (as in the memorial shown in Figure 25). These losses conjoin migrants journeying to and through the island to those who live there and whose community functions as a gateway to mainland territories. The memorial to the SIEV X (Figure 25) on Christmas Island is much smaller, but no less powerful, as is another SIEV X memorial several thousand kilometers away in the Australian national capital, Canberra. As symbolized in the memorials, the sculptures themselves constitute a countervailing act to the violence of confinement in those very locations. Rather than capture and confine bodies, the memorials invite visitors and residents to witness and remember by traveling and gathering at a site that conjoins people at the island border.

Though important expressions of loss and grief, these formal memorials are not the only material forms of remembering on the islands. On Lampedusa, for example, many forms of remembering are apparent, as the island is a location imbued with the politics of erasure, location, haunting, and collective emotional struggles with trauma and meanings of migration. As the Mediterranean Sea becomes a cemetery for migrant crossings, as it was called by the prime minister of Malta (BBC News 2013), the island of Lampedusa becomes a location entangled with collective emotional struggles with the trauma of loss and the site of a powerful memorial: an archway on the beach.

Where national and multinational struggles over both disappearance and triumph unfold cyclically on Lampedusa (Cuttitta 2014), formal and informal sites of memorialization of people and their journeys to the island include a gateway memorial sculpture dedicated to those who died en route; the boat cemetery introduced in chapter 2 where ships that carried migrants are lain to rest; a small museum filled with personal effects gathered from ships at the cemetery to remember those who traveled through the island (Sperandio 2019, 92); and an international memorial event organized by activists across Europe in October 2014. In the cemetery, shells of boats attested to the presence of migrants gone missing, whether before or after their arrival, at which point many are returned to Libya or Tunisia or moved quickly to one of eight facilities in Sicily. In 2010, for example, Italy was undercounting arrivals. Government authorities excluded people on boats intercepted in landings data to keep reported numbers low. In contravention of international law, identities of individuals were recorded incorrectly to facilitate the return of third-party nationals to Tunisia, where Italy had bilateral return agreements in place.

In stark contrast with our experience of Sicilian residents reporting no crossings are Frontex interception data gathered with freedom of information requests by Williams (2018) and other scholars.[3] By 2014, the number of arrivals on Lampedusa grew precipitously to historic highs. According to Frontex data, EU authorities intercepted 110,508 migrants en route to Lampedusa in 2014 (Frontex 2015a). The IOM estimated that by July 2015, some 150,000 migrants had crossed the Mediterranean, greatly surpassing crossings in the previous years (IOM 2015). In its data, Frontex reported 1,033,103 interceptions in 2015 across the Mediterranean and Canary Islands (Frontex 2015a). By 2016, deaths at sea were increasing, with IOM (2019) estimating a total of 33,686 deaths between 2014 and 2019.

Alongside increases in deaths were significant increases in enforcement operations by Italy, Malta, Greece, and other EU member states through Frontex operations. Frontex spent at least €67.11 million on maritime operations in 2015 (Frontex 2016).

While erasures were happening on Lampedusa as authorities quickly shuttled migrants to other destinations, Italy and Frontex continued to push enforcement farther offshore and deeper into North Africa (Bialasiewicz 2012; Williams 2018), along transit routes. Research conducted by MSF on the border between Libya and Tunisia in 2011 found evidence of widespread, systematic torture in detention facilities in Libya (Médecins Sans Frontières 2011a). The team's findings draw out direct links between the return of migrants from the EU and their physical abuse as both deterrent and form of sexual and economic exploitation in detention facilities in Libya (Médecins Sans Frontières 2011a, 4), which is not a signatory to the Convention. The report provides testimonies of migrants and doctors, showing in detail how detainees are "denied basic human dignity as a result of their migrant status" (Médecins Sans Frontières 2011a, 4). This silence and complicity surrounding physical violence and the violence of erasure reinforce the devaluation of human life offshore.

Memorials and other forms of remembering become even more important in the context of historical and biographical erasure, denial, and contestation where they are built. Lampedusa's boat cemetery serves as a case in point. Although a small and marginalized place on a small island distant from the heart of the EU, the boat cemetery—and its destruction—symbolized a significant location in the struggle to humanize and value lives lived and lost crossing the Mediterranean. The failure to determine the cause of the fire that destroyed the cemetery left open the trauma of loss, followed by embodied recovery work carried out by activists, followed by more loss, in a tragic cycle that migrants, Lampedusans, and front-line workers live out.

To call attention to the island as a gateway site of crossing, confinement, and death in remote zones, Lampedusa was chosen as the site where activists met in October 2014 to fight the exclusionary EU border enforcement practices. They did so one year after the sinking of the boat, to remember.

MAPPING

In recent years, mapping for social justice has taken off, assisted by the opening of technology to the public and community organizations in ways that were not possible even ten years ago. Mapping has also become a salient, politicized, and contested tool for both sides in border struggles: for enforcement agencies seeking to thwart unauthorized migration and in antidetention activist movements.

As Walters (2012) and others note, maps are never simple and always represent political exercises. In the case of hidden violence and enforcement, one finds highly politicized projects of location (Maillet et al. 2016). In regions where states have invested in opacity to hide information, the simple act of locating people on a map can be profound.

Some of these mapping efforts have been highly organized, national and international in scope. Some have drawn on participatory mapping principles reliant on a kind of guerilla public engagement in gathering information. Others have engaged governing authorities more formally through access to information requests. A prime example of the former is the detention-mapping project of the Detention Watch Network, a U.S.-based, member-driven coalition of NGOs working on advocacy and activism pertaining to detention, in existence in some fashion since 1996. Given the sheer size, scope, reach, and opacity of detention facilities in the United States (Detention Watch Network 2015), the DWN set up its mapping project to solicit input from the public. The network invited people to add information to the map about the location of facilities where people were being held, including the names and addresses of facilities as well as any information available on advocacy groups working in the area. Given the frequent transfers of detainees across the country, often without prior notice to the detainee herself, let alone friends, family members, or legal counsel, this contact information became crucial in the process of locating people lost into a system that Hiemstra (2013) has characterized as "chaotic."

In a 2008 meeting with staff at DWN headquarters in Washington, D.C., I learned the history of their mapping project, a response to the fact that detainees were so often hidden either in remote locations or in unmarked locations in plain sight, often in warehouses (as in Elizabeth, New Jersey, for example). At the time that the mapping project began, ICE would provide advocates only with the names of facilities around the country and the associated government field office; they did not provide the address or telephone number. While it was difficult to locate detainees held in large, dedicated federal facilities, it was even more difficult to find out about small numbers of people being held in rural county jails run by local and state authorities.

DWN's mapping project used open source technology. Although it began with the basics—showing the locations of facilities across the country—these basics proved immediately helpful for people searching for individuals who had been detained. The basic information provided included address, phone number, and local organizations working in geographical proximity to the facility. Subsequent work involved gathering more detailed information, such as visiting hours, conditions, and mailing requirements to assist family, friends, and advocates.

The Global Detention Project is a relatively small outfit headquartered in Geneva, with a more global mission in scope: to map detention around the world. The founders and staff running the project pursued a more formal model in their efforts to map detention internationally, by country, relying primarily on access to information requests to research the latest figures, locations, policies, and laws pertaining to detention. The result is a comprehensive listing of detention facilities around the world, organized by country and updated periodically. Particularly controversial and policy-changing migration-related events and court battles are often included in the short narratives on each country website. The national organization of the site means that in-between spaces, such as islands, do not necessarily feature centrally, unless they are included in national databases and records.

Still other projects are smaller but no less influential. One important resource is a migration atlas designed by Migreurop (2015). Like the DWN, this group claims its role in advocacy and activism as its mission. Just as the DWN maps proved a catalyst for U.S. advocates, Migreurop's mapping efforts have been equally important and influential in raising awareness and building movements to challenge detention across the EU. Increasingly, as the surge in migration from the southern to northern EU intensified in 2015 and 2016, migrants used social media to map and share information about route openings and closures.

These endeavors to map are at times the basic but essential first steps in gathering information needed for advocacy.[4] People must first be located to be counted, accounted for, visited, and joined in the fight for freedom. In fact, liaising is key for the gathering and sharing of information, making the building of networks, campaigns, and coalitions a foundational part of activist movements designed to fight detention and support those on the inside.

BUILDING COALITIONS AND NETWORKS

Whether in the United States or Australia, advocates, activists, and detainees must overcome great, shifting distances of enforcement, whether working with people held in facilities on mainland or island territories. To overcome the distance, remarkable coalitions are formed, networks built, and campaigns undertaken. They frequently have used basic technology such as mobile telephones and email listserves to share information from site to site, to locate detainees transferred from one place to another. Like the DWN and the Global Detention Project, more local groups constructed tight networks to share and circulate information about and among people intentionally detached and hidden from view.

This has been especially pronounced in Australia, where a smaller population confronts a smaller detention system (than in the United States) across great distances. Networks developed through various campaigns: telephoning those too far to be reached in person, letter-writing campaigns, rooms for refugees, phone call campaigns in Australia. Still other campaigns in Australia were also highly localized, including the declaration of welcoming towns and visitors' groups in rural Australia. Christmas Islanders, for example, formed a volunteer network that worked to support asylum seekers detained on the island in the early years when detention began there, before the number of people grew beyond the capacity of exhausted volunteers.

For every isolating mechanism of exclusion deployed by the Australian federal government, activists countered geographies of detachment with tightly knit networks designed to overcome distances. I spent several weeks in Australia in 2006 conducting semistructured interviews with those involved in antidetention and antideportation movements. These were a diverse set of people who became involved for a variety of reasons, all leading to their engagement with social justice around the issue of the treatment of refugees. They pursued different strategies and offered distinct contributions, organizations, and networks, stitching together the threads of social justice movements.

These began with efforts to challenge the violent hegemony of homogenizing discourses about people in detention as security threats and bogus asylum seekers. Advocates and activists, in response, began campaigns with the not-so-simple efforts of identification. This is a process politicized in the legal regulation of asylum because a person must be identified properly to make an asylum claim and to be deported; they must also be identified to be located and visited in detention. In Australia, activists would form relationships with sympathetic guards. They gathered and shared information and maintained their own statistics on details related to detention. They specialized in smuggling information in and out. Daring nuns proved especially successful at sneaking in phone cards, identity documents in their bras, food, medicine, tape players, and even a camera in a cake—in the case of one nun we interviewed—in their efforts to help build legal cases.

To contest the efforts to hide and homogenize, to detach and distance detainees from sources of support, activist groups compiled their own statistics and embarked on their own campaigns to identify and track detainees and to provide information and legal advocacy. Only once identities of detainees had been established could they then be contacted. Advocacy networks embarked on letter-writing campaigns (e.g., Burnside 2003) and even telephone campaigns. I met Australians who had identified children in detention and then made telephone calls to them every day for months, sometimes years before—if ever—meeting them.

Still others tried more literally to reach asylum seekers. Lawyers, priests, advocates, and journalists faced aggressive campaigns by the federal government to restrict access by not granting visas to visit Nauru, for example. In cases where they had been granted, they had their visa applications revoked and, in some cases, were forcibly removed from planes bound for Nauru (interview, Sydney, May 2006). Those who were successful often went undercover as tourists to do so.[5]

Conversely, others carried out public campaigns to call attention to hidden and remote sites of enforcement. One group of activists embarked on a very public "freedom bus tour" that traversed the Australian outback to travel to remote detention centers along the western coast. They filmed their journey and produced a documentary that portrays harassment by the police.

Often, once particular detainees had garnered the support of advocates, the federal government would again attempt to hide them, sending people in chartered flights overnight westward across the country to even more remote detention centers. One respondent called this the "chasing" of detainees all over the country, from detention center to center. Detainees would disappear for several hours while being moved, only to reappear elsewhere. The Department of Immigration and Multicultural Affairs (DIMA), in fact, was one of largest consumers of chartered flights. Once activists were organized, such disappearances would prompt a flurry of email messages across list servers and telephone calls among organizations and individuals in remote locations until the detainees could again be located. Another part of the campaign was to call attention to their plights: to counter homogenization with histories and information. A poll conducted after the Tampa incident found that 85 percent of Australians supported government policies. Activists mobilized to confront this 85 percent and the reelection of Prime Minister Howard, who catalyzed fear and anti–asylum seeker xenophobia in service of his political campaign.

The activist movements that arose in the early 2000s, some of which continue today, involved exciting coalition politics. Many of those leading the way in activist and advocacy networks were women, sometimes retired, sometimes children of refugees or immigrants. Some were young, urban university students and graduates, others rural Australians. Among those involved were large numbers of lawyers, social workers, psychologists, and medical doctors who would provide services. Nuns were particularly successful at raising funds for bail, hiding identity documents, pressuring the government, and sheltering those released or escaped. With the devolution of the state's social welfare role to religious groups, NGOs, and individual volunteers, a substantial amount of pro bono "care" work transpired—and also meant advocates and activists experienced fatigue and burnout.[6]

Some helped detainees to escape, while others harbored escapees secretly or ran more "formalized" and publicized programs, such as Spare Rooms for Refugees. This program solicited urban dwellers to volunteer rooms for refugees who had succeeded in getting out of detention. Once released, "freedom" from incarceration often involved new restrictions in the form of visa conditions. Most former detainees do not hold permanent visas but rather one of a dizzying array of temporary protection visas (TPVs), a title that in itself suggests a reluctance to commit to protection, and which became more prevalent statistically with each passing year.[7] Thousands of people holding TPVs could move freely but did not have the right to work or even volunteer. In a classic case of the devolution of the welfare to the neoliberal state, they were forced, therefore, to rely on others. They lived with volunteers, with nuns who raised and posted bail, and with other former detainees.

Meanwhile, still other activist campaigns worked the media strategically to call attention to children in detention. A Sydney-based group called Chilout, for example, led a successful campaign to publicize the detention of children by Australia. They repeatedly released photographs to the press that depicted children in detention centers, emphasizing their isolation and lack of access to health care, education, and other services and support. This campaign was followed by other national campaigns, including extensive research in the form of the National Inquiry into Children in Immigration Detention 2014 by the Australian Human Rights Commission (2014). Chilout's publicity of the study and the children themselves resulted in successful policy change and the release of children from detention in 2005.[8] Many children were moved into alternatives to detention in communities. Despite this progress, a statement released in January 2016 shows the Commission's continued concern: "the Commission continues to have serious concerns about the impact of Australia's mandatory immigration detention system on children, and Australia's compliance with its obligations under the *Convention on the Rights of the Child*" (Australian Human Rights Commission 2016).

VISITING

Visiting is often the next step and crucial to bringing activism across the boundaries dividing people located within and beyond facilities. Visitors' campaigns often emerge out of the building of networks, coalitions, and organizations. Visits require traversing distances and other significant barriers to make it inside facilities to visit detainees with enough frequency to build relationships. Authorities deter people in Australia and the United States from visiting detainees due to the sheer distance they must travel and the bureaucracy they must navigate to reach them. Costs to fly to places such as Christmas Island, Guam, or even across the country are prohibitive. Only one charter airline flies to Christmas Island, a few times a week. The four-and-a-half-hour flights depart the western city of Perth a few times a week and cost more than AUS$1,000. The twelve-hour flights from California to Guam (most with stop-offs in Japan) run more frequently and cost more. Most people cannot afford these flights. As a result, local advocacy at home was needed.

In contrast, government authorities have significant funds to invest in moving detainees and authorities great distances. Since the inception of its remote detention regime, the Australian government has proven one of the largest clients of charter flight companies in recent years, due to its geographically dispersed detention regime. As a recent example, the government flew 365 asylum seekers on eleven flights at a cost of AU$31.7 million when it reopened Nauru's detention center in 2012.

One of the largest, most interesting, and atypical for geographical and political reasons was a group called Rural Australians for Refugees (RAR), whom I interviewed in 2006. RAR calls itself an "anarchic network" (Coombs 2004) organizing rurally in the politically conservative small farming towns of Australia to support, attract, shelter, and employ refugees. The group had formed to support refugees and contest authorities' assumptions that Australians living in rural areas would hold antirefugee perspectives and would welcome detention centers over refugees in their communities. Some of their strategies included the declaration of welcoming towns, letter-writing campaigns, and visits. They strategically funded groups near detention centers who would share information and sponsor those released. They successfully mobilized in remote locations to show the government that people in less populated parts of the country would not stand for its inhumane treatment. Said one settlement worker interviewed, "that group more than anything scared the shit out of the government" (interview, Sydney, May 2006) precisely because of its political unpredictability in the Australian geographic context.

Whereas RAR and nuns were people who identified more quietly as advocates, still others who identified as activists organized collective protests in places like Woomera and Curtin detention centers. There were momentous occasions and visits that involved the pushing down of fences and the subsequent escape of hundreds of detainees.

Finally, much support work was taken up by former detainees themselves, who bring phone cards, mobile phones, and food. Networks constituted by former detainees also moved information across fences—also destabilizing isolation and the idea that no information or currency moves in or out of the space of detention. Omar and Adham are two friends who met in at the Villawood Immigration Detention Centre in Sydney. Each was imprisoned for longer than five years, a significant percentage of their adult lives at thirty-two and thirty-six. Omar is from Kuwait, Adham from Palestine. They have very different histories that began to converge once each arrived in Australia. Omar is stateless, though to his mind, he fits all five conditions, only one of which would be required for refugee status. After five years in detention, he was finally released on a temporary bridging visa that allowed him to stay only until another country accepted him as a refugee, at which point he would be removed.[9] The day he was released from Villawood, two hundred detainees brought him on a victory march around the compound. He then applied to go to eighty-three countries and was denied everywhere. Once released, he visited Adham nearly daily and helped him to start a mobile phone business that traversed the walls of the detention center. As he walked away from the outdoor visiting space at the end of each visit back to friends, Omar would throw a mobile phone over in a sock that Adham would collect and sell. Omar lost his socks while Adham made money. When Adham was finally released, the two started a successful painting business together in Sydney. Still, neither has any promise of permanent status in Australia.

On a visit to Villawood with Adham and Omar on the industrial outskirts of Sydney one Saturday afternoon, we brought new underwear, cigarettes, chocolate, clothes, and food to their friends on the inside. Omar and Adham prepared fresh salad and halal meats and rice, food that their friends who were still detained would not get on the inside. The weekly visits were difficult for them. Their friends discussed the stress of not sleeping, not eating, pacing at night, confronting anger, depression, uncertainty, and boredom. They felt abandoned and forgotten by the world, and Adham and Omar attempted to keep them going and connected to the outside world during their visits. As we left, Omar tossed a mobile phone over to two friends, who quietly walked over to retrieve it.

Similar visitors' campaigns exist wherever there is detention, some more formal and institutionalized than others. In the United Kingdom, for example, the Association of Visitors to Immigration Detention is a registered charity based in Oxford with members across England and is especially active in communities that have detention facilities. In 2006, the group had sixteen member groups in England and Scotland.

A few years later, in the United States, the DWN drew on the Australian experience in building a visitors' training campaign to assist small groups to build the capacity, consistency, resources, and skills needed to run a sustained visitors' campaign, particularly in communities—both urban and rural—where detention facilities are located.

These social movements that I only here begin to document represent creative efforts to transcend and challenge isolation and detachment. In Australia, a people's inquiry was undertaken by many of the same networks to revisit detention practices and the lack of accountability on the part of government during this recent era.

PROTESTING AND THE BODY AS TECHNOLOGY OF POLITICAL PROTEST

Increasingly, people on the inside are working to call attention to their plight in collaboration with people enjoying freedom outside of facilities to use any tools available to them, whether technologies of social media or performance art and music (Marciniak and Tyler 2014). Some protests are more traditional, and many times during the course of the research, I was told memorable histories of walls being pushed down around Woomera and in Italy as detainees exited and flooded nearby towns in peaceful celebration. More often, more harmful violence has occurred, whether at the scale of riots within facilities or individual acts of self-harm, starvation, or suicide—employing the body as tool and space of political protest during confinement.

In each case, and in different ways, people utilize their own bodies as a political space of protest and technology of resistance. Here I briefly discuss a range of kinds of protests, with attention to the role of the body as political site and technology of resistance in each.

People turn to their bodies to protest as the last political space remaining. They may be isolated in any number of ways, whether held remotely, far away, or in a place that is unknown to community, family, or friends. Even in high-security, remote locations such as Christmas Island, solitary confinement is often a tool used to separate people who are deemed threatening troublemakers or suicide risks. In many facilities, people are prevented from using mobile phones or computers with access to the internet. Confronted with profound isolation, and often experiencing the despair of limbo, many turn to self-harm and suicide attempts. The deleterious effects of isolation on mental health have been well documented (e.g., Coffey et al. 2010; Neave 2013) and are exacerbated by detention in remote locations and the use of solitary confinement. Statistics show, for example, that a disproportionate number of incidents of self-harm in the overall system took place on Christmas Island: more than 50 percent (Bastians 2011). Of course, it is not lost on migrants themselves that they have been so devalued as to be reduced to the management of their bodies. The body becomes a site of conflict and contestation over territorial control, where political value is lost and regained. Forms of self-harm not only may seem the only space and means of political protest remaining but they also immediately hail the resources that have been lacking, such as medical attention.

Alternatively, the body can be seen as an expansive tool used in conjunction with technology for resistance. Although people who are detained remotely and confined to small spaces often feel that their space and chances to protest are reduced to the body as political space, they are sometimes able to extend this space through use of technology. Social media becomes especially useful.[10] People detained remotely, while spatially isolated, were also highly connected to people in other parts of Australia, in other facilities, and around the world with social media. As Kate Coddington and I (2014) argued, they are able to use technology to counter or mediate (if not end) the isolating effects of remote detention with tools such as social media, which give them access to join in the building of transnational networks, share information, facilitate advocacy across facility boundaries and international borders, and assist in building transnational social movements.

Even people we visited who had been detained on very remote Christmas Island for several months shared updated statistics and outcomes of the cases of fellow passengers and passengers on other boats and in detention in other places. People on Nauru tweeted about their arrival and conditions in detention. Facebook became an important resource and a way to reach out to convey, *I am here, where are you? What is happening there?* Technology itself becomes a key part of transnational activism designed to use the body to reduce the harm of isolation. When the Nauruan government banned all local access to Facebook in 2015, it was criticized and accused of doing so to shut down outsiders' knowledge and insider sharing of conditions of detention (*Oceania* 2015).

From the time of the journey by boat, such technology proves helpful. Even when banned, travelers and detainees often find access. Where possible, travelers use cell phones and other technology to communicate their journey and arrival. In a notorious case that took place in Indonesia in 2009, a boat carrying Sri Lankan Tamils was intercepted by Indonesian authorities and docked at Merak on the coast of Java (*Al Jazeera* 2010). People on board refused to disembark, instead using mobile phones to broadcast their plight to a global audience. While authorities succeeded in confining them to a small spit of land, they still could not hide their plight from the global community.

Activists and advocates located outside of facilities also use technologies such as mapping and social media to fight detention. A recent example is known as the Carta di Lampedusa, or the Lampedusa charter, published and signed online in 2014. Families of the victims who died when the ship sank met with members of European civil society, including migration and trade union activists, to commemorate those who died and ask questions about why they had lost their lives (Reuter 2014). The charter was released in the lead-up to the EU-wide memorial organized on the island in October 2014. Researchers are also part of these efforts in their work to count, document, and broadcast deaths, as in work by No More Deaths along the Mexico–United States border and the work overseen by Spijkerboer (Spijkerboer et al. 2015). They too are part of the collective refusal circulated in November 2014.

Australia's Let Them Stay Campaign offers an important example of the precarity and import of bodies. In 2016, the Supreme Court of Papua New Guinea deemed detention on Manus Island illegal, resulting in tension between governments about how to close the facility. Subsequently, 267 people (including 37 babies born in Australia) who had been flown to the mainland for medical care filed a suit asking to stay. The court denied the request, and the decision gave rise to the citizens' movement known as the Let Them Stay campaign (Hodge 2019). Campaigners were successful in achieving at least a temporary stay for many, if not all. In contrast with the detention center supervisor's statement that "no one cares" to visit people confined remotely, Let Them Stay demonstrated clearly that people care across great distances, but that those with the resources and power to turn their passion into effective action are located in greater numbers on mainland territory.

If the topological border produces topographies of confinement and isolation, transnational social movements building on feminist countertopographies draw a diverse politics of location. They seek to locate exclusion and its attendant violence by locating, documenting, and publicizing those lost to state violence.

HAUNTING SOVEREIGNTIES AND DETENTION AS A LOSS OF LIFE THAT POLITICIZES

In this chapter, I have mapped some of the many local, national, and transnational activist responses to enforcement archipelagoes. The archipelago operates as a spatial fetish that traffics in in/visibility, capitalizing on insecurity and fear. Activists, in contrast, have sought to restore humanity by understanding and publicizing the corporeal violence of exclusion, the racialized bodies enforced.

The prolonged uncertainty and violence embedded in the enforcement archipelago mirror Gordon's (2008, xvi) argument that oppression haunts and destabilizes reality:

> Haunting is one way in which abusive systems of power make themselves known and their impacts felt in everyday life, especially . . . when their oppressive nature is denied. . . . I used the term

haunting to describe those singular yet repetitive instances when home becomes unfamiliar, when your bearings on the world lose direction, when the over-and-done-with comes alive, when what's been in your blind spot comes into view.

As a result of the complexity of present and past, sovereign and non-sovereign territory, it is difficult to trace accountability for violence carried out across interstitial zones. Yet wherever one travels, there sovereign power acts in some form, even where the state appears absent. Sovereign powers extend outward like tentacles, moving the border to intercepted bodies, carrying out detention in ambiguous places between states through third parties, IOM, or Libyan officials acting on behalf of Italy. Haunting sovereignties link the enforcement archipelago to migrant bodies. State authorities too often seem to assume that this violence can be hidden in plain sight. But activists working locally and transnationally operate on a premise that what has been hidden must be revealed if social change is to happen.

In the realm of migration and asylum seeking, Butler's call for accountability holds meaning not only in the physical deaths of those lost at sea and along the border but for those experiencing the limbo of living death and deathly living in detention.

Butler (2004, 31–35) frames the loss of those whom she argues cannot be mourned through three kinds of death: the physical death of the body, the political death of the subject who can be forgotten, and the ontological death of the person. In the introduction, I explored these three deaths to understand the death of asylum. But Butler's analysis also engages a potential political response to death, understanding us all to be socially constituted beings attached to others through loss and vulnerability. She asks that loss and mourning be politicizing: "it furnishes a sense of political community of a complex order, and it does this first of all by bringing to the fore the relational ties that have implications for theorizing fundamental dependency and ethical responsibility" (22). It is through this relative form of precarity that we can read contemporary processes of securitization and engage Butler's call to use precarity as a basis for the formation of political community, to "guard against injury and violence" in the deathly living and loss of life in detention and beyond in the archipelago.

Rather than disappearing through Butler's three deaths, migrants survive and linger—in real life and as ghostly figures who themselves haunt through the forensic tracing of their present absence. Though demonized in national politics, they haunt the national psyche, prompting Italy to grant postmortem citizenship to those hundreds who most recently lost their lives. These travelers also haunt the international state system as ghostly figures out of place, in various states of not belonging, refusing either to adapt to the territorial desires of nation-states or to disappear from view.

CONCLUSIONS

In early discussions of the enforcement archipelago in this book, I discussed human smuggling and border enforcement as geographically relational phenomena. Through engagement with protest campaigns, I have shown activism and border enforcement also to be socially relational phenomena. This chapter linked the unforgivable deaths of migrants with "tick-tock regularity" and the death of asylum with the most salient countervailing force that I have found in my research: the life of activism. The death of asylum is being fought by activism, evident in this chapter across a diverse array of transnational social movements built on the politics of location. Given the isolation and distance put to use in containing people across the enforcement archipelago (onshore and offshore), and the substantial resources invested in keeping people and information about them hidden, the work of location proves central in the fight against remote detention. In the strategies used by activists and advocates discussed in this chapter—counting, documenting, remembering, building networks, visiting, and protesting—the work of location proved a central organizing theme across them. I have positioned these movements and campaigns as countertopographical forces designed to fight the topological bordering that shows endless capacity to isolate and confine, creating islands within islands and mobilizing islands beyond islands.

In contrast, the life of activism understands the work of location as geographical and social, with all people embedded in social relations and accountable to and for one another, in Butler's terms. Activists are engaged in Tolia-Kelly's (2006) "embodied recovery work," work that builds on a Butlerian politics of grieving and accountability. Memorialization and mapping mobilize the politics of location and emotion to document death, catalyzing and mobilizing emotions of grief toward political ends. A powerful example is the Let Them Stay campaign discussed here and started in Australia in 2016. The Let Them Stay campaign involved protests and the provision of sanctuary in homes, churches, and states that stood to contest the exclusionary actions of the federal government (Doherty 2016). It gave rise to a broader subsequent movement.

Many catalyzing events, such as boat losses at sea and deaths in facilities, have exposed the poor conditions and violence built into enforcement operations and detention facilities, causing them to be shut down in light of tipping points in public opinion. These include stories of negligence by denying medical care, suicide, and self-harm as well as riots. And yet the body—like the body politic—proves resilient in these stories, a key site of political struggle with many roles in the contestation of detention.

The body figured prominently in political protest in three ways in this chapter, at first the object and subject of efforts to count and account through documenting and mapping. Those confined often find their political space of protest reduced to the body. Yet the body also simultaneously, in conjunction with technology, becomes an expansive space of political protest through social media. These roles of the body in antidetention politics are distinct but reconcilable, even nourishing to one another. What they hold in common is their use of technologies, such as mapping, social media, and mobile phones, to exercise rights to locate, map, share information, move, stay, and protest (self-harm, suicide, hunger strikes, pushing down walls, destroying facilities).

At the same time that political protest happens in ways that show the reduction of political struggle to the physical body—such as hunger strikes, lip sewing, and suicides attempted and completed—people simultaneously find ways to broadcast these plights of the physical and emotional body to transnational communities and audiences using technology such as mobile phones and social media. Like the body, technology proves central to the fight against remote forms of isolation in the archipelago and the death of asylum.

Conclusions

The island is like an idea lifted out of the sea's brooding.

The island is an idea of itself—an imaginary island and a real one—real and imaginary reflecting together in the mirror of the water.

Look in the mirror. What can you see?

—JEANETTE WINTERSON, *The Powerbook*

The search for asylum has not disappeared; those seeking protection continue to haunt the global community and an international state system that largely refuses recognition of their plight, whether in life or in death. As scholars of haunting argue (Cho 2008; Gordon 2008), repression and violence suppressed never disappear but continually reappear. Haunting continues as those hidden and lost in the enforcement archipelago continually reappear, their absence ever present in the continuum of life and death.

As Butler (2004, 33–34) notes, the dead who lack recognition remain spectral:

> They cannot be mourned because they are always already lost or, rather, never "were," and they must be killed, since they seem to live on, stubbornly, in this state of deadness. . . . The derealization of the "Other" means that it is neither alive nor dead, but interminably spectral.

As Gordon writes, "the ghost is not simply a dead or missing person, but a social figure, and investigating it can lead to that dense site where history and subjectivity make social life" (as cited in Cho 2008, 29).

Adrift in the politics of migration and border enforcement, the physical and ontological deaths of asylum advance its political death. The more ludicrous responses to asylum seeking now under way are spectral; they are ghostlike images that are difficult to fathom, even when witnessed firsthand. Consider Spanish soldiers shooting at hundreds of migrants as they climb the fences around the Spanish exclaves of Ceuta and Melilla; people on boats on the Mediterranean, heavily monitored by surveillance yet still "left to die" as they are abandoned by officials from several countries at once; naval pushbacks and towbacks that kill those they feign to protect; and the negotiation of trade deals between Australia and the United States that traffic in refugees as though they were commodities, a de-valuation of human life at the precise moment of "rescue." While memorials to the dead—discussed in chapter 6—exist all over islands, an equally heavy specter of the living dead hangs behind the bars of detention and in the interstitial legal geographies of administrative proceedings.

In February 2014, I accompanied activists to witness court hearings held daily at the federal courthouse in downtown Tucson, Arizona. Part theater, part macabre shell of justice, these hearings were organized as part of the U.S. federal government's Operation Streamline. In place since 2005 (Borderlands Autonomous Collective 2012; Boyce and Launius 2013, 2), this operation accelerates processing and deportation of people arrested and charged with "illegal entry" into the United States over its southern border with Mexico. One activist group called this "Assembly Line Injustice for Corporate Profit" in its clever "illustrated guide to the criminalization of migrants." The Operation was in effect in eight of nine Border Patrol sectors in the U.S. Southwest, with the exception of San Diego (Boyce and Launius 2013, 1). I sat next to activist scholars Sarah Launius and Matthew Lowen, who brought me to the hearing on a visit to Tucson. ICE detainees who had recently been picked up while crossing the border were marched into the room in a line. They were primarily men, many very young, with only a few women among them. Most had traveled from Mexico, Guatemala, El Salvador, and Honduras. They wore faded clothing that had likely been on for several weeks or months of the journey. They were shackled around the hands and feet, with the shackles attached at the waist. The sound of chains clanging as each line entered and exited the room still haunts me as a racialized remnant of U.S. historical uses of forced migration in the shackling of transatlantic trade in African slave labor. Clear plastic dispensers of hand sanitizer sat on every table, their smell permeating the room—as if dealing with people arrested in this manner along the border was essentially dirty, diseased work threatening contagion. The sound of chains, the smell of sanitizer, and the speed of justice erased any lingering whiff of humanity and human dignity that might remain for these sojourners.

Activists aptly labeled this hearing an "assembly line," with proceedings organized to administer punishment with swift efficiency. Men were lined up in a row and asked to stand, several standing simultaneously before efficiently spaced microphones. Their government-appointed lawyers stood behind them. The judge would pose a question, which was quickly translated into Spanish. In response, each person would step to the microphone, one by one. Their answers never varied, as each man responded in a sequence repeated down the line: yes, yes, yes, yes, yes, yes. These were responses to questions about whether they understood their rights and that they would be sentenced to up to 180 days in prison and barred reentry to the United States. They signaled quick acceptance of a plea bargain associated with charges of "illegal entry" that would go on a permanent criminal record (End Streamline Coalition 2014).

We sat right of stage front, where people entered and exited the room in line. Many kept eyes cast downward or on the back of the person whom they followed, whether in shame, dismay, or fear. Some looked up and saw us, however, brief eye contact our only connection to the architecture of exclusion and the carcass of justice served. The entire affair was over in about an hour. As Boyce and Launius (2013, 2) note in their observations of the mass trials, "the results undermine due process in ways that are deeply unsettling." These include pressure to conform and failure to translate into languages other than Spanish, inadequate information about cases or rights, and inadequate access to legal counsel knowledgeable about immigration (Boyce and Launius 2013, 2). The attorneys representing migrants may spend up to twenty minutes acquainting themselves with clients and their cases. Once the proceedings begin, up to seventy people can be convicted within a few hours (End Streamline Coalition 2014).

Operation Streamline is further evidence of the death of political asylum and the more general foreclosure upon access to legal representation and meaningful legal proceedings in the United States. While Operation Streamline takes place in close proximity to the southern border, its sociolegal dimensions are by no means confined to border spaces or border regions. Rather, they are mimicked across the country in stilted proceedings that rely on geographical isolation and lack of legal representation (National Immigrant Justice Center 2010; Hiemstra 2013; Echavarri 2020).

In the years following these observations, assembly-line exclusion of people seeking asylum was extended south of the border into Mexico as the Trump administration threw its geopolitical weight into crafting bilateral arrangements with Mexico and Guatemala to detain people en route to seeking asylum in the United States. The spectacle of the border wall between the United States and Mexico was accompanied by aggressive measures to intercept and detain people migrating north in search of safe haven long before they actually reached that border.

Daily, myriad forms of cruelty and dehumanization continue in the enforcement archipelago, offshore and on mainland territory. States traffic in distance and isolation, investing in enforcement that makes life more precarious and death more likely. In the U.S. Southwest, and in other borderlands, expulsion has become not only predictable and punitive but industrialized to respond to increases in migration. People are "processed" and "managed" on islands and in transit zones as beds proliferate in mainland facilities to fuel capitalist expansion of the detention industry, capitalizing on the intimate economy of the body (Conlon and Hiemstra 2016). Since President Trump took office in 2017, ICE intensified its cruelty vis-à-vis creative uses of detention, isolation, and policing, with the strategic campaign carried out to separate families in detention as punitive tool. Enforcement is a business with a capitalist hunger for continuous expansion, operating at a cost of $3.3 billion for detention and deportation in the United States in 2016 (DHS 2016, 5). No one simple story line suffices to explain this growth in detention and border enforcement budgets. This business privatizes the biopolitical management of people, fueling the intimate politics of their mobility with confinement of the body, contracting out detention and asylum along the way (see Hiemstra and Conlon 2017). Policies build on a heightened politics of fear, with practices of intimate bodily threats—such as separation of parents and children—designed to contain, order, punish, and traumatize racialized people scripted as security threats, detained and invisibilized at great distances. Sovereign power is exercised ever more remotely amid the historically well-rehearsed desire to control territory, people, and their mobility.

In 2017, as new-to-office President Trump blustered and bungled the "huge," "beautiful wall" that occupied his geographical imagination, investments in walls built to confine on remote islands farther afield continued apace. Catherine Benoit (2019) argues that the walling of the EU begins in the French territories of Mayotte and St. Martin. States aggressively denied the right to seek asylum with these investments in offshore enforcement in ever more remote locations. Islands became flashpoints within the borderlands where legal struggles over entry and exclusion transpired. Migrants and aspiring asylum seekers encountered proliferating spaces of confinement en route and found themselves in extended forms of limbo. States increasingly treated mobile bodies as islands by mobilizing search-and-rescue areas, designing detention facilities, and setting in motion a range of other technologies that fueled evolving topologies designed and deployed to deter.

STUDYING GHOSTS OF VIOLENCE IN THE ARCHIPELAGO

Migration scholars must take up Grace Cho's (2008) demand that we study the ghosts of violence; this task is paramount to any fight against the death of asylum. Cho asks, "How does one detect a haunting that has been so dislocated and finely dispersed? How does one study that which is unseen and unspoken, that which has been lost, forgotten, made to disappear? How does one tell a story about something that cannot fully be known?" (41). While Cho was writing about the silent persistence of violence experienced by Korean women who were sex workers for U.S. military personnel, this endeavor to understand the unspoken applies also to the exclusions that lead to the deaths of asylum and asylum seekers in the present. Policy makers refuse to acknowledge the overwhelming body of empirical evidence that proves without question that border enforcement is a deadly form of state violence.

The primary argument offered for excessive shows of migration-related enforcement relies on the idea of deterrence: the notion that more border enforcement and more aggressive interception, detention, and deportation will deter future migrants from crossing borders. And yet, research consistently shows that more aggressive enforcement, interception, and detention do not serve as deterrents (Nadig 2002; Nevins 2010; Hiemstra 2012; Andersson 2014). On the contrary, enforcement measures prove damaging, disruptive, and unsustainable in countless ways. They prolong experiences of insecurity, often retraumatizing those who have fled. They cut off participation in social and economic life and livelihoods.

Yet politicians and policy makers persist in promoting the idea that detention succeeds as rescue and deterrent. Narratives of deterrence, meanwhile, obscure the fact that detention and interception practices enact violence on present migrant bodies and absent family members (Coutin 2016). Enforcement measures are often linked to the interests of national security, a narrative that obscures the human insecurity they so often cause (Hiemstra 2019a). Recurring calls for stricter border enforcement, too, ignore and obscure evidence that enforcement intensifies precarity. Still, the shrill discourse of threat to security and imagined geographies of violence continue to obscure the real and present danger of prolonged containment and the violent geographies it too imposes. Throughout the archipelago, enforcement measures along the border, in ports, at sea, on islands, and in airports obscure the mundane yet life-sustaining human relations that they disrupt, the lives that they render insecure.

Despite being one of the greatest public policy failures of our time, deterrence remains a popular political response to displacement and migration. Though morally corrupt, deterrence through enforcement continues to be politically palatable and stunningly well resourced, one of the most expensive and failed public policies of our time. The great wall of Donald Trump's geographical imagination already exists the world over. Researchers have documented the growth in physical barriers along borders and associated border deaths and disappearances. Although the positive correlation between border enforcement and border deaths is well documented, states continue to design politically popular policies and invest resources in enforcement, development, and other budget lines to stop people en route. As authorities dislodge traditional borders and affix them to mobile bodies, people struggle to survive, experiencing greater violence as the enforcement archipelago expands offshore.

I have tracked development and growth of enforcement archipelagoes across regions, mapping their origin in border externalization and its genealogy in chapter 1 and contemporary expressions throughout the book. In chapter 2, I drew out the spectacular and performative nature of border enforcement in the archipelago as well as the precarity it sows and the violent geographies it hides. Chapter 3 tracked the growth of detention on islands exploited by Australia, and chapter 4 explored the growth of remote detention onshore in the United States. Chapter 5 turned to Canada, a site where the death of asylum unfolds more quietly, with geopoliticized fields of exceptionalism that mobilize borders as islands to migrant bodies in law, policy, and practice. In chapter 6, I discussed activist movements happening locally, nationally, and transnationally, designed to counter the death of asylum with the life of activism.

Many of the examples explored throughout the book demonstrate the movement of border enforcement from the scale of domestic bordering at land borders to the finer scale and material, intimate political geographies of the body. Detention itself represents one such bordering practice, premised on isolated confinement of bodies and separation of families (Barrick 2018). Time and again, authorities treat the body as island, in law as in space. Activists, cognizant of these body politics, respond with tactics premised on body mobility: the right to move, the right to stay, the right to freedom.

I have found and shared inspiration in transnational social movements that build on a politics of location to counter the isolation, hidden geographies, and daily violence transpiring in the archipelago with a transnational politics rooted in place. By working to map, document, remember, visit, and transgress the boundaries around detention facilities and sovereign territories, activists, detainees, and other members of civil society are fighting back. These movements are at once highly local and global. They are happening in remote locations of border crossing and in the urban epicenters of power, such as in the courtrooms where cases are decided.

The enforcement archipelago has functioned in this book as material stage and spatial metaphor for the death of asylum. An island is a unique place, like any other, whose particular history and geography inform its use as a site of detention. Indeed, states continue to advance this empirical trend. In December 2018, the Danish Parliament passed legislation to detain asylum seekers on a small island about eighty kilometers from Copenhagen. The proposed facilities under renovation were formerly used as a laboratory for experimentation on diseased animals. At the same time, the Bangladeshi government hired British and Chinese engineers to actualize a plan initially proposed in January

2017 to build up a silt island. This would force remote location from the mainland to Thengar Char, a vulnerable island in the Bay of Bengal that is inundated during monsoon season—the latest expression of the search for islands as the last remaining sites in the humanitarian-enforcement spectrum (BBC 2017). As the plan developed, authorities suggested moving one hundred thousand Rohingya refugees from Cox's Bazaar at the outset, with the capacity to move up to one million. This plan was heavily criticized because of the island's vulnerability to flooding due to its location in the path of tropical storms. According to the plans, those relocated to the island would only be allowed to leave it if agreeing to return home.

In exploring this global trend in the use of islands to detain, I have also found the spatial form of the island reproduced everywhere in relation to state enforcement practices, isolating racialized bodies as islands through changes to policy and legislation. On mainland territories, enforcement and detention facilities are often hidden from view, again separating and isolating people through their remote confinement, restricting their access to rights and protections. Meanwhile, island communities, landscapes, and infrastructure have transitioned from safe haven to carceral space—as on Lampedusa and Christmas Island—with those detained increasingly isolated and segregated from each other in situ. I have argued that we are seeing a significant transformation from border crossing to island, as border enforcement is intensified onshore and offshore. This shift raises new lines of research driven by empirical and conceptual inquiry to determine patterns where island detention and island bordering are happening.

Given the continuum of violence and death made apparent in this book, we must continue the collective struggle to make good on Butler's calls for discovery of political community in the shared experiences of grief and mourning. Hidden geographies of enforcement require ontologies of exclusion and politics of inclusion that restlessly ask how we know what is known about offshore enforcement and how more can be known about what is happening along the peripheral and precarious edges of the nation-state. Given that most violent episodes only rarely reach the international community, more intense scrutiny of border-lands transited between states is needed. Although remote, islands in the enforcement archipelago are far from marginal. They require greater attention, lest activists and critical scholars find themselves distracted by the continuous spectacles of enforcement at land borders (Coleman 2019).

As we witness the death of asylum, we must ask who *we* are in relation to its passing. From what historical and contemporary vantage points can Mbembe's (2003) necropolitics be witnessed and not witnessed, and what are the immediate implications for social change that prioritizes the preservation of human and political life? As feminist performance scholar Diana Taylor (1998, 182) writes in her essay "Border Watching," "it is the spectators/witnesses' job to challenge the plot, interrupt the action, and reinterpret events." Taylor politicizes witnessing and challenges the spectator to transform looking from orientalizing act to political action. The shift from orientalism to action is especially necessary in the placement of islands in our collective lives. Islands—and island detentions—remain both geographically and socially distant from most people's daily lives in larger mainland populations. And yet none among us is an island, to return to Dunne, and we are all privy to holding the death of asylum and its memorialization as public record. Disruption is precisely the work that researchers and activists have been doing around the globe to call attention to the machinery of exclusion, from activists who chained themselves to the wheels of G4S security buses carrying detainees to one of the Operation Streamline hearings in downtown Tucson to nuns holding vigils for years outside the facilities in Chicago.

On May 6, 2015, I found myself in the midst of one such challenge, in yet another courtroom, this one twenty-two hundred miles northeast of Tucson at the Provincial Court in downtown Toronto. There legal counsel Barbara Jackman argued an appeal on behalf of detainees being held indefinitely under Canada's new immigration laws implemented in 2012. End Immigration Detention and No One Is Illegal had organized an event designed to "crowd the court," an example of the transformation from witnessing as looking to political action. The idea was to let the three judges who heard the case know that the detainees held support and that the judges' decision mattered not only to the plaintiffs but to broad communities of people supporting them. In her appeal, Jackman noted that the EU would hold people in detention only for six months and then make presumptive release and that the United States would hold people only for nine days and then make presumptive release. She framed Canada as extreme and extraordinary in upholding indefinite detention that had kept her clients imprisoned in Lindsay, Ontario, for up to ten years in one case. As Jackman built a meticulous case against indefinite detention in Canada, she challenged the devastating effects of time and life suspended in the form of indefinite detention and opined that lawyers involved in Operation Streamline and judges in Canada participated in distinct yet flimsy shells of legal justice. In both cases, the death of asylum could be located in state manipulations of time, space, geography, and law: in an effort to hold people far away, to devalue their membership in society through invisibility, to minimize their contact with juridical procedures designed to protect their rights, and to extend this limbo to the possibility of forever.

ISLANDS AND THE DEATH OF ASYLUM

When I began work on this book years ago, I remained tentative in my assessment of asylum. I wondered then if we were witnessing its erosion or disappearance. Over time, as I researched what was happening in the nation-states that had once led the world in robust asylum and refugee resettlement programs, I arrived at the death of asylum. In conversation with Butlerian ideas about dehumanization and the politics of mourning and scholarship on social death (Cacho 2012; Kralova 2015) and necropolitics (Mbembe 2003), I understood the death of asylum as physical, ontological, political, and social. Some readers might find this mere provocation. Could asylum actually disappear? As time goes on, in addition to the empirical evidence presented in this book, daily news propels this argument forward. By the time of completion, protests against the kinds of exclusion detailed in this book had spilled out into the streets in Europe, Britain, and the United States and in Stockholm and Paris, cities where those admitted still find themselves isolated and invisibilized. Lawyers remained central to legal and political struggles, but courts were not the only place where people were fighting border violence and hidden exclusions.

Whereas Hannah Arendt (1958) understood the plight of refugees and stateless persons as key to understanding modern politics (Ramadan 2012), other scholars posit the camp as the key location through which to read modern politics—albeit in distinct ways (Agamben 1998; Minca 2005; Ramadan 2012). For de Leon (2015), deserts are spaces of death and dehumanization. This book has positioned islands within this genealogy as a key geographical location through which to understand not only modern spatial politics and forms of sovereignty but, more specifically, global trends in migration: the precarity of asylum seeking, the global growth in detention, and new spatial and sociolegal forms of exclusion and what they portend for the future of human migration and asylum seeking. I have argued that islands be moved from margin to center to understandings of contemporary politics of displacement and the more specific crisis of asylum.

Highly lucrative security industries profit from the proliferation of detention facilities and the continuous intensification of border enforcement—even in the face of overwhelming evidence that deterrence fails (Detention Watch Network 2015). This expansion contributes to deaths of border crossers at numbers growing at alarming rates. Detention is now a large, transnational industry consolidated into a small handful of corporations that run facilities around the world. With the largest among these corporations based in the United States, and the United States staging a historically unprecedented expansion of detention infrastructure, numbers reached a historic high in 2019. These trends show no sign of imminent reversal. Border enforcement and detention budgets in the countries discussed in this book have reached historic highs. In Australia, this pinnacle resulted in no boat arrivals and no asylum seeking on mainland territory by those traveling by boat in search of protection in 2015. In the United States, with the nascent administration of President Trump in early 2017, the highest border enforcement budget in the world was destined to increase by executive order with the hiring of fifteen thousand new Border Patrol and ICE personnel to carry out a potentially drastic expansion of detention, deportation, and border wall construction. Everywhere immigration enforcement operations are unfolding, security industries are working nearby. G4S vans are running and IOM offices are operational in Tucson, Toronto, and Rome. According to its own website, in 2016, GEO Group managed 104 facilities with eighty-seven thousand beds worldwide (GEO Group 2016)—an increase of eight facilities and fourteen thousand beds in four years since 2012 (GEO Group 2015).[1]

Border walls are thriving, with the cost for Trump's "beautiful wall," in one incarnation, estimated at $21 billion, according to leaked documents. Most fortified barriers were constructed after World War II (Hassner and Wittenberg 2009), with significant expansion and construction of the vast majority since 9/11. Whereas there existed only fifteen walls in 1989, by 2017 there were approximately seventy (Vallet, cited in Jones and Johnson 2017).

This thriving is remarkable given the proven, recurring failure of detention and deterrence as public policy. Greater enforcement has never been an effective solution or even a feigned effort to address the root causes of migration and displacement: deprivation, poverty, and conflict. The collective failure to meaningfully address these root causes means that they will continue. The astounding collective investment in enforcement as the main response means that things will continue to get worse for people on the move, making deterrence one of the most expensive and sustained policy failures of our time—and yet one with strong public support and political will. The remote detention of people on islands and mainland territories neither fixes the problems of economic disparity and displacement nor erases the existence of those fighting to survive their burden. Distancing understood as a form of dehumanization and devaluation, a removal from the frame in Butlerian terms, means that humanization and a return to the frame of political life are needed. Reading Butler and extending her politics to the crises of asylum, I understand activists working to counter deathly forms of living in detention with the enactment of public processes of grief and mourning that can humanize and politicize.

Many have written about the figure of the asylum seeker or person without status as stranger, the response to asylum seekers as hospitality or hosting (e.g., Derrida 2000; Khanna 2006). The enforcement archipelago that I have depicted constitutes a strange land in which we now collectively arrive, one populated not by strangers or hospitality but by strange behavior. In 2014, for example, the *Sydney Morning Herald* (2014) published figures on the cash incentives that the Australian government was providing to asylum seekers detained on Nauru and Manus islands who volunteered to return home, yet another series of controversial "return packages" administered by the International Organization for Migration (whose Assisted Voluntary Return Program I discussed in the Canadian context in chapter 5). The amounts offered varied by country, making a mockery of ample provision of access to asylum processes determined by individual histories of persecution. According to the newspaper, Lebanese asylum seekers were offered the largest incentive, at AU$10,000; Iranians and Sudanese were offered AU$7,000; Afghans were given AU$4,000; and Pakistani, Nepalese, and Burmese were offered the smaller package of AU$3,300.

A few months later, in September 2014, Australia announced quietly a deal to pay AU$40 million to Cambodia over a four-year period to resettle asylees from Nauru and Papua New Guinea. At that time, approximately twenty-five hundred people were being held in detention on the two islands (*Brisbane Times* 2014; Carmichael 2014). Two years later, fewer than five people were resettled through this program, and in 2016, a Cambodian official declared the agreement a failure. In 2016, Australia and the United States agreed to a people trade during President Obama's final months in office: the United States would accept some portion of the 1,150 remaining refugees detained on Nauru and Manus islands. During President Trump's first few weeks in office, a reportedly terse telephone call with Australian prime minister Malcolm Turnbull threw this deal into question. Despite that spectacle, at the time of publication, some seven hundred have been resettled in the United States.

During this same period of escalated migration and exclusion, authorities intercepted 169,264 people en route to Italy in 2014 and another 149,390 in 2015 (Frontex 2015b, 2015c). In October 2014, the IOM estimated that 3,072 people were lost while trying to reach southern member states of the EU by sea. By the end of its one-year existence, on November 1, 2014, Italy's humanitarian–enforcement Operation Mare Nostrum had rescue-intercepted some 150,000 people in the Mediterranean Sea (Mainwaring 2015). Although fewer people attempted to cross the Mediterranean in 2016, more died in the process, bringing estimated border deaths on the Mediterranean from thirty-seven hundred in 2015 to five thousand in 2016 (Saeed 2017).

Rather than a robust exercise of the mandate to protect encoded in the Convention, we are witnessing a chipping away of the right even to seek asylum through the creative interplay between geography and legality evident throughout this book. I have shown the persistent exploitation, construction, and mobilization of islands everywhere in the archipelago. The ever-expansive nature of the archipelago involves the proliferating capacity of states to reproduce islands that further isolate. The proliferating islands within the archipelago are a testament to the death of asylum and its location, ultimately, on the bodies of those confined.

But the death of asylum is also happening beyond the enforcement archipelago offshore with the creation of islands beyond islands. If asylum is dying physically and ontologically offshore, this disease is also reaching mainland territories where power is concentrated, as the Canadian case demonstrates. Reminiscent of Foucault's (2003) "boomerang effect," mainland moves to isolate through law, discourse, and securitization take their cues from historical and contemporary experimentation on islands:

> While colonization, with its techniques and its political and ju-ridical weapons, obviously transported European models to other continents, it also had a considerable boomerang effect on the mechanisms of power in the West, and on the apparatuses, institutions, and techniques of power. A whole series of colonial models was brought back to the West, and the result was that the West could practice something resembling colonization, or an internal colonialism, on itself. (103)

Within the archipelago, islands become sites of policy development and transfer. Australia moves all processing offshore, converting Australian territory to not-Australia and non-Australian islands to processing centers for seekers of asylum in Australia; the EU effectively displaces Mediterranean crossings to the African continent and Central America; and Canada imports Australian policies, while the United States imports Australia's refugees. Would-be seekers of asylum themselves become part of the boomerang effect, traversing well-trodden racialized routes of slavery and colonialism with new forms of forced migration and exploitation, continuous reminders of the displacement caused by conflicts that Western states sow or support.

As this book goes to press, eruptions along borders of humanity grow worse, not better. Shrill xenophobic politics and political parties moved from margin to center, making their ascent in parts of Europe, Australia, and the United States and Canada. In the United States, moves that resemble progress to regularize and legalize were met with con-tinuous resistance in recent years, through the Obama administration. Discourse and policy cannot seem to move beyond the stranglehold of the largest border enforcement budget in the world, the largest deten-tion and deportation system in the world, and the intractable issue of legality. Overlain upon this intractability, President Trump's arrival in office led to drastic changes to landscapes of migration, asylum, and border enforcement, as he signed executive orders to halt various forms of immigration and slow refugee resettlement, increase detention and deportation, staff the border with military personnel, and hire new CBP and ICE employees, who proceeded on a ruthless campaign to separate families in their zeal to detain and deport.

Over the last five years, as the globe experienced its highest rates of dislocation, states retreated from their refugee resettlement programs. At the same time that the highest crossings were recorded on the Mediterranean, some sixty-eight thousand unaccompanied Central American minors made perilous journeys across the border between Mexico and the United States, most fleeing recurring cycles of violence and deprivation in Central America. Detention centers and shelters were opened and new facilities constructed as NGOs and government agencies confronted a humanitarian crisis. Children were separated from families and detained in newly recycled carceral spaces, including tent cities and former super-Walmart centers along the southern border.

As children crossed borders, news coverage and politicians alike framed their arrival not as a humanitarian crisis with causes tied to U.S. geopolitical histories in Central America but as evidence of the abuse of a "generous" immigration and asylum system that had failed to deter. The U.S. government designed new policies to move people and infrastructure south of the border to countries of origin where people were encouraged and eventually required to seek asylum from home. Within the United States, detention facilities were reopened and built, and processing accelerated. In the wake of this arrival, the U.S. government opened its largest detention facility, in Dilley, Texas, designed to hold families, with a capacity of more than two thousand. At the same time that families were transported to isolated sites of detention on military bases and elsewhere across the country, Americans protested their presence in their communities, from southern California to New York. Although the violence in Central America continued, asylum claims dropped significantly.

Subsequently, asylum seeking traveled north of the United States. After Trump's executive orders set a new agenda for aggressive enforcement, many continued north into Canada, filling shelters and overwhelming border communities (CBC 2017). By 2019, nearly forty thousand people had crossed the Canada–United States land border on foot in search of a safe haven. The Canadian government extended its Safe Third Country Agreement and implemented changes in Canadian refugee law to restrict access.

From Operation Sovereign Borders to Brexit to Trump, the rising tide of nationalism around the globe remained inextricably linked to enhanced forms of border policing as states refashioned themselves as walled islands. The *New York Times* editorial board observed in 2017 this geographical standpoint in "President Trump's Island Mentality." This island thinking—treating the state, its citizens, and their fortune as though they existed remotely in relation to others—had ramifications for immediate neighbors and distant travelers alike.

RESISTING THE ARCHIPELAGO? LAMPEDUSA IN BERLIN, THE ISLAND IN THE CITY

As John Dunne famously wrote in the epigraph with which this book opened, "no man is an island." People are not islands, yet migrants are treated as islands as they face proliferating spaces of confinement on their journeys. As authorities dislodge borders and affix them to mobile, racialized bodies, migrants struggle to survive, experiencing greater violence as the enforcement archipelago expands.

As systemic fixes and viable policy alternatives recede into the horizon of entrenched politics and resurgent nationalism, critical migration scholars find themselves reduced to body counts and documentation of deaths. We find ourselves in continuous reaction, scrambling to assemble and disseminate further empirical evidence of a broken system and distracted by the latest enforcement spectacle.

Meanwhile, people in detention and former detainees themselves are leading the way in antidetention and antideportation movements that call out the boomerang effect and haunting colonial ligatures of geopoliticized repression. Germany, for example, is a destination for many asylum seekers who entered at points along the southern EU, such as Lampedusa, years earlier, were released from detention, made asylum claims, and continue to hold temporary status. As a result of extended legal limbo without status, they live increasingly precarious lives on city streets. One group of people from various African and Middle

Eastern countries of origin mobilized their shared histories of doing time on the island for political means, organizing campaigns around the monikers "Lampedusa in Hamburg" and "Lampedusa in Berlin." Because of the Dublin Conventions, asylum seekers to the EU must, by law, make a claim for asylum in the first country where they land. And yet those countries along the southern EU border, including Italy and Greece, feature low acceptance rates and few chances for employment. After surviving journeys that involve years of limbo in revolving doors of detention and expulsion as people enter and reenter the EU by sea, many face subsequent years of precarity once they have entered. This time often involves movement across the EU in the search for refuge as both legal recognition and livelihood.

In 2013, I met members of the group Lampedusa in Berlin and attended one of their regular performances in Oranienplatz in the gentrifying neighborhood of Kreuzberg. The group had established a thriving, festive, and highly organized encampment in a city park in Berlin, one block from the location where the Berlin wall once formally divided East from West. During the several-month occupation of the park, the group staged performances of geopoliticized journeys across the Mediterranean, through Lampedusa and southern Europe, only to reach lives of limbo and few rights in Germany, where they still held interstitial legal status (depicted in Figure 26). Although this particular encampment was taken down in 2014, Lampedusa in Berlin continued, campaigning with other asylum advocacy groups and radical queer organizers elsewhere in Berlin and Germany.

These assemblies of people who have passed through Lampedusa are bringing geopolitics and national politics to the cities where they reside, connecting precarious daily living to the geopolitical and geoeconomic relations causing their displacement. They convert shared island histories of detention into political mobilization, demanding to be remembered and heard, not disappeared as they occupy the heart of public space in the city. Facing the absence of legal recognition by Germany or the EU, they build on a politics of location to demand rights to the city, including recognition, political participation, and opportunities for livelihood and shelter. These demands are evident in this 2014 appeal from Lampedusa in Hamburg: "A lot of people are living on the streets or under terrible conditions in this city. Refugees who fled from war are excluded from social rights and declared as 'illegals.' People have no

FIGURE 26. Lampedusa in Berlin performance in Berlin, 2013. Photograph by Jennifer Hyndman.

right to work because they have the wrong papers, while employers profit from their unprotected status. The rents are rising and many people are pushed out of their neighborhoods" (Lampedusa in Hamburg 2014).

Lampedusa in Berlin and Lampedusa in Hamburg challenge local, national, and international communities to recognize their accountability for precarious and liminal status in Germany (nationally) and in German cities. They reject the geopolitical order that fails to recognize their membership in political communities. Group members are Libyan, Somali, and Nigerian. They speak of the involvement of Western powers and NATO in conflict and colonial histories in countries they fled. They do so by occupying public spaces located on geopoliticized, historical grounds of division. Their campaigns intentionally elide and shine light on the correspondence between local and international borders and their devastating effects on precarious, racialized others seeking refuge. Members of Lampedusa in Berlin and Lampedusa in Hamburg forge refuge and welcoming campaigns while themselves remaining without formal recognition or acceptance.

People are fighting the perpetual isolation of recurring islands in the archipelago by carrying shared island histories into the highly visible centers of power in the metropole: Berlin, Sydney, Toronto, and Rome. They refuse to disappear or be silenced, despite the lack of legal status, the death of asylum, and the substantial resources invested in their distant exclusion. Their presence and political struggle provide hope that the life of humanity and of activism will survive the death of empathy that seems crucial to the death of asylum.

These are emotional landscapes where the depth of trauma transmitted from colonial past to colonial present—to detainees, authorities, and future generations—remains yet unknown. Future research must explore more deeply the historical context on which these archipelagoes are built, the people and communities exploited there (see, e.g., Teaiwa 2015), and the effects of detention that will haunt future generations. This research will uncover the continual eruption of the past in the present and violence happening inside detention facilities to the outside world. These eruptions are themselves provocative entry points demanding deeper exploration of the colonial and militarized grounds on which contemporary enforcement is carried out in the archipelago.

By early 2017, when President Trump signed executive orders that upended many of the underpinnings of several decades of immigration and refugee policy in the United States, these battles spilled from the courts into the streets and airports (Kocher 2017). Trump temporarily blocked entry of all immigrants—including those with legal status—from seven countries with majority Muslim populations and resettlement of all refugees for four months—and for those from Syria, indefinitely. In 2019, the Department of Homeland Security implemented the Migrant Protection Protocols, requiring asylum seekers to wait in Mexico for the duration of their legal proceedings (Blitzer 2019). Internally, on mainland sovereign territory, ICE unleashed the full force of the detention and deportation infrastructure. Trump's offshore plans to curtail protection also continued apace: "Trump tries out an idea that's been graining ground globally" (Peterson 2017). In his first address to Congress in February, Trump suggested that "the only solution for refugee crises . . . 'is to create the conditions where displaced persons can safely return home'" (Peterson 2017). Taking cues from contemporary forms of offshoring carried out by Australia, Canada, and the EU, the Trump administration stepped up returns to Mexico and revived earlier archipelagic carceral spaces in the Caribbean— having promised during his campaign to "fill" the Guantánamo Bay naval base with "bad dudes" (Peterson 2017; Rosenberg 2017). The externalization policies once originating in the United States moved and evolved abroad, now returning home as new forms of offshoring with euphemistic names like "safe third," amounting to containment of displaced people outside the gates.

The spatial patterns identified in this book have intensified, and the death of asylum persists: in France's closure of makeshift shelters at Calais and fortification of processing abroad in Niger; in the EU's attempts to regulate all human mobility in Turkey and deeper into the African continent (Landau 2019); in Australia's continued use of islands despite formal condemnation by the international community; in the United States' refusal to allow entry, its willingness to trade airplanes of refugee claimants, and its fervor to separate children from their parents.

These exclusionary moves have exposed the topological border in action again, both within the United States and well beyond sovereign borders, targeting racialized bodies and mobilities with mobile border enforcement. They have also ignited new forms of political resistance hewn from broad coalitions of everyday people not content to idly witness the death of asylum. People used social media to converge on airports where people were being detained and returned home, barred from entry. They called media attention to the topological border in action, a task perhaps easier at airports inside domestic U.S. territory than offshore on the Guantánamo Bay naval base and at black sites also reinvigorated by Trump offshore.

This book goes to press amid a global pandemic brought on by COVID-19. The virus intensified inequality, rendering marginalized people more vulnerable, including people in detention. In the United States COVID-19 spread through detention centers, infecting people detained, workers, and surrounding communities. Some countries released people from detention, while others like Malta detained on ships, producing more islands at sea. The United States accelerated transfers and deportations, making both mechanisms for further spread. The pandemic continues, as do seismic social, economic, and political shifts, the outcomes still unknown.

What we do know is that asylum has never been more politicized or imperiled. Yet creative forms of resistance and refusal continue apace, the obituary not yet published.

Acknowledgments

I am grateful to the many inspiring people I have the privilege to meet on a daily basis in the work that I do: those who share their time and insights as participants, researchers, and activists. I am especially humbled by people I have met who are surviving detention, who somehow have not lost their spirit and will to live and change the world—in spite of it all.

I am very fortunate to experience friendships wherein intellectual engagement, support, and laughter are beautifully intertwined. For this I thank Ishan Ashutosh, Lisa Bhungalia, Laura Bisaillon, Jennifer Chun, Alison Crosby, Win Curran, Rowan Flad, Chris Gabriel, Judy Han, Roberta Hawkins, Jenna Hennebry, Suzan Ilcan, Sean Lockwood, Jenna Loyd, Audrey Macklin, Rianne Mahon, Ray Martinez, Lisa Molomot, Beverley Mullings, Jackie Orr, Raul Pacheco, In Paik, Celine Park, William Payne, Gerry Pratt, Momin Rahman, Kim Rygiel, Farhana Sultana, William Walters, Helen Watkins, Graham Webber, and Richard Wright. Years of conversation with Jennifer Hyndman fueled this work. Close friends and colleagues *also* generously provided feedback on chapters; thank-yous to Nancy Hiemstra, Sarah Hughes, Jennifer Hyndman, Cetta Mainwaring, Margaret Walton-Roberts, and Kira Williams. Thanks to Tara Vinodrai for discussions in interstitial spaces afforded by our commute. Other friends and colleagues inspired as I wrote and engaged: Feyzi Baban, Ranu Basu, Daniele Belanger, Emily Billo, Alice Bloch, Pablo Bose, Mary Bosworth, Christina Clark-Kazak, Mat Coleman, Michael Collyer, Deirdre Conlon, Catherine Dauvergne, Patricia Ehrkamp, Emily Gilbert, Paul Hodge, Loren Landau, David Ley, Lauren Martin, Jacque Micieli-Voutsinas, Sharon Pickering, Mark Salter, Anna Secor, Stephanie Silverman, Rachel Silvey, and Imogen Tyler.

I am indebted to scholars who worked as research assistants (Kate Coddington, Emily Mitchell-Eaton, Tina Catania) and postdoctoral fellow (Jenna Loyd) on the Island Detention Project. Kira Williams also assisted with data on losses and enforcement operations and bibliographic research. Tanzeel Hakak, Karla Acevedo, Ellen Fowler, and Ana Visan also provided research assistance. Shiva Mohan provided crucial assistance with the bibliography and index. Rob Fiedler and Trina King created beautiful maps. Thanks also to Ileana Díaz, Pauline Maillet, Kate Motluk, and Monica Romero. Conversations with students, past and present, sustain and stir my research and writing.

Chapters of this book benefited from collegial feedback from audiences in various institutions and at conferences where I was invited and hosted to give lectures. The book took a long time to complete, making my gracious hosts and their institutions too numerous to mention. I am very grateful for these opportunities to share and discuss ideas.

This work was funded generously by the National Science Foundation, the Canada Research Chair program, Wilfrid Laurier University, and the Balsillie School for International Affairs. I found colleagues and support at Laurier's International Migration Research Centre. I also thank Harvard's Canada Program and staff and colleagues at the Weatherhead Center for International Affairs. This material is based on work supported by the National Science Foundation under award 0847133 (Principal Investigator: Alison Mountz). Any opinions, findings, and conclusions or recommendations expressed in this material do not necessarily reflect the views of the National Science Foundation.

Thanks to the Global Detention Project for permission to reproduce Canada maps in chapter 5.

I am grateful to the University of Minnesota Press staff, especially to editor Jason Weidemann, for the right combination of comradery, encouragement, and patience, and to editorial assistant Gabe Levin for his editorial labor. Reviewers generously provided thoughtful, engaging, and helpful feedback on earlier versions of this manuscript. All mistakes are my own.

Last, but not least, I thank my family, near and far, chosen and not, for love, support, humor, and understanding.

Notes

PREFACE

1 Here I build on Bejarano et al.'s (2012) argument that border places and workers are exploited by the border enforcement industry through what they call "border sexual conquest."

2 These figures are compiled using Frontex data on expenditures and losses garnered from information released to the public and posted at AsktheEU.org.

3 According to data available from U.S. Immigration and Customs Enforcement (ICE), the number of facilities in use over the last several years has varied widely. In 2008, for example, 552 facilities were in use. In 2015, the number of facilities in use was 209. These data are available on the ICE website.

INTRODUCTION

1 There is a selection bias attached to this statistic, given that many people who arrive on Greek soil choose not to apply for asylum there, attempting instead to move on to other countries to file claims—given low chances of acceptance compared with other EU member states.

2 Jennifer Hyndman and I (Hyndman and Mountz 2008) have written about this as *neo-refoulement,* or a way of evading the legal obligation not to return people to places where they may be at risk of harm.

3 These are contested numbers, unstable due to the uncertainty surrounding disappearances and the distinct statistical methods used by organizations and researchers to document and analyze losses. Most researchers who collect these data agree that they are conservative estimates that undercount actual losses (e.g., Last et al. 2017; Williams and Mountz 2018).

4 These countries have been sharing intelligence since the end of World

War II, and the Five Country Conference is a contemporary arrangement that formalizes biometric data sharing for the purposes of immigration enforcement: "The Five Country Conference ('FCC') is a forum for immigration and border security—involving Canada, Australia, the United Kingdom (U.K.), the United States (U.S.) and New Zealand" (New Zealand Immigration Lawyer 2010).

5 Ruthie Gilmore (2007) shows how the "golden gulag" imprisons across the globalized California economy.

1. EXTERNALIZING ASYLUM

1 The robust contributions of EU-based political scientists also contribute to the focus in literature on externalization of EU migration controls (e.g., Haddad 2008).

2 I am grateful to Ariel and Kira Williams for assistance with research on this point.

3 Waiting zones in international airports also came into existence in the 1980s (Makaremi 2009). These are liminal zones where noncitizens enter legal, spatial, and temporal limbo, where they may in fact be present on sovereign territory but not yet admitted into the country, as Pauline Maillet (2017) demonstrates in the case of France's waiting zones.

4 Carling (2007a) notes that readmission agreements between Spain and Morocco date back to 1992.

3. THE ISLAND WITHIN THE ARCHIPELAGO

1 This information is not publicly available, so this estimate of twelve to fourteen facilities is based on field research in Indonesia in 2011. The number is a range because it includes two sites of detention not currently in use at the time of writing, to the best of my knowledge.

2 I was contacted by the Australian Broadcasting Corporation as a result of this claim and did an interview the following day on the same radio show to share my recent meetings with asylum seekers held in detention in Indonesia on behalf of Australia.

4. REMOTE DETENTION

1   Language is constraining and violent in its categorizations that divide and distinguish, haunted by legibilities of the state. People without citizenship who are held in detention fall into a broad array of legal categories. Some are asylum seekers asking for protection; some are undocumented migrants, who are often picked up for working without valid work papers; and still others may have been arrested on criminal charges but find themselves funneled into national detention and deportation regimes. Unless referring to a specific population, I use *migrant* as an inclusive term signifying those without citizenship in the country where they are detained.

2   Similar critiques of frequent, unannounced transfers have been levied by critics of the Australian and U.K. detention systems (e.g., Gill 2009a, 2009b).

3   Because the Buffalo Federal Detention Facility (located in the small town of Batavia) is a men's facility, women were usually placed in detention among "mainstream" populations in county jails across western New York.

4   In Sodus, a small town near Rochester, the U.S. Border Patrol arrested migrant workers on their way to church services. They also surrounded the trailer homes of migrant workers in local apple orchards; adults and children were then roused from bed and arrested in early-morning raids. For more information, see http://detentiontaskforce.org/en/node/13.

5   Not surprisingly, much research on the effects of remote detention has been conducted in Australia (e.g., Green and Eager 2010; Neave 2013) and to a lesser extent in the United States (e.g., Hiemstra 2012).

6   One group even created a video game to protest treatment at the facility called Escape from Woomera.

7   Where possible, No More Deaths keeps various counts of deaths along the United States–Mexico border; see http://www.nomoredeaths.org /index.php/Information/deaths.html. These are contested figures and reflect only the number of bodies that were actually found.

8   Detention Watch Network map, http://www.detentionwatchnetwork .org/dwnmap.

9   See http://www.globaldetentionproject.org/.

10 These groups reported on their campaigns at the annual meeting of the Detention Watch Network in Washington, D.C., in September 2009.

6. THE STRUGGLE

1   This department has undergone several changes in name in the time since. At the time of writing in 2019, it is the Department of Immigration and Border Protection.

2   This case was under consideration in February 2017, when the U.S. Supreme Court heard arguments regarding the rights of people *not* located on U.S. soil to sue U.S. authorities responsible for extraterritorial deaths in court (O'Dell 2017).

3   All data released in response to access to information requests are then posted online, where requests can also be made; see "Ask the EU," http://www.asktheeu.org/.

4   Still other researchers and activists are embarking on countermapping projects that prioritize migrants' worldviews, migration journeys, and spatial perspectives, eschewing more traditional political maps (e.g., Tazzioli and Garelli 2019).

5   One example is a moving essay authored by an artist and a journalist who snuck onto Nauru posing as "housewives" on vacation.

6   There are important links between gender, activism, and "care" work (see Coddington 2017). Whereas a large percentage of organizers are women, a large percentage of those detained are men. In Australia, women volunteers discussed their adoption of "boys," as they called them, and fought simultaneously and in particular for the release of women and children. Familial relationships developed between detainees and older women, who would correspond "Dear Mom" and "Dear Son" (Burnside 2003). Still other alliances grew more romantic in nature, with marriages between male detainees and female advocates—an interesting example of the notion that women reproduce the nation.

7   Australia ended the TPVs for a few years, only to reinstate them again under Prime Minister Tony Abbott.

8   Once released, there were no policies in effect to support these children, even for legal guardianship, once again signaling the devolution of state responsibilities to local communities construed as caregivers.

9   Additional research should explore Australia's excessive visa regime. DIMA administers so many different kinds of visas with different conditions attached that it excessively difficult for those with temporary status to understand what they could or could not do once released from detention. Many, for example, were denied the right to work or volunteer

while having access to no social or health-related benefits, essentially relegating them to reliance on charitable donations or unauthorized work for which they were likely to be exploited, found noncompliant, and returned to detention.

10   One change that occurred between when I researched detention practices in Australia in 2006 and again in 2010 and 2011 was that detainees were allowed to use internet access and mobile phones in facilities.

CONCLUSIONS

1   In 2012, GEO managed seventy-three thousand beds in ninety-six facilities (GEO Group 2015).

Bibliography

Aas, Katja Franko, and Helene Gundhus. 2015. "Policing Humanitarian Borderlands: Frontex, Human Rights and the Precariousness of Life." *British
Journal of Criminology* 55, no. 1: 1–18.

Afouxenidis, Alex, Michalis Petrou, George Kandylis, Angelo Tramountanis,
and Dora Giannaki. 2017. "Dealing with a Humanitarian Crisis: Refugees
on the Eastern EU Border of the Island of Lesvos." *Journal of Applied
Security Research* 12, no. 1: 7–39.

Agamben, Giorgio. 1998. *Homo Sacer: Sovereign Power and Bare Life.* Stanford,
Calif.: Stanford University Press.

Agamben, Giorgio. 2005. *State of Exception.* Chicago: University of Chicago
Press.

Al Jazeera. 2010. "Sri Lanka Asylum Seekers in Limbo: Group Stranded in
Indonesian Port for More than Five Months." March 10. https://www
.aljazeera.com/news/asia-pacific/2010/03/201031054731247310.html.

American Immigration Council. 2019. "The Cost of Immigration Enforcement
and Border Security." https://www.americanimmigrationcouncil.org/sites
/default/files/research/the_cost_of_immigration_enforcement_and_bor
der_security.pdf.

Amnesty International. 2012. *S.O.S. Europe: Human Rights and Migration
Control.* London: International Secretariat, United Kingdom.

Amnesty International. 2013. "This Is Breaking People: Human Rights
Violations at Australia's Asylum Seeker Processing Center on Manus
Island, Papua New Guinea." https://www.amnesty.org.au/wp-content
/uploads/2016/09/Amnesty_International_Manus_Island_report-1.pdf.

Amoore, Louise. 2006. "Biometric Borders: Governing Mobilities in the War
on Terror." *Political Geography* 25, no. 3: 336–51.

Amoore, Louise, and Marieke de Goede, eds. 2008. *Risk and the War on Terror.* New York: Routledge.

Anderson, Kay J. 1991. *Vancouver's Chinatown: Racial Discourse in Canada,
1875–1980.* Montreal: McGill-Queen's University Press.

Anderson, Kay, and Susan J. Smith. 2001. "Emotional Geographies." *Transactions of the Institute of British Geographers* 26, no. 1: 7–10.

Andersson, Ruben. 2014. *Illegality, Inc.: Clandestine Migration and the Business of Bordering Europe.* Oakland: University of California Press.

Andreas, Peter. 2009. *Border Games: Policing the U.S.–Mexico Divide.* 2nd ed. Ithaca, N.Y.: Cornell University Press.

Andreas, Peter, and Ethan Nadelmann. 2006. *Policing the Globe: Criminalization and Crime Control in International Relations.* Oxford: Oxford University Press.

Andrijasevic, Rutvica. 2006. "How to Balance Rights and Responsibilities on Asylum at the EU's Southern Border of Italy and Libya." Working Paper 27. http://idcoalition.org/news/libya-report-how-to-balance-rights-and-responsibilities-on-asylum-at-the-eu-southern-border-of-italy-and-libya/.

Andrijasevic, Rutvica. 2010. "From Exception to Excess: Detention and Deportations across the Mediterranean Space." In *The Deportation Regime: Sovereignty, Space, and the Freedom of Movement,* edited by Nicholas De Genova and Nathalie Peutz, 147–65. Durham, N.C.: Duke University Press.

Andrijasevic, Rutvica, and William Walters. 2010. "The International Organization for Migration and the International Government of Borders." *Environment and Planning, Part D* 28, no. 6: 977–99.

Anzaldúa, Gloria. 1987. *Borderlands/La Frontera: The New Mestiza.* San Francisco: Aunt Lute.

Applebaum, Anne. 2003. *Gulag: A History.* New York: Anchor Books.

Arbel, Efrat, and Alletta Brenner. 2013. *Bordering on Failure: Canada–U.S. Border Policy and the Politics of Refugee Exclusion.* Cambridge, Mass.: Harvard Immigration and Refugee Law Clinical Program. http://harvard immigrationclinic.files.wordpress.com/2013/11/bordering-on-failure -harvard-immigration-and-refugee-law-clinical-program1.pdf.

Arendt, Hannah. 1958. *The Origins of Totalitarianism.* Cleveland, Ohio: Meridian Books.

Ashutosh, Ishan, and Alison Mountz. 2011. "Managing Migration for the Benefit of Whom? Interrogating the Work of the International Organization for Migration." *Citizenship Studies* 15, no. 1: 21–38.

Atak, Idil, and François Crépeau. 2013. "The Securitization of Asylum and Human Rights in Canada and the European Union." In *Contemporary Issues in Refugee Law,* edited by Satvinder Singh Juss and Colin Harvey, 227–57. Cheltenham, U.K.: Edward Elgar.

Australian Broadcasting Corporation. 2011. "Christmas Island Funerals Anger Relatives." http://www.abc.net.au/news/2011-02-15/christmas -island-funerals-anger-relatives/1942970?site=sydney.

Australian Human Rights Commission. 2010. *Immigration Detention on Christmas Island.* Sydney: AHRC.

Australian Human Rights Commission. 2011. "Joint Select Committee on Australia's Immigration Detention Network, Final Report." http://www .aph.gov.au/~/media/wopapub/senate/committee/immigration_deten tion_ctte/report/report_pdf.ashx.

Australian Human Rights Commission. 2014. "National Inquiry into Children in Immigration Detention 2014." https://www.humanrights.gov.au/our -work/asylum-seekers-and-refugees/projects/national-inquiry-children -immigration-detention-index.

Australian Human Rights Commission. 2016. "Information about Children in Immigration Detention." https://www.humanrights.gov.au/information -about-children-immigration-detention.

Baban, Feyzi, Suzan Ilcan, and Kim Rygiel. 2017. "Syrian Refugees in Turkey: Pathways to Precarity, Differential Inclusion, and Negotiated Citizenship Rights." *Journal of Ethnic and Migration Studies* 43, no. 1: 41–57.

Baldacchino, Godfrey. 2004. "The Coming of Age of Island Studies." *Tijdschrift voor Economische en Sociale Geografie* 95, no. 3: 272–83.

Baldacchino, Godfrey. 2007. "Islands as Novelty Sites." *Geographical Review* 97, no. 2: 165–74.

Baldacchino, Godfrey, and David Milne. 2006. "Exploring Sub-national Island Jurisdictions: An Editorial Introduction." *The Round Table* 95, no. 386: 487–502.

Balibar, Étienne. 2002. *Three Concepts of Politics: Emancipation, Transformation, Civility, in Politics and the Other Scene.* Verso: London.

Barnes, Richard. 2004. "Refugee Law at Sea." *International and Comparative Law Quarterly* 53, no. 1: 47–77.

Barrick, Leigh. 2018. "Central American Displacement and the Politics of United States Deterrence Strategy." PhD diss., Geography, University of British Columbia.

Basaran, Tugba. 2011. *Security, Law, and Borders: At the Limits of Liberties.* London: Routledge.

Bashford, Alison, and Carolyn Strange. 2002. "Asylum-Seekers and National Histories of Detention." *Australian Journal of Politics and History* 48, no. 4: 509–27.

Bastians, Kate. 2011. "Christmas Island Self-Harm on Rise." *Sydney Morning Herald*, May 23. https://www.smh.com.au/national/christmas-island-self-harm-on-rise-20110522-1eyyq.html.

Bastos, Cristiana. 2008. "Migrants, Settlers and Colonists: The Biopolitics of Displaced Bodies." *International Migration* 46, no. 5: 27–54.

BBC News. 2013. "Mediterranean 'a Cemetery'—Maltese PM Muscat." http://www.bbc.co.uk/news/world-europe-24502279.

BBC News. 2017. "Rohingya Refugees in Bangladesh Face Relocation to an Island." http://www.bbc.com/news/world-asia-38799586.

Bejarano, Cynthia, Maria Cristina Morales, and Said Saddiki. 2012. "Understanding Conquest through a Border Lens: A Comparative Analysis of the Mexico–U.S. and Morocco–Spain Regions." In *Beyond Walls and Cages: Prisons, Borders, and Global Crisis*, edited by Jenna Loyd, Matt Mitchelson, and Andrew Burridge, 27–41. Athens: University of Georgia Press.

Belcher, Oliver, and Lauren Martin. 2013. "Ethnographies of Closed Doors: Conceptualising Openness and Closure of US Immigration and Military Institutions." *Area* 45, no. 4: 403–10.

Belcher, Oliver, Lauren Martin, Anna Secor, Stephanie Simon, and Tommy Wilson. 2008. "Everywhere and Nowhere: The Exception and the Topological Challenge to Geography." *Antipode* 40, no. 4: 499–503.

Benoit, Catherine. 2008. "St. Martin's Change of Political Status: Inscribing Borders and Immigration Laws onto Geographical Space." *New West Indian Guide* 82, no. 3/4: 211–35.

Benoit, Catherine. 2019. "Fortress Europe's Far-Flung Borderlands: 'Illegality' and the 'Deportation Regime' in France's Caribbean and Indian Ocean Territories." *Mobilities*. doi:10.1080/17450101.2019.1678909.

Benton, Lauren. 2010. *A Search for Sovereignty: Law and Geography in European Empires, 1400–1900*. Cambridge: Cambridge University Press.

Bernardie-Tahier, Nathalie, and Camille Schmoll. 2014. "Opening Up the Island: A 'Counter-islandness' Approach to Migration in Malta." *Island Studies* 9, no. 1: 43–56.

Bernstein, Nina. 2008. "Detention Center Facing Inquiries Will Get No More Immigrant Detainees." *New York Times*, December 5. http://www.nytimes.com/2008/12/06/nyregion/06detain.html.

Bernstein, Nina. 2010. "Officials Hid Truth of Immigration Deaths in Jails." *New York Times*, January 9. http://www.nytimes.com/2010/01/10/us/10detain.html.

Berry, Joanna. 2012. "Primer on the 'Designated Countries of Origin' Scheme." http://www.carl-acaadr.ca/our-work/issues/DCO#Primer.

Betts, Alexander. 2004. "The International Relations of the 'New' Extraterritorial Approaches to Refugee Protection: Explaining the Policy Initiatives of the UK Government and UNHCR." *Refuge* 22, no. 1: 58–70.

Betts, Alexander, ed. 2010. *Global Migration Governance.* Oxford: Oxford University Press.

Bhandari, Aparita, and Amarnath Amarasingam. 2014. "Has Canada Seen the Last of the Boat People?" *Globe and Mail,* October 18, F3.

Bialasiewicz, Luiza. 2012. "Off-shoring and Out-sourcing the Borders of Europe: Libya and EU Border Work in the Mediterranean." *Geopolitics* 17, no. 4: 843–66.

Bigo, Didier. 2000. "When Two Become One: Internal and External Securitizations in Europe." In *International Relations Theory and the Politics of European Integration,* edited by Morten Kelstrup and Michael Williams, 171–204. New York: Routledge.

Bigo, Didier. 2002. "Security and Immigration: Toward a Critique of the Governmentality of Unease." *Alternatives* 27: 63–92.

Binelli, Mark. 2016. "10 Shots across the Border." *New York Times,* March 6, MM36.

Blitzer, Jonathan. 2019. "How the U.S. Asylum System Is Keeping Migrants at Risk in Mexico." *New Yorker,* October 1. https://www.newyorker.com/news/dispatch/how-the-us-asylum-system-is-keeping-migrants-at-risk-in-mexico.

Bloch, Alice, and Liza Schuster. 2005. "At the Extremes of Exclusion: Deportation, Detention and Dispersal." *Ethnic and Racial Studies* 28, no. 3: 491–512.

Boltanski, Luc. 1999. *Distant Suffering: Morality, Media, and Politics.* Cambridge: Cambridge University Press.

Bonds, Anne. 2009. "Discipline and Devolution: Constructions of Poverty, Race, and Criminality in the Politics of Rural Prison Development." *Antipode* 41, no. 3: 416–38.

Bon Tempo, Carl J. 2008. *Americans at the Gate: The United States and Refugees during the Cold War.* Princeton, N.J.: Princeton University Press.

Border Crossing Observatory. 2015. http://artsonline.monash.edu.au/thebordercrossingobservatory/.

Border Deaths. 2015. "Human Costs of Border Control: Deaths at the Borders of Southern Europe." http://www.borderdeaths.org/.

Borderlands Autonomous Collective. 2012. "Resisting the Security Industrial Complex: Operation Streamline and the Militarization of the Arizona–Mexico Border." In *Beyond Walls and Cages: Bridging Immigration Enforcement and the Prison Industrial Complex,* edited by A. Burridge, J.

Loyd, and M. Michelson, 190–208. Athens: University of Georgia Press.

Boswell, Christina. 2003. "The External Dimension of EU Immigration and Asylum Policy." *International Affairs* 79, no. 3: 619–38.

Bosworth, Mary. 2014. *Inside Immigration Detention.* Oxford: Oxford University Press.

Boyce, Geoffrey, and Sarah Launius. 2013. "Warehousing the Poor: How Federal Prosecution Initiatives Like 'Operation Streamline' Hurt Immigrants, Drive Mass Incarceration and Damage U.S. Communities." *Different Takes* 82, Fall. http://popdev.hampshire.edu/projects/dt/82.

Bradimore, Ashley, and Harald Bauder. 2011. "Mystery Ships and Risky Boat People: Tamil Refugee Migration in the Newsprint Media." *Canadian Journal of Communication* 36, no. 4: 637–61.

Brigden, Noelle K. 2016. "Improvised Transnationalism: Clandestine Migration at the Border of Anthropology and International Relations." *International Studies Quarterly* 60, no. 2: 343–54.

Brigden, Noelle. 2018. *The Migrant Passage: Clandestine Journeys from Central America.* Ithaca, N.Y.: Cornell University Press.

Briskman, Linda, Susie Latham, and Chris Goddard. 2008. *Human Rights Overboard: Seeking Asylum in Australia.* Victoria: Scribe.

Brochmann, Grete. 2002. "Citizenship and Inclusion in European Welfare States: The EU Dimension." In *Migration and the Externalities of European Integration,* edited by Sandra Lavenex and Emek M. Uçarer, 179–92. Oxford: Lexington Books.

Bronskill, Jim. 2014. "CBSA's Treatment of Detainees Criticized: Opposition Challenges Government after Red Cross Report Finds Some Are Housed in Jails, Mixed in with Criminals in Crowded Cells." *Globe and Mail,* September 26, A8.

Brouwer, Andrew. 2003. "Attack of the Migration Integrity Specialists! Interdiction and the Threat to Asylum." Canadian Council for Refugees. http://ccrweb.ca/sites/ccrweb.ca/files/static-files/interdictionab.htm.

Brown, Wendy. 2010. *Walled States, Waning Sovereignty.* Brooklyn, N.Y.: Zone Books.

Brown, Wendy. 2017. "Interventions on the State of Sovereignty at the Border." *Political Geography* 59, July, 1–10.

Burnett, Christina D. 2005. "The Edges of Empire and Limits of Sovereignty: American Guano Islands." *American Quarterly* 57, no. 3: 779–803.

Burnside, Janet. 2003. *From Nothing to Zero: Letters from Refugees in Australia's Detention Centres.* Melbourne: Lonely Planet.

Burridge, Andrew. 2009. "Differential Criminalization under Operation Streamline: Challenges to Freedom of Movement and Humanitarian Aid Provision in the Mexico–US Borderlands." *Refuge* 26, no. 2: 78–91.

Burridge, Andrew, Nick Gill, Austin Kocher, and Lauren Martin. 2017. "Polymorphic Borders." *Territory, Politics, Governance* 5, no. 3: 239–51.

Burroughs, Elaine, and Kira Williams, eds. 2018. *Contemporary Boat Migration: Data, Geopolitics, and Discourses.* London: Rowman and Littlefield.

Butler, Judith. 2004. *Precarious Life: The Powers of Mourning and Violence.* New York: Verso.

Butler, Judith. 2010. *Frames of War.* New York: Verso.

Cacho, Lisa. 2012. *Social Death: Racialized Rightlessness and the Criminalization of the Unprotected.* New York: New York University Press.

Cader, Fathima. 2010. "Rocking the Boat: A Brief History of Anti-migrant Hysteria in Canada." *Pacific Free Press,* August 16. https://pulsemedia.org/2010/08/19/rocking-the-boat-a-brief-history-of-anti-migrant-hysteria-in-canada/.

Camacho, Keith L. 2012. "After 9/11: Militarized Borders and Social Movements in the Mariana Islands." *American Quarterly* 64, no. 4: 685–713.

Campesi, Giuseppe. 2011. "The Arab Spring and the Crisis of the European Border Regime. Manufacturing Emergency in the Lampedusa Crisis." EUI Working Paper RSCAS 59. http://cadmus.eui.eu/bitstream/handle/1814/19375/RSCAS_2011_59.pdf?sequence=1.

Campesi, Giuseppe. 2014. "Frontex, the Euro-Mediterranean Border and the Paradoxes of Humanitarian Rhetoric." *South East European Journal of Political Science* 2, no. 3: 126–34.

Canadian Association of Refugee Lawyers. 2012. "Designated Country of Origin Scheme Is Arbitrary, Unfair, and Unconstitutional." Press release, December 14. http://www.carl-acaadr.ca/our-work/issues/DCO.

Canadian Border Services Agency. 2012. "Marine Migrants: Program Strategy for the Next Arrival. For the Vice-President." http://ccrweb.ca/files/atip-cbsa-sun-sea-strategy-next-arrival.pdf.

Canadian Border Services Agency. 2014. "2013–14 Departmental Performance Report." https://www.cbsa-asfc.gc.ca/agency-agence/reports-rapports/dpr-rmr/2013-2014/report-rapport-eng.pdf.

Canadian Border Services Agency. 2015. "Assisted Voluntary Return and Reintegration (AVRR) Pilot Program." https://www.cbsa-asfc.gc.ca/agency-agence/reports-rapports/pia-efvp/atip-aiprp/avrr-arvr-eng.html.

Canadian Council for Refugees. 2003. "Interdiction and Refugee Protection:

Bridging the Gap." Paper presented at the International Workshop, Ottawa, Canada, May 29.

Canadian Council for Refugees. 2012. "Protect Refugees from Bill C-31: Joint Statement." March. http://ccrweb.ca/en/protect-refugees-c31-statement.

Canadian Council for Refugees. 2015. "Sun Sea: Five Years Later." August. http://ccrweb.ca/sites/ccrweb.ca/files/sun-sea-five-years-later.pdf.

Carling, Jørgen. 2007a. "Migration Control and Migrant Fatalities at the Spanish–African Borders." *International Migration Review* 41, no. 2: 316–43.

Carling, Jørgen. 2007b. "Unauthorized Migration from Africa to Spain." *International Migration* 45, no. 4: 3–37.

Carling, Jørgen, and Hernandez-Carretero, María. 2011. "Protecting Europe and Protecting Migrant? Strategies for Managing Unauthorised Migration from Africa." *British Journal of Politics and International Relations* 13, no. 1: 42–58.

Carmichael, Robert. 2014. "Australia to Pay Cambodia $35 Million in Refugee Deal." September 26. http://www.voanews.com/content/australia-to-pay-cambodia-35-million-refugee-deal/2463073.html.

Carta di Lampedusa. 2014. http://www.lacartadilampedusa.org/.

Castles, Stephen. 2008. "The Politics of Exclusion: Asylum and the Global Order." *Metropolis World Bulletin* 8: 3–6.

Cave, Damien. 2018. "Why the U.S. Is Taking 58 Refugees in a Deal Trump Called 'Dumb.'" *New York Times,* January 23. https://www.nytimes.com/2018/01/23/world/australia/manus-refugees-trump.html.

Chak, Tings. 2014. *Undocumented: The Architecture of Migrant Detention.* Amsterdam: Architectural Observer.

Chin, Ko-lin. 1999. *Smuggled Chinese: Clandestine Immigration to the United States.* Philadelphia: Temple University Press.

Cho, G. 2008. *Haunting the Korean Diaspora: Shame, Secrecy, and the Forgotten War.* Minneapolis: University of Minnesota Press.

Cho, Grace M. 2009. *Haunting the Korean Diaspora: Shame, Secrecy, and the Forgotten War.* Minneapolis: University of Minnesota Press.

Citizenship and Immigration Canada. 2001. News release. February 21.

Citizenship and Immigration Canada. 2016. "Designated Countries of Origin." http://www.cic.gc.ca/english/refugees/reform-safe.asp.

Coddington, Kate. 2014. "Geographies of Containment: Logics of Enclosure in Aboriginal and Asylum Seeker Policies in Australia's Northern Territory." PhD diss., Syracuse University.

Coddington, Kate. 2017. "Contagious Trauma: Reframing the Spatial Mobility of Trauma within Advocacy Work." *Emotion, Space, and Society* 24: 66–73.

Coddington, Kate, and Jacque Micieli-Voutsinas. 2017. "On Trauma, Geography, and Mobility: Towards Geographies of Trauma." *Emotion, Space, and Society* 24, no. 1: 52–56.

Coddington, Kate, and Alison Mountz. 2014. "Countering Isolation with Use of Technology: How Asylum-Seeking Detainees on Islands in the Indian Ocean Use Social Media to Transcend Their Confinement." *Journal of the Indian Ocean Region* 10, no. 1: 97–113.

Coffey, Guy, Ida Kaplan, Robyn Sampson, and Maria Tucci. 2010. "The Meaning and Mental Health Consequences of Long-Term Immigration Detention for People Seeking Asylum." *Social Science and Medicine* 70, no. 12: 2070–79.

Coleman, Matthew. 2005. "US Statecraft and the US–Mexico Border as Security/Economy Nexus." *Political Geography* 24, no. 2: 185–209.

Coleman, Matthew. 2007. "Immigration Geopolitics beyond the US–Mexico Border." *Geopolitics* 39, no. 1: 54–76.

Coleman, Matthew. 2009. "What Counts as the Politics and Practice of Security, and Where? Devolution and Immigrant Security after 9/11." *Annals of the Association of American Geographers* 99, no. 5: 904–13.

Coleman, Mattew. 2019. "Jenna Loyd and Alison Mountz's Boats, Borders, and Bases, Authors Meet Critics." Paper presented at the conference of the Association of American Geographers, Washington, D.C.

Collett, Elizabeth. 2017. "The Paradox of the EU–Turkey Refugee Deal." Migration Policy Institute. http://www.migrationpolicy.org/news/paradox-eu-turkey-refugee-deal.

Collyer, Michael. 2007. "In-Between Places: Trans-Saharan Transit Migrants in Morocco and the Fragmented Journey to Europe." *Antipode* 39, no. 4: 668–90.

Collyer, Michael. 2010. "Stranded Migrants and the Fragmented Journey." *Journal of Refugee Studies* 23, no. 3: 273–93.

Collyer, Michael. 2012. "Migrants as Strategic Actors in the European Union's Global Approach to Migration and Mobility." *Global Networks* 12, no. 4: 505–24.

Collyer, Michael, and Russell King. 2015. "Producing Transnational Space: International Migration and the Extra-territorial Reach of State Power." *Progress in Human Geography* 39, no. 2: 185–204.

Conlon, Deirdre. 2007. "The Nation as Embodied Practice: Women, Migration and the Social Production of Nationhood in Ireland." PhD diss., City University of New York.

Conlon, Deirdre. 2011. "Waiting: Feminist Perspectives on the Spacings/

Timings of Migrant (Im)mobility." *Gender, Place, and Culture* 18, no. 3: 353–60.

Conlon, Deirdre, and Nancy Hiemstra. 2014. "Examining the Everyday Microeconomies of Migrant Detention in the United States." *Geographica Helvetica* 69, no. 5: 335–44.

Conlon, Deirdre, and Nancy Hiemstra, eds. 2016. *Intimate Economies of Immigration Detention: Critical Perspectives.* New York: Routledge.

Coombs, Anne. 2004. "Mobilising Rural Australia." *Griffith Review* 3, Autumn: 96–106.

Cornelius, Wayne A. 2001. "Death at the Border: Efficacy and Unintended Consequences of US Immigration Control Policy." *Population and Development Review* 27, no. 4: 661–85.

Council of the European Union. 2008. "European Pact on Immigration and Asylum." https://www.refworld.org/docid/48fc40b62.html.

Coutin, Susan B. 2016. *Exiled Home: Salvadoran Transnational Youth in the Aftermath of Violence.* Durham, N.C.: Duke University Press.

Crawley, Heaven, Frank Düvell, Simon McMahon, Katharine Jones, and Nando Sigona. 2018. *Unraveling Europe's "Migration Crisis": Journeys over Land and Sea.* Bristol, U.K.: Policy Press.

Cresswell, Tim. 2006. *On the Move: Mobility in the Modern Western World.* New York: Routledge.

Crock, Mary, and Daniel Ghezelbash. 2010. "Do Loose Lips Bring Ships? The Role of Policy, Politics and Human Rights in Managing Unauthorised Boat Arrivals." *Griffith Law Review* 19, no. 2: 238–87.

Cuttitta, Paolo. 2014. "Borderizing the Island and Narratives of the Lampedusa 'Border Play.'" *ACME* 13, no. 2: 196–219.

Das, Veena, and Deborah Poole eds. 2004. *Anthropology in the Margins of the State.* New York: American Research Advanced Seminar Series.

Dastyari, Azadeh. 2015. *United States Migrant Interdiction and the Detention of Refugees in Guantánamo Bay.* New York: Cambridge University Press.

Davidson, Robert. 2003. "Spaces of Immigration 'Prevention': Interdiction and the Non-place." *Diacritics* 33, nos. 3–4: 205–7.

Davies, Lizzy, and Arthur Nelson. 2014. "Italy: End of Ongoing Sea Rescue Mission 'Puts Thousands at Risk.'" *Guardian,* October 31. http://www.theguardian.com/world/2014/oct/31/italy-sea-mission-thousands-risk.

Davis, Sasha. 2011. "The US Military Base Network and Contemporary Colonialism: Power Projection, Resistance and the Quest for Operational Unilateralism." *Political Geography* 30, no. 4: 215–24.

Dear, Michael. 2013. *Why Walls Won't Work: Repairing the US–Mexico Divide.* New York: Oxford University Press.

De Bruycker, Philippe, Anna Di Bartolomeo, and Philippe Fargues. 2013. *Migrants Smuggled by Sea to the EU: Facts, Laws, and Policy Options.* Florence, Italy: European University Institute, Migration Policy Center.

De Genova, Nicholas. 2002. "Migrant 'Illegality' and Deportability in Everyday Life." *Annual Review of Anthropology* 31, no. 1: 419–47.

De Genova, Nicholas. 2013. "Spectacles of Migrant 'Illegality': The Scene of Exclusion, the Obscene of Inclusion." *Ethnic and Racial Studies* 36, no. 7: 1180–98.

Delaney, David. 2010. *Nomospheric Investigations: The Spatial, the Legal and the Pragmatics of World-Making.* Abingdon, U.K.: Routledge.

Delano, Alexandra, and Benjamin Nienass. 2014. "Invisible Victims: Undocumented Migrants and the Aftermath of September 11." *Politics and Society* 42, no. 3: 399–421.

De Leon, Jason, and Michael Wells. 2015. *The Land of Open Graves: Living and Dying on the Migrant Trail.* Berkeley: University of California Press.

Department of Foreign Affairs and Trade. 2015. "Regional Resettlement Agreement between Australia and Papua New Guinea." http://dfat.gov.au/geo/papua-new-guinea/Documents/regional-resettlement-arrangement-20130719.pdf.

Department of Immigration and Border Protection [Australia]. 2014. *Quarterly Report on Detention.* Available from author.

Department of Immigration and Multicultural and Indigenous Affairs [Australia]. 2006. *Managing the Border: Immigration Compliance, 2004–2005 Edition.* https://www.homeaffairs.gov.au/ReportsandPublications/Documents/annual-reports/diac-annual-report-2004–05-full-version.pdf.

Detention Watch Network. 2015. "About the U.S. Detention and Deportation System." http://www.detentionwatchnetwork.org/resources.

Doherty, Ben. 2015a. "Almost 200 Refugees on Nauru Arrested as Police Crack Down on Peaceful Protests." *Guardian,* March 5. http://www.theguardian.com/world/2015/mar/04/up-to-70-refugees-nauru-arrested-police-crack-down-peaceful-protests.

Doherty, Ben. 2015b. "Manus Island Asylum Seekers Declare End to Two-Week Long Hunger Strike." *Guardian,* January 27. http://www.theguardian.com/australia-news/2015/jan/27/manus-island-asylum-seekers-end-hunger-strike.

Doherty, Ben. 2016. "'Let Them Stay': Backlash in Australia against Plans to Send Asylum Seekers to Detention." *Guardian,* February 10. https://www.theguardian.com/australia-news/2016/feb/10/let-them-stay-australia-backlash-267-asylum-seekers-island-detention-camps.

Doherty, Ben. 2018. "Scathing UN Migration Report Mars Australia's First Week

on Human Rights Council." *Guardian*, March 1. http://www.theguardian
.com/asutralia-news/2018/mar/02/scathing-un-migration-report-not-ide
al-start-to-australias-human-rights-council-tenure?CMP=share_btn
_link.

Donne, John. 1839. "Devotions upon Emergent Occasions: Meditation XVII."
In *The Works of John Donne*, edited by Henry Alford, 3:574–75. London:
John W. Parker.

Dow, Mark. 2004. *American Gulag: Inside U.S. Immigration Prisons*. Berkeley:
University of California Press.

Durieux, Jean-François, and Jane McAdam. 2004. "*Non-Refoulement* through
Time: The Case for a Derogation Clause to the Refugee Convention in
Mass Influx Emergencies." *International Journal of Refugee Law* 16, no. 1:
4–24.

Echavarri, Fernanda. 2020. "'A Fucking Disaster That Is Designed to Fail': How
Trump Wrecked America's Immigration Courts." *Mother Jones*, February
6. https://www.motherjones.com/politics/2020/02/trump-immigration
-court-backlog-migrant-protection-protocols/.

End Streamline Coalition. 2014. *End Operation Streamline: Assemblyline Injustice for Corporate Prophet—An Illustrated Guide to the Criminalization
of Migrants*. Available from the author.

Eugenio, Haidee V. 2013. "Kilili Eyes CW Extension to 2019." *Saipan Tribune*,
December 17. https://sablan.house.gov/kilili-eyes-cw-extension-2019.

Euractiv. 2011. "Court Exposes Appalling Detention Conditions in Greece."
January 24. https://www.euractiv.com/section/justice-home-affairs/news
/court-exposes-appalling-detention-conditions-in-greece/.

Euronews. 2017. "Italy, Libya Sign Agreement to Curb Flow of Migrants to
Europe." February 2. http://www.euronews.com/2017/02/02/italy-libya
-sign-agreement-to-curb-flow-of-migrants-to-europe.

European Commission. 2015. *The Hotspot Approach to Managing Exceptional
Migratory Flows*. Brussels: European Commission. http://ec.europa.eu
/dgs/home-affairs/what-we-do/policies/european-agenda-migration
/background-information/docs/2_hotspots_en.pdf.

European Parliament. 2016. "On the Front Line: The Hot Spot Approach to
Managing Migration." http://www.europarl.europa.eu/RegData/etudes
/STUD/2016/556942/IPOL_STU%282016%29556942_EN.pdf.

European United Left. 2005. "Lampedusa and Melilla: Southern Frontier
of Fortress Europe." http://www.guengl.eu/uploads/_old_cms_files/EN
_Lampedusa.pdf.

Eurostat. 2016. European Commission's Asylum and Managed Migration Da-

tabase. http://ec.europa.eu/eurostat/web/asylum-and-managed-migration
/data/database?p_p_id=NavTreeportletprod_WAR_NavTreeportletprod
_INSTANCE_sFp6GUtIbBHg&p_p_lifecycle=0&p_p_state=normal&p
_p_mode=view&p_p_col_id=column-2&p_p_col_count=1#.

Faiola, Anthony, and Griff White. 2016. "E.U. Strikes Deal to Return New
Migrants to Turkey." *Washington Post,* March 18. https://www.washing
tonpost.com/world/europe/europe-offers-deal-to-turkey-to-take-back
-migrants/2016/03/18/809d80ba-ebab-11e5-bc08-3e03a5b41910_story.html.

Fan, Mary. 2008. "When Deterrence and Death Mitigation Fall Short: Fan-
tasy and Fetishes as Gap-Fillers in Border Regulation." *Law and Society
Review* 42, no. 4: 701–34.

Fassin, Didier. 2013. "The Precarious Truth of Asylum." *Public Culture* 25,
no. 1: 39–63.

Flynn, Michael, and Cecilia Cannon. 2009. "The Privatization of Immi-
gration Detention: Towards a Global View." Global Detention Project
Working Paper. http://www.globaldetentionproject.org/fileadmin/docs
/GDP_PrivatizationPaper_Final5.pdf.

Flynn, Michael, and Matthew Flynn. 2017. *Challenging Immigration Detention:
Academics, Activists, and Policy-Makers.* Cheltenham, U.K.: Edward Elgar.

Forensic Architecture. 2016. "The Left-to-Die Boat." http://www.forensicz
-architecture.org/case/left-die-boat/.

Foucault, Michel. (1978) 1995. *Discipline and Punish: The Birth of the Prison.*
New York: Vintage Books.

Foucault, Michel. 2003. *Society Must Be Defended: Lectures at the Collège de
France, 1975–1976.* London: Allen Unwin.

Frelick, Bill. 2009. *Pushed Back, Pushed Around: Italy's Forced Return of Boat
Migrants and Asylum Seekers, Libya's Mistreatment of Migrants and Asylum
Seekers.* New York: Human Rights Watch.

Frelick, Bill, Ian Kysel, and Jennifer Podkul. 2016. "The Impact of Externalization of Migration Controls on the Rights of Asylum Seekers and Other
Migrants." *Journal on Migration and Human Security* 4, no. 4: 190–220.

Frontex. 2015a. "Number of Border Crossings by Year, Country of Origin,
Location of Detection." http://www.asktheeu.org/en/request/number_of
_border_crossings_by_ye#incoming-7682.

Frontex. 2015b. "Re: JORA Variables for Incidents during JO EPN-HERMES
and JO TRITON, 2011–2014." European Union. http://www.asktheeu.org/.

Frontex. 2015c. "Re: JORA Variables for Incidents during JO Hermes, Aeneas
and Triton, March 2015–Present." European Union. Freedom of information request at www.asktheeu.org/.

Frontex. 2016. "Archive of Operations." European Union. http://frontex
.europa.eu/operations/archive-of-operations/.

Gammeltoft-Hansen, Thomas. 2011. *Access to Asylum: International Refugee Law and the Globalisation of Migration Control.* Cambridge: Cambridge University Press.

Gavreau, Catherine, and Glynis Williams. 2003. "Detention in Canada: Are We on the Slippery Slope?" *Refuge* 20, no. 3: 68–70.

Geiger, Martin. 2013. "The Transformation of Migration Politics: From Migration Control to Disciplining Mobility." In *Disciplining the Transnational Mobility of People,* edited by Martin Geiger and Antoine Pécoud, 15–40. Basingstoke, U.K.: Palgrave Macmillan.

Geiger, Martin. 2016. "Policy Outsourcing and Remote Management: The Present and Future of Border Migration Politics." In *Externalizing Migration Management: Europe, North America and the Spread of "Remote Control" Practices,* edited by Ruben Zaiotti, 261–79. London: Routledge.

Geiger, Martin, and Antoine Pécoud, eds. 2010. *The Politics of International Migration Management.* New York: Palgrave Macmillan.

GEO Group. 2016. "Our Locations." http://www.geogroup.com/locations.

Giannacopoulos, Maria, and Claire Loughnan. 2019. "'Closure' at Manus Island and Carceral Expansion in the Open Air Prison." *Globalizations.* doi:https://doi.org/10.1080/14747731.2019.1679549.

Giddens, Anthony. 1991. *Modernity and Self-Identity: Self and Society in the Late Modern Age.* Stanford, Calif.: Stanford University Press.

Gilbert, Emily. 2005. "The Inevitability of Integration? Neoliberal Discourse and the Proposals for a New North American Economic Space after September 11." *Annals of the Association of American Geographers* 95, no. 1: 202–22.

Gilbert, Emily. 2007. "Leaky Borders and Solid Citizens: Governing Security, Prosperity and Quality of Life in a North American Partnership." *Antipode* 39, no. 1: 77–98.

Gilbert, Emily. 2012. "Borders and Security in North America." In *North America in Question,* edited by Jeffrey Ayers and Laura Macdonald, 196–218. Toronto: University of Toronto Press.

Gilbert, Liette. 2013a. "Canada's Visa Requirement for Mexicans and Its Political Rationalities." *NorteAmérica: Revista Académica del CISAN-UNAM* 8, no. 1: 139–61.

Gilbert, Liette. 2013b. "The Discursive Production of Mexican Refugee Crisis in Canadian Media and Policy." *Journal of Ethnic and Migration Studies* 39, no. 5: 827–43.

Gill, Nicholas. 2009a. "Governmental Mobility: The Power Effects of the Movement of Detained Asylum Seekers around Britain's Detention Estate." *Political Geography* 28, no. 3: 186–96.

Gill, Nicholas. 2009b. "Longing for Stillness: The Forced Movement of Asylum Seekers." *M/C Journal: A Journal of Media and Culture* 12, no. 1: 10–15.

Gilmore, Ruth W. 2007. *Golden Gulag: Labor, Land, State, and Opposition in Globalizing California*. Berkeley: University of California Press.

Gleeson, Madeline. 2017. "Offshore Processing: An Overview." Andrew and Renata Kaldor Centre for International Refugee Law, University of New South Wales. https://www.kaldorcentre.unsw.edu.au/publication/offshore -processing-overview.

Global Detention Project. 2020. "Canada Immigration Detention." https:// www.globaldetentionproject.org/countries/americas/canada.

Goldring, Luin, Carolina Berinstein, and Judith Bernhard. 2009. "Institutionalizing Precarious Migratory Status in Canada." *Citizenship Studies* 13, no. 3: 239–65.

Gordon, Avery. 2008. *Ghostly Matters: Haunting and the Sociological Imagination*. Minneapolis: University of Minnesota Press.

Gordon, Avery. 2011. "Some Thoughts on Haunting and Futurity." *Borderlands* 10, no. 2: 1–21.

Gordon, Colin, ed. 1980. *Power/Knowledge: Selected Interviews and Other Writings by Michel Foucault, 1972–1977*. New York: Pantheon Books.

Gordon, Michael. 2006. *Freeing Ali*. Sydney: University of New South Wales Press.

Government of Canada. 2019. "Asylum Claims by Year—2011–2016." https:// www.canada.ca/en/immigration-refugees-citizenship/services/refugees /asylum-claims/processed-claims.html.

Grabbe, Heather. 2000. "The Sharp Edges of Europe: Extending Schengen Eastwards." *International Affairs* 76, no. 3: 519–36.

Grant, Angus, and Sean Rehaag. 2016. "Unappealing: An Assessment of the Limits on Appeal Rights in Canada's New Refugee Determination System." *UBCL Review* 49: 203.

Green, Janette P., and Kathy Eager. 2010. "The Health of People in Australian Immigration Detention Centres." *Medical Journal of Australia* 192, no. 2: 65–70.

Gregory, Derek. 2004. *The Colonial Present*. Malden, Mass.: Blackwell.

Gregory, Derek. 2006. "The Black Flag: Guantánamo Bay and the Space of Exception." *Geografiska Annaler* 88, no. 4: 405–27.

Gregory, Derek. 2007. "Vanishing Points: Law, Violence, and Exception in the Global War Prison." In *Violent Geographies: Fear, Terror, and Political Violence,* edited by Derek Gregory and Allan Pred, 205–36. London: Routledge.

Gregory, Derek. 2011. "The Everywhere War." *The Geographical Journal* 177, no. 3: 238–50.

Gros, Hanna, and Paloma van Groll. 2015. *"We Have No Rights": Arbitrary Imprisonment and Cruel Treatment of Migrants with Mental Health Issues in Canada.* Toronto: International Human Rights Program, University of Toronto Faculty of Law. http://ihrp.law.utoronto.ca/sites/ihrp.law.utoronto .ca/files/PUBLICATIONS/IHRP%20We%20Have%20No%20Rights%20 Report%20web%20170615.pdf.

Gupta, Anil, and Aradhana Sharma, eds. 2006. *Anthropology of the State.* London: Blackwell.

Gutting, Gary. 2014. "Michel Foucault." In *The Stanford Encyclopedia of Philosophy,* edited by Edward N. Zalta. Metaphysics Research Lab, Stanford University. https://plato.stanford.edu/archives/win2014/entries/foucault/.

Haddad, Emma. 2008. "The External Dimension of EU Refugee Policy: A New Approach to Asylum?" *Government and Opposition* 43, no. 2: 190–205.

Hall, Bianca. 2013. "Minister Wants Boat People Called Illegals." *Brisbane Times,* October 20. http://www.brisbanetimes.com.au/federal-politics /political-news/minister-wants-boat-people-called-illegals-20131019-2vtlo .html.

Hall, Bianca, and Michael Gordon. 2013. "'Cruelty' in Nauru Camp Slammed by Whistleblowers." *Canberra Times,* July 25, A4.

Harris, Kathleen. 2017. "Nearly Half of Illegal Border-Crossers into Canada Are from Haiti." *CBC News,* November 22. http://www.cbc.ca/news /politics/haiti-border-crossers-canada-irregular-1.4414781.

Harvey, D. 1989. *The Condition of Postmodernity: An Enquiry into the Origins of Cultural Change.* Oxford: Basil Blackwell.

Hassner, Ron, and Jason Wittenberg. 2009. "Barriers to Entry: Who Builds Fortified Boundaries and Are They Likely to Work?" Paper presented at Fences and Walls in International Relations Conference, University of Quebec at Montreal.

Hathaway, James C. 1998. "Can International Refugee Law Be Made Relevant Again?" *Law Quad. Notes* 41, no. 3: 106–8.

Hawke, Allan, and Helen Williams. 2011. "An Independent Review of the Incidents at the Christmas Island Immigration Detention Centre and Villawood Immigration Detention Centre." http://www.immi.gov.au /media/publications/independent-review-incidents.htm.

Helleiner, Jane. 2016. *Borderline Canadianness: Border Crossings and Every-*

day Nationalism in Niagara. Toronto: University of Toronto Press.

Helsinki Times. 2014. "New Operation Could Hide Major Shift in Europe's Immigration Control Policy." September 11. http://www.helsinkitimes .fi/world-int/11969-new-operation-could-hide-major-shift-in-europe-s -immigration-control-policy-2.html.

Hepworth, Kate. 2015 *At the Edges of Citizenship: Security and the Constitution of Non-citizen Subjects*. Farnham, U.K.: Ashgate.

Hiemstra, Nancy. 2012. "The View from Ecuador: Security, Insecurity, and Chaotic Geographies of U.S. Migrant Detention and Deportation." PhD diss., Syracuse University.

Hiemstra, Nancy. 2013. "'You Don't Even Know Where You Are': Chaotic Geographies of U.S. Migrant Detention and Deportation." In *Carceral Spaces: Mobility and Agency in Imprisonment and Migrant Detention*, edited by Dominique Moran, Nick Gill, and Deirdre Conlon, 57–75. Farnham, U.K.: Ashgate.

Hiemstra, Nancy. 2019a. *Detain and Deport: The Chaotic U.S. Immigration Enforcement Regime*. Athens: University of Georgia Press.

Hiemstra, Nancy. 2019b. "Pushing the US–Mexico Border South: United States' Immigration Policing throughout the Americas." *International Journal of Migration and Border Studies* 5, no. 1/2: 44–63.

Hiemstra, Nancy, and Deirdre Conlon. 2017. "Beyond Privatization: Bureau-cratization and the Spatialities of Immigration Detention Expansion." *Territory, Politics, Governance* 5, no. 3: 252–68.

Hier, Sean, and Joshua Greenberg. 2002. "Constructing Discursive Crisis: Risk, Problematization and Illegal Chinese in Canada." *Ethnic and Racial Studies* 25, no. 3: 490–513.

Hodge, Paul. 2015. "A Grievable Life? The Criminalisation and Securing of Asylum Seeker Bodies in the 'Violent Frames' of Australia's *Operation Sovereign Borders*." *Geoforum* 58: 122–31.

Hodge, Paul. 2019. "#LetThemStay#BringThemHere: Embodied Politics, Asylum Seeking, and Performativities of Protest Opposing Australia's Operation Sovereign Borders." *Environment and Planning C: Politics and Space* 37, no. 3: 386–406.

Hughes, Sarah M. 2016. "Beyond Intentionality: Exploring Creativity and Resistance within a UK Immigration Removal Centre." *Citizenship Studies* 20, no. 3–4: 427–43.

Hugo, Graeme. 2001. "From Compassion to Compliance? Trends in Refugee and Humanitarian Migration in Australia." *GeoJournal* 56, no. 1: 27–37.

Human Rights Watch. 2008. "Stuck in a Revolving Door: Iraqis and Other Asylum Seekers and Migrants at the Greece/Turkey Entrance to the

European Union." https://www.hrw.org/sites/default/files/reports/greece
turkey1108web_0.pdf

Human Rights Watch. 2009. "Locked Up Far Away: The Transfer of Immigrants to Remote Detention Centers in the United States." http://www
.hrw.org/en/reports/2009/12/02/locked-far-away.

Human Rights Watch. 2011. "The EU's Dirty Hands: Frontex Involvement in Ill-Treatment of Migrant Detainees in Greece." http://www.hrw.org/sites
/default/files/reports/greece0911webwcover_0.pdf.

Hussein, Muhammad, Awnesh Singh, and Than Aung. 2011. "Rise and Fall of Sea Level in Nauru Area over a Nodal Cycle." *The South Pacific Journal of Natural and Applied Sciences* 28, no. 1: 63–68.

Hutton, Marg. 2015a. "Database of Asylum Seeker Boats." http://sievx.com
/dbs/boats/.

Hutton, Marg. 2015b. "Drownings on the Public Record of People Attempting to Enter Australia Irregularly by Boat since 1998." http://sievx.com
/articles/background/DrowningsTable.pdf.

Huysmans, Jef. 2000. "The European Union and the Securitization of Migration." *Journal of Common Market Studies* 38, no. 5: 751–77.

Huysmans, Jef. 2006. *The Politics of Insecurity: Fear, Migration and Asylum in the EU.* London: Routledge.

Hyndman, Jennifer. 2000. *Managing Displacement.* Minneapolis: University of Minnesota Press.

Hyndman, Jennifer. 2007. "The Securitization of Fear in Post-tsunami Sri Lanka." *Annals of the Association of American Geographers* 97, no. 2: 361–72.

Hyndman, Jennifer, Silvia D'Addario, and Matt Stevens. 2014. "Refugee Research Synthesis 2009–2013." Citizenship and Immigration Canada. http://ceris.ca/wp-content/uploads/2015/01/CERIS-Research-Synthesis
-on-Refugees.pdf.

Hyndman, Jennifer, and Wenona Giles. 2011. "Waiting for What? The Feminization of Asylum in Protracted Situations." *Gender, Place, and Culture* 18, no. 3: 361–79.

Hyndman, Jennifer, and Wenona Giles. 2014. "From Nexus to Nothing: The Rare Reception of Asylum Seekers in Canada." Paper presented at Smart Borders, Smart Reception workshop, Carleton University, Ottawa.

Hyndman, Jennifer, and Wenona Giles. 2016. *Refugees in Extended Exile: Living on the Edge.* New York: Routledge.

Hyndman, Jennifer, and Alison Mountz. 2007. "Refuge or Refusal: The Geography of Exclusion." *Violent Geographies: Fear, Terror, and Political Violence,* January, 390.

Hyndman, Jennifer, and Alison Mountz. 2008. "Another Brick in the Wall? 'Neo-refoulement' and the Externalisation of Asylum in Australia and Europe." *Government and Opposition* 43, no. 2: 249–69.

Ibrahim, Maggie. 2005. "The Securitization of Migration: A Racial Discourse." *International Migration* 43, no. 5: 163–87.

Immigration, Refugees, and Citizenship Canada. 2019. "Canada Ends the Designated Country of Origin Practice." May 17. https://www.canada.ca /en/immigration-refugees-citizenship/news/2019/05/canada-ends-the -designated-country-of-origin-practice.html.

Immigroup. 2013. "Immigration News: Citizenship and Immigration Canada's List of High Risk Countries." https://www.immigroup.com/news /citizenship-and-immigration-canadas-list-high-risk-countries.

Index Mundi. 2018. "Guam Demographics Profile 2018." https://www.index mundi.com/guam/demographics_profile.html.

International Organization for Migration. 2014. "Fatal Journeys: Tracking Lives Lost during Migration." http://www.iom.int/files/live/sites/iom/files/pbn /docs/Fatal-Journeys-Tracking-Lives-Lost-during-Migration-2014.pdf.

International Organization for Migration. 2015. "Migrant Boat Arrivals in Europe Top 150,000 in 2015." http://www.iom.int/news/migrant-boat -arrivals-europe-top-150000-2015.

International Organization for Migration. 2016. "IOM Counts 3,771 Migrant Fatalities in Mediterranean in 2015." https://www.iom.int/news/iom -counts-3771-migrant-fatalities-mediterranean-2015.

International Organization for Migration. 2019. "Missing Migrants Project." Migration Data Portal. https://migrationdataportal.org/themes/migrant -deaths-and-disappearances.

Irvine, Sandy. 2011. "Canadian Refugee Policy: Understanding the Role of International Bureaucratic Networks in Domestic Paradigm Change." In *Policy Paradigms, Transnationalism, and Domestic Politics,* edited by Grace Darlene Skogstad, 171–201. Toronto: University of Toronto Press.

Jones, Reece. 2012a. *Border Walls: Security and the War on Terror in the United States, India, and Israel.* London: Zed Books.

Jones, Reece. 2012b. "Spaces of Refusal: Rethinking Sovereign Power and Resistance at the Border." *Annals of the Association of American Geographers* 102, no. 3: 685–99.

Jones, Reece, and Corey Johnson. 2016. "Border Militarisation and the Re-articulation of Sovereignty." *Transactions of the Institute of British Geographers* 41, no. 2: 187–200.

Jones, Reece, Corey Johnson, Wendy Brown, Gabriel Popescu, Polly Pallister-Wilkins, Alison Mountz, and Emily Gilbert. 2017. "Interventions on the State of Sovereignty at the Border." *Political Geography* 59, July: 1–10.

Kaplan, Amy. 2005. "Where Is Guantánamo?" *American Quarterly* 57, no. 3: 831–58.

Karp, Paul, and Paul Farrell. 2016. "Refugees Held in Australian Offshore Detention to Be Resettled in US." *Guardian*, November 13. https://www.theguardian.com/australia-news/2016/nov/13/refugees-held-in-australian-offshore-detention-to-be-resettled-in-us.

Kasparek, Bernd. 2010. "Borders and Populations in Flux: Frontex's Place in the European Union's Migration Management." In *The Politics of International Migration Management*, edited by Martin Geiger and Antoine Pécoud, 1–20. London: Palgrave Macmillan.

Kasparek, Bernd. 2016. "Routes, Corridors, and Spaces of Exception: Governing Migration and Europe." http://nearfuturesonline.org/routes-corridors-and-spaces-of-exception-governing-migration-and-europe/.

Katz, Cindi. 2001. "On the Grounds of Globalization: A Topography for Feminist Political Engagement." *Signs* 26, no. 4: 1213–34.

Katz, Cindi. 2004. *Growing Up Global: Economic Restructuring and Children's Everyday Lives*. Minneapolis: University of Minnesota Press.

Katz, Cindi. 2007. "Banal Terrorism." In *Violent Geographies*, edited by D. Gregory and A. Pred, 349–61. New York: Routledge.

Kaushal, Asha, and Catherine Dauvergne. 2011. "The Growing Culture of Exclusion: Trends in Canadian Refugee Exclusions." *International Journal of Refugee Law* 23, no. 1: 54–92.

Kazimi, Ali. 2012. *Undesirables: White Canada and the Komagata Maru—An Illustrated History*. Vancouver: Douglas and McIntyre.

Keep Talking Greece. 2015. "Farmakonisi Tragedy: Greece Dismiss Claims, Coast Guard Was Towing Migrants' Boat Back to Turkey." http://www.keeptalkinggreece.com/2014/01/23/farmakonisi-tragedy-greece-dismiss-claims-coast-guard-was-towing-migrants-boat-back-to-turkey/.

Kernerman, Gerald. 2008. "Refugee Interdiction before Heaven's Gate." *Government and Opposition* 43, no. 2: 230–48.

Keung, Nicholas. 2019. "Canada's Refugee Claim Acceptance Rate Falls amid Record Backlog of Asylum Seekers." *Toronto Star*, June 19. https://www.thestar.com/news/gta/2019/06/19/canadas-refugee-acceptance-rate-falls-amid-record-backlog-of-asylum-claims.html.

Kevin, Tony. 2004. *A Certain Maritime Incident: The Sinking of SIEV X*. Melbourne: Scribe.

Khalili, Laleh. 2012. *Time in the Shadows: Confinement in Counterinsurgencies.* Palo Alto, Calif.: Stanford University Press.

Khanna, Ranjana. 2006. "Asylum." *Texas International Law Journal* 41, no. 3: 471–90.

Khosravi, Shahram. 2010. *"Illegal" Traveller: An Auto-ethnography of Borders.* New York: Palgrave Macmillan.

Kim, Caroline, and Jenna Loyd. 2008. "Is Riding the Bus a Ticket to Jail?" *Colorlines,* June 12. http://www.colorlines.com/article.php?ID=304.

Koh, Harold H. 1994. "America's Offshore Refugee Camps." *University of Richmond Law Review* 29, no. 1: 139–73.

Koser, Khalid. 2000. "Asylum Policies, Trafficking and Vulnerability." *International Migration* 38, no. 3: 91–111.

Koser, Khalid. 2010. "Introduction: International Migration and Global Governance." *Global Governance* 16, no. 3: 301–15.

Králová, Jana. 2015. "What Is Social Death?" *Contemporary Social Science* 10, no. 3: 235–48.

Krishnamurti, Sailaja. 2013. "Queue-Jumpers, Terrorists, Breeders: Representations of Tamil Migrants in Canadian Popular Media." *South Asia Diaspora* 5, no. 1: 139–57.

Kronick, Rachel, Cécile Rousseau, and Janet Cleveland. 2015. "Asylum-Seeking Children's Experiences of Detention in Canada: A Qualitative Study." *American Journal of Orthopsychiatry* 85, no. 3: 287–94.

La Guardia, Anton. 2015. "Wave after Wave." *Economist,* November 21, 77.

Lampedusa in Hamburg. 2014. Facebook home page. https://de-de.facebook.com/lampedusainhamburg/.

Landau, Loren. 2019. "A Chronotope of Containment Development: Europe's Migrant Crisis and Africa's Reterritorialisation." *Antipode* 51, no. 1: 169–86.

Larsen, Mike. 2014. "Indefinitely Pending: Security Certificates and Permanent Temporariness." In *Liberating Temporariness: Migration, Work, and Citizenship in an Age of Insecurity,* edited by Leah Vosko, Valerie Preston, and Robert Latham, 76–96. Montreal: McGill-Queen's University Press.

Last, Tamara, Giorgia Mirto, Orçun Ulusoy, Ignacio Urquijo, Joke Harte, Nefeli Bami, Marta Pérez Pérez, Flor Macias Delgado, Amélie Tapella, Alexandra Michalaki, Eirini Michalitsi, Efi Latsoudi, Naya Tselepi, Marios Chatziprokopiou, and Thomas P. Spijkerboer. 2017. "Deaths at the Borders Database: Evidence of Deceased Migrants' Bodies Found along the Southern External Borders of the European Union." *Journal of Ethnic and Migration Studies* 43, no. 5: 693–712.

Lavenex, Sandra. 1999. *Safe Third Countries: Extending the EU Asylum and*

Immigration Policies to Central and Eastern Europe. Budapest: Central European University Press.

Le Espiritu, Yen. 2014. *Body Counts: The Vietnam War and Militarized Refugees.* Berkeley: University of California Press.

Lipman, Jana. 2012. "'Give Us a Ship': The Vietnamese Repatriate Movement on Guam, 1975." *American Quarterly* 64, no. 1: 1–31.

Lipman, Jana. 2013. "'The Fish Trusts the Water, and It Is in the Water That It Is Cooked': The Caribbean Origins of the Krome Detention Center." *Radical History Review* 115, Winter: 115–41.

Loyd, Jenna, Matthew Mitchelson, and Andrew Burridge, eds. 2012. *Beyond Walls and Cages: Prisons, Borders, and Global Crisis.* Athens: University of Georgia Press.

Loyd, Jenna, and Alison Mountz. 2018. *Boats, Borders, and Bases: Race, the Cold War, and the Rise of Migration Detention in the United States.* Berkeley: University of California Press.

Lutterbeck, Derek. 2009. "Small Frontier Island: Malta and the Challenge of Irregular Immigration." *Mediterranean Quarterly* 20, no. 1: 119–44.

MacCharles, Tonda. 2015. "Ottawa Hiding Details of Secret Terror Watch with Five Eyes Allies." *Toronto Star,* February 13. http://www.thestar.com/news /canada/2015/02/13/secrecy-shrouds-information-sharing-agreement -with-five-eyes-allies.html.

Macklin, Audrey. 2003. "The Value(s) of the Canada–US Safe Third Country Agreement. Caledon Institute of Social Policy." https://maytree.com/wp -content/uploads/558320703.pdf.

Macklin, Audrey. 2005. "Disappearing Refugees: Reflections on the Canada– U.S. Safe Third Country Agreement." *Columbia Journal of Human Rights Law Review* 36: 365–426.

Macklin, Audrey. 2015. "The Return of Banishment: Do the New Denationalization Policies Weaken Citizenship?" http://eudo-citizenship.eu /commentaries/citizenship-forum/citizenship-forum-cat/1268-the-return -of-banishment-do-the-new-denationalisation-policies-weaken-citizen ship?showall=&limitstart=.

Magner, Tara. 2004. "A Less than 'Pacific' Solution for Asylum Seekers in Australia." *International Journal of Refugee Law* 16, no. 1: 53–90.

Maillet, Pauline. 2017. "Exclusion from Rights through Extra-territoriality at Home: The Case of Paris Roissy-Charles de Gaulle Airport's Waiting Zone." PhD diss., Wilfrid Laurier University.

Maillet, Pauline, Alison Mountz, and Kira Williams. 2016. "Researching Detention, Asylum-Seeking, and Unauthorized Migration: The Challenges of, and Limits to, Field Work in Confined Locations and Wide-Open Spaces." *Social and Cultural Geographies* 18, no. 7: 927–50.

Maillet, Pauline, Alison Mountz, and Kira Williams. 2018. "Exclusion through *imperio*: Entanglements of Law and Geography in the Waiting Zone, Excised Territory and Search and Rescue Region." *Social and Legal Studies* 27, no. 2. http://journals.sagepub.com/doi/10.1177/0964663917746487.

Mainwaring, Cetta. 2012a. "Constructing a Crisis: The Role of Immigration Detention in Malta." *Population, Space, and Place* 18, no. 6: 687–700.

Mainwaring, Cetta. 2012b. "Resisting Distalization? Malta and Cyprus' Influence on EU Migration and Asylum Policies." *Refugee Studies Quarterly* 31, no. 4: 38–66.

Mainwaring, Cetta. 2014. "Small States and Nonmaterial Power: Creating Crises and Shaping Migration Policies in Malta, Cyprus, and the European Union." *Journal of Immigrant and Refugee Studies* 12, no. 2: 103–22.

Mainwaring, Cetta. 2015. "Mourning the Mediterranean Dead and Locking Up Survivors." *Open Democracy,* April 27. https://www.opendemocracy.net/can-europe-make-it/cetta-mainwaring/mourning-mediterranean-dead-and-locking-up-survivors.

Mainwaring, Cetta. 2019. *At Europe's Edge: Migration and Crisis in the Mediterranean.* Oxford: Oxford University Press.

Mainwaring, Cetta, and Noelle Brigden. 2016. "Beyond the Border: Clandestine Migration Journeys." *Geopolitics* 21, no. 2: 243–62.

Makaremi, Chowra. 2009. "Governing Borders in France: From Extraterritorial to Humanitarian Confinement." *Canadian Journal of Law and Society* 24, no. 3: 411–32.

Marciniak, Katarzyna, and Imogen Tyler, eds. 2014. *Immigrant Protest: Politics, Aesthetics, and Everyday Dissent.* Albany: SUNY Press.

Mares, Peter. 2001. *Borderline.* Sydney: UNSW Press.

Marr, David. 2009. "The Indian Ocean Solution." *Monthly.* https://www.themonthly.com.au/monthly-essays-david-marr-indian-solution-christmas-island-1940.

Marr, David, and Ana Secor. 2014. "Towards a Post-mathematical Topology." *Progress in Human Geography* 38, no. 3: 420–38.

Martin, Susan, Sanjula Weerasinghe, and Abbie Taylor. 2014. "What Is Crisis Migration?" *Forced Migration Review* 45: 5–9. http://www.fmreview.org/sites/fmr/files/FMRdownloads/en/crisis/martin-weerasinghe-taylor.pdf.

Marwah, Sonal, Stephen Cornish, and Carol Devine. 2016. "The Less-Told Migration Story and Its Humanitarian Consequences." MSF Report.

Available from the author. Summary at https://www.doctorswithoutborders
.ca/node/3202.

Mason, Jana. 1999. "Where America's Day Begins: Chinese Asylum Seekers
on Guam." *Refugee Reports (U.S. Committee for Refugees)* 20, no. 8. http://
www.refugees.org/world/articles/asylum_rr99_8.htm.

Mbembe, Achille. 2003. "Necropolitics." *Public Culture* 15, no. 1: 11–40.

McBride, Michael J. 1999. "Migrants and Asylum-Seekers: Policy Responses
in the United States to Immigrants and Refugees from Central America
and the Caribbean." *International Migration* 37, no. 1: 289–317.

McElwee, Sean. 2018. "It's Time to Abolish ICE: A Mass-Deportation Strike
Force Is Incompatible with Democracy and Human Rights." *Nation*, March
9. https://www.thenation.com/article/its-time-to-abolish-ice/.

Médecins Sans Frontières. 2004. Press release, October 3. http://www.msf
.org/msfinternational/invoke.cfm?objectid=C3AF4D0F-DDCB-4191
-96A8FD95DC0491BA&component=toolkit.pressrelease&method=full
_html.

Médecins Sans Frontières. 2011a. "From North Africa to Italy: Seeking Refuge,
Finding Suffering." May. http://www.doctorswithoutborders.org/publica
tions/reports/2011/MSF_From%20North%20Africa%20to%20Italy.pdf.

Médecins Sans Frontières. 2011b. "Torture, Exploitation and Abuse of Migrants
in North Africa." May. Available from the author.

Migrants at Sea. 2011. "Italian Coast Guard: 44,000 Migrants Reach Italy by
Boat in First Half of 2011." July 1. https://migrantsatsea.org/2011/07/01
/italian-coast-guard-44000-migrants-reach-italy-by-boat-in-first-half
-of-2011/.

Migreurop. 2013a. *The Atlas of Migration in Europe: A Critical Geography of
Migration Policies*. Oxford: New Internationalist.

Migreurop. 2013b. "Launch of the Atlas of Migration in Europe: A Critical
Geography of Migration Policies." http://www.migreurop.org/article2311
.html?lang=fr.

Migreurop. 2015. *Atlas of Migration in Europe: A Critical Geography of Migration Policies*, 2nd ed. Oxford: New Internationalist.

Minca, Claudio. 2005. "The Return of the Camp." *Progress in Human Geography* 29, no. 4: 405–12.

Minca, Claudio. 2007. "Agamben's Geographies of Modernity." *Political Geography* 26, no. 1: 78–97.

Ministero dell'Interno. 2011. "Informativa al Senato sui flussi migratori a
Lampedusall sottosegretario: Viale: 'L'emergenza che stiamo gestendo
coinvolge tutta l'Europa; bisogna comprendere ciò se vogliamo un unico

grande sistema di governo del fenomeno dell'immigrazione.'" https://www1
.interno.gov.it/mininterno/export/sites/default/it/sezioni/sala_stampa
/notizie/_sottosegretarioxprecedenti/2100_505_sottosegretario_viale
/0000070_2011_09_29_informativa_Viale_al_Senato.html_109962327
.html.

Missbach, Antje. 2017. "Accommodating Asylum Seekers and Refugees in Indonesia: From Immigration Detention to Containment in 'Alternatives to Detention.'" *Refuge* 33, no. 2: 32–44.

Mitchell, Katharyne. 2006. "Geographies of Identity: The New Exceptionalism." *Progress in Human Geography* 30, no. 1: 95–106.

Molloy, James, and James Simeon. 2016. "Introduction: The Indochinese Refugee Movement and the Launch of Canada's Sponsorship Program." *Refuge* 32: 2–8.

Moore, Robert. 2000. "The Debris of Empire: The 1981 Nationality Act and the Oceanic Dependent Territories." *Immigrants and Minorities* 19, no. 1: 1–24.

Moran, Dominique, Nick Gill, and Deirdre Conlon, eds. 2013. *Carceral Spaces: Mobility and Agency in Imprisonment and Migrant Detention*. Aldershot, U.K.: Ashgate.

Moran, Dominique, Laura Piacentini, and Judith Pallot. 2013. "Liminal Trans-Carceral Space: Prison Transportation for Women in the Russian Federation." In *Carceral Geographies: Mobility and Agency in Imprisonment and Migrant Detention*, edited by Dominique Moran, Nick Gill, and Deirdre Conlon, 109–24. Aldershot, U.K.: Ashgate.

Mountz, Alison. 2004. "Embodying the Nation-State: Canada's Response to Human Smuggling." *Political Geography* 23, no. 3: 323–45.

Mountz, Alison. 2006. "Human Smuggling and the Canadian State." *Canadian Foreign Policy* 13, no. 1: 59–80.

Mountz, Alison. 2010. *Seeking Asylum: Human Smuggling and Bureaucracy at the Border*. Minneapolis: University of Minnesota Press.

Mountz, Alison. 2011a. "The Enforcement Archipelago: Detention, Haunting, and Asylum on Islands." *Political Geography* 30, no. 3: 118–28.

Mountz, Alison. 2011b. "Specters at the Port of Entry: Understanding State Mobilities through an Ontology of Exclusion." *Mobilities* 6, no. 3: 317–34.

Mountz, Alison. 2011c. "Where Asylum-Seekers Wait: Feminist Counter-topographies of Sites between States." *Gender, Place, and Culture* 18, no. 3: 381–99.

Mountz, Alison. 2012. "Mapping Remote Detention: Dis/location through Isolation." In *Beyond Walls and Cages: Prisons, Borders, and Global Crisis,* edited by Jenna Loyd, Matthew Mitchelson, and Andrew Burridge, 27–41. Athens: University of Georgia Press.

Mountz, Alison. 2013. "Political Geography I: Reconfiguring Geographies of Sovereignty." *Progress in Human Geography* 37, no. 6: 829–41.

Mountz, Alison, and Nancy Hiemstra. 2014. "Chaos and Crisis: Dissecting the Spatio-temporal Logics of Contemporary Migrations and State Practices." *Annals of the Association of American Geographers* 104, no. 2: 382–90.

Mountz, Alison, and Jenna Loyd. 2014. "Transnational Productions of Remoteness: Building Onshore and Offshore Carceral Regimes across Borders." *Geographica Helvetica* 69, no. 5: 389–98.

Nadig, Aninia. 2002. "Human Smuggling, National Security, and Refugee Protection." *Journal of Refugee Studies* 15, no. 1: 1–25.

National Immigrant Justice Center. 2010. "Isolated in Detention: Limited Access to Legal Counsel in Immigration Detention Facilities Jeopardizes a Fair Day in Court." https://immigrantjustice.org/sites/default/files /uploaded-files/no-content-type/2017-04/Isolated-in-Detention-Report -FINAL_September2010.pdf.

Nazario, Sonia. 2015. "The Refugees at Our Door: We Are Paying Mexico to Keep People from Reaching Our Border, People Who Are Fleeing Central American Violence." *New York Times,* October 11, SR1.

Neave, Colin. 2013. *Suicide in the Immigration Detention Network.* Canberra: Commonwealth Ombudsman. http://www.ombudsman.gov.au/__data /assets/pdf_file/0022/30298/December-2013-Suicide-and-self-harm-in -the-Immigration-Detention-Network.pdf.

Nelson, Diane. 2009. *Reckoning: The Ends of War in Guatemala.* Durham, N.C.: Duke University Press.

Nemeth, Charles. 2010. *Homeland Security: An Introduction to Principles and Practice.* Boca Raton, Fla.: CRC Press.

Nethery, Amy, Brynna Rafferty-Brown, and Savitri Taylor. 2013. "Exporting Detention: Australia-Funded Immigration Detention in Indonesia." *Journal of Refugee Studies* 26, no. 1: 88–109.

Nevins, Joseph. 2010. *Operation Gatekeeper and Beyond: The Rise of the "Illegal Alien" and the Making of the U.S.–Mexico Boundary.* 2nd ed. London: Routledge.

Nevins, Joseph, and Mizue Aizeki. 2008. *Dying to Live: A Story of U.S. Immigration in an Age of Global Apartheid.* San Francisco: Open Media/ City Lights Books.

Newland, Kathleen. 2005. "Drop in Asylum Numbers Shows Changes in

Demand and Supply." Migration Policy Institute. https://www.migra
tionpolicy.org/article/drop-asylum-numbers-shows-changes-demand
-and-supply.

New York Civil Liberties Union. 2011. "Just Derailed: What Raids on New
York's Trains and Buses Reveal about Border Patrol's Interior Enforce-
ment Practices." http://familiesforfreedom.org/sites/default/files/images
/FFFNYUNYCLU_justicederailedweb.pdf.

New York Times. 2007. "Gitmos across America." June 27, A22.

New York Times. 2013. "Gitmo Is Killing Me." April 15, A19.

New York Times. 2017. "President Trump's Island Mentality." March 4, SR12.

New York University Law. 2015. "Complaint for Declaratory and Injunctive Relief." http://www.law.nyu.edu/sites/default/files/ECM_PRO_066796.pdf.

New Zealand Immigration Lawyer. 2010. "Immigrant Fingerprints Checks
Introduced between Oz and New Zealand as Part of Fraud Drive That
Will Be Extended to Other Countries." https://immigratenz.wordpress
.com/2010/08/29/immigrant-fingerprints-checks-introduced-between
-oz-and-new-zealand-as-part-of-fraud-drive-that-will-be-extended-to
-other-countries/#comments.

Nicolson, Adam. 2007. "The Islands." Geographical Review 97, no. 2: 153–64.

Ngai, Mae. 2008. Impossible Subjects: Illegal Aliens and the Making of Modern
America. Princeton, N.J.: Princeton University Press.

Noble, Dennis. 2011. The U.S. Coast Guard's War on Human Smuggling.
Gainesville: University Press of Florida.

Noll, Gregor. 2003. "Visions of the Exceptional: Legal and Theoretical Issues
Raised by Transit Processing Centres and Protection Zones." European
Journal of Migration and Law 5, no. 3: 303–41.

Nossiter, Adam. 2018. "French Outpost in African Migrant Hub, Asylum
for a Select Few." New York Times, February 25. https://www.nytimes
.com/2018/02/25/world/africa/france-africa-migrants-asylum-niger.html.

Nyers, Peter. 2005. Rethinking Refugees beyond States of Emergency. New
York: Routledge.

Oceania. 2015. "Facebook Ban in Nauru Criticized." May 13. http://www
.oceaniatv.net/2015/05/13/facebook-ban-in-nauru-criticized/.

O'Dell, Rob. 2017. "Supreme Court: Can Mexican Citizens Sue Border Patrol Agents in Cross-Border Killings?" Arizona Republic, February 19.
http://www.azcentral.com/story/news/politics/border-issues/2017/02/19
/supreme-court-mexican-sue-border-patrol-killings-jose-antonio-elena
-rodriguez-sergio-adrian-hernandez-guereca/97875736/.

Office of Immigration Statistics. 2009. "Immigration Enforcement Actions: 2008." https://www.dhs.gov/sites/default/files/publications/Enforcement _Actions_2008.pdf.

Office of Immigration Statistics. 2010. "Immigration Enforcement Actions: 2009." https://www.dhs.gov/sites/default/files/publications/Enforcement _Actions_2009.pdf.

Office of Immigration Statistics. 2011. "Immigration Enforcement Actions: 2011." http://www.dhs.gov/sites/default/files/publications/immigration -statistics/enforcement_ar_2011.pdf.

Office of Immigration Statistics. 2016a. "2015 Yearbook of Immigration Statistics." https://www.dhs.gov/sites/default/files/publications/Yearbook_Im migration_Statistics_2015.pdf.

Office of Immigration Statistics. 2016b. "FY 2019 Budget in Brief." https:// www.dhs.gov/sites/default/files/publications/DHS%20BIB%202019.pdf.

Owen, Amy. 2010. "Guam Culture, Immigration and the US Military Build-Up." *Asia Pacific Viewpoint* 51, no. 3: 304–18.

Paglen, Trevor, and A. C. Thompson. 2006. *Torture Taxi: On the Trail of the CIA's Rendition Flights.* Hoboken, N.J.: Melville House.

Paik, Naomi. 2013. "Carceral Quarantine at Guantánamo: Legacies of US Imprisonment of Haitian Refugees, 1991–1994." *Radical History Review* 115, Winter: 142–68.

Paik, Naomi. 2016. *Rightlessness: Testimony and Redress in U.S. Prison Camps since World War II.* Chapel Hill: University of North Carolina Press.

Pain, R., and L. Staeheli. 2014. "Introduction: Intimacy-Geopolitics and Violence." *Area* 46, no. 4: 344–47.

Painter, Joe. 2006. "Prosaic Geographies of Stateness." *Political Geography* 25, no. 7: 752–74.

Pallister-Wilkins, P. 2017a. "Humanitarian Borderwork: Actors, Spaces, Categories." *Political Geography* 59: 1–10.

Pallister-Wilkins, P. 2017b. "Humanitarian Rescue/Sovereign Capture and the Policing of Possible Responses to Violent Borders." *Global Policy* 8: 19–24.

Parkes, Roderick, and Steffen Angenendt. 2009. "The Re-nationalization of Migration Policy-Making? EU Cooperation after the Immigration Pact." Working Paper FG 1. http://swp-berlin.org/common/get_document .php?asset_id=5681.

Pastore, Ferruccio. 2001. "Reconciling the Prince's 'Two Arms': Internal–External Security Policy Coordination." Occasional Papers 30. Institute for Security Studies, Western European Union. https://www.iss.europa .eu/sites/default/files/EUISSFiles/occo30.pdf.

Peck, Jamie, and Nik Theodore. 2015. *Fast Policy: Experimental Statecraft at the Thresholds of Neoliberalism*. Minneapolis: University of Minnesota Press.

Pécoud, Antoine. 2014. *Depoliticizing Migration: Power and Ideas in International Migration Narratives*. New York: Palgrave Macmillan.

Perera, Suvendrini. 2002. "What Is a Camp . . . ?" *Borderlands E-Journal* 1, no. 1: 1–10. http://www.borderlandsejournal.adelaide.edu.au/vol1no1_2002 /perera_camp.html.

Perera, Suvendrini. 2009. *Australia and the Insular Imagination: Beaches, Borders, Boats, and Bodies*. New York: Palgrave Macmillan.

Perera, Suvendrini. 2013. "Oceanic Corpo-graphies, Refugee Bodies, and the Making and Unmaking of Waters." *Feminist Review* 103, no. 1: 58–79.

Perkel, Colin. 2016. "Another Death in Immigration Custody Draws Ire from Human Rights Groups." *Globe and Mail,* March 9. https://www .theglobeandmail.com/news/national/another-death-in-immigration -custody-draws-ire-from-rights-groups/article29100441/.

Peters, Kimberley. 2010. "Future Promises for Contemporary Social and Cultural Geographies of the Sea." *Geography Compass* 4, no. 9: 1260–72.

Peterson, Matt. 2017. "The Rise of Refugee Offshoring." *Atlantic,* March 1. https://www.theatlantic.com/international/archive/2017/03/refugee -offshoring-trump/518331/.

Pickering, Sharon. 2014. "Floating Carceral Spaces: Border Enforcement and Gender on the High Seas." *Criminology and Penology* 16, no. 2: 187–205.

Pilger, John. 2007. *Freedom Next Time*. New York: Nation Books.

Planas, Roque. 2015. "Family Detention Center in Texas Is 'Utterly Unncecessary,' Says Immigration Attorney." *Huffington Post,* January 14. http://www .huffingtonpost.com/2015/01/14/dilley-texas-detention-center_n_6473274 .html.

Popescu, Gabriel. 2017. "Making Space for Digital Technologies: The Digital, the Limit, and the Sovereign." *Political Geography* 59: 1–10.

Pratt, Geraldine. 2005. "Abandoned Women and Spaces of Exception." *Antipode* 37, no. 5: 1052–78.

Pratt, Geraldine, and Victoria Rosner. 2006. "Introduction: The Global and the Intimate." *Women's Studies Quarterly* 34, no. 1/2.

PRO ASYL. 2012. "Walls of Shame: Accounts from Inside the Detention Centres of Evros." http://www.proasyl.de/fileadmin/fm-dam/q_PUB LIKATIONEN/2012/Evros-Bericht_12_04_10_BHP.pdf.

Pskowski, Martha. 2016. "Detained in Dilley: Deportation and Asylum in Texas." *Counterpunch,* June 27. http://www.counterpunch.org/2016/06/27 /detained-in-dilley-deportation-and-asylum-in-texas/.

Public Safety Canada. 2018. "Beyond the Border: A Shared Vision for Perimeter Security and Economic Competitiveness." https://www.publicsafety .gc.ca/cnt/brdr-strtgs/bynd-th-brdr/index-en.aspx.

Pugh, Jonathan. 2013. "Island Movements: Thinking with the Archipelago." *Island Studies Journal* 8, no. 1: 9–24.

Puumala, Eeva, and Anitta Kynsilehto. 2016. "Does the Body Matter? Determining the Right to Asylum and the Corporeality of Political Communication." *European Journal of Cultural Studies* 19, no. 4: 352–68.

Ramadan, Adam. 2012. "Spatialising the Refugee Camp." *Transactions of the Institute of British Geographers* 38, no. 1: 65–77.

Razack, Sherene. 1999. "Making Canada White: Law and the Policing of Bodies of Colour in the 1990s." *Canadian Journal of Law and Society* 14, no. 1: 159–84.

Refugee Action Collective. 2005. "Howard's Forgotten People: Ninety-two Asylum Seekers Left to Rot on Lombok." Media release, October 10. http://www.rac-vic.org/html/media_05_10_10. Available from the author.

Refugee Action Collective. 2010. "International Day of Action to Free Tamil Refugees in Indonesia." Media release, January 18. http://www.scoop .co.nz/stories/WO1001/S00345.htm.

Reid-Henry, Simon. 2007. "Exceptional Sovereignty? Guantánamo Bay and the Re-colonial Present." *Antipode* 39, no. 4: 627–48.

Reilly, Alex, and Sara Davies. 2013. "Are Australia's Refugee Acceptance Rates High When Compared with Other Nations?" *Guardian*, August 20. http://www.theguardian.com/world/2013/aug/20/are-australia-refugee -acceptance-rates-high-compared-with-other-nations.

Reuter, Conny. 2014. "Hong Kong—Lampedusa—Brussels." October 3. http:// europeanmovement.eu/news/solidar-weekly-round-up-03-10-2014/.

Robjant, Katy, Ian Robbins, and Victoria Senior. 2009. "Psychological Distress amongst Immigration Detainees: A Cross-Sectional Questionnaire Study." *British Journal of Clinical Psychology* 48, no. 3: 275–86.

Rogers, Robert. 1995. *Destiny's Landfall: A History of Guam.* Honolulu: University of Hawai'i.

Rosenberg, Carol. 2017. "It's Only a Drill: Guantánamo Trains for a Caribbean Migrant Crisis." *Miami Herald,* March 1. http://www.miamiherald.com /news/nation-world/world/americas/guantanamo/article135673913.html.

Saeed, Saim. 2017. "Fewer Migrants, but More Deaths: Amnesty Report." http://www.politico.eu/article/fewer-migrants-but-more-deaths-amnesty -report/.

Salter, Mark. 2004. "Passports, Mobility, and Security: How Smart Can the Border Be?" *International Studies Perspectives* 5, no. 1: 71–91.

Sampson, Robyn. 2013. "Embodied Borders: Biopolitics, Knowledge Mobilization and Alternatives to Immigration Detention." PhD diss., La Trobe University.

Sanchez, Lisa. 2004. "The Global E-rotic Subject, the Ban, and the Prostitute-Free Zone: Sex Work and the Theory of Differential Exclusion." *Environment and Planning D: Society and Space* 22, no. 6: 861–83.

Sassen, Saskia. 1996. *Losing Control? Sovereignty in an Age of Globalization.* New York: Columbia University Press.

Schalansky, Judith. 2009. *Atlas of Remote Islands: Fifty Islands I Have Never Set Foot On and Never Will.* New York: Penguin Books.

Schriro, Dora. 2009. "Immigration Detention Overview and Recommendations." Homeland Security, Immigration and Customs Enforcement. http://documents.nytimes.com/immigration-detention-overview-and-recommendations#p=1.

Schuster, Liza. 2005. "The Realities of a New Asylum Paradigm." COMPAS Working Paper 20. University of Oxford, Policy Documentation Centre. https://www.compas.ox.ac.uk/media/WP-2005-020-Schuster_New_Asylum_Paradigm.pdf.

Seelke, Clare, and Kristin Finklea. 2016. "U.S.–Mexican Security Cooperation: The Mérida Initiative and Beyond." Congressional Research Service Report. https://www.fas.org/sgp/crs/row/R41349.pdf.

Sharpe, Christina. 2016. *In the Wake: On Blackness and Being.* Durham, N.C.: Duke University Press.

Sheller, Mimi. 2009. "Infrastructures of the Imagined Island: Software, Mobilities, and the Architecture of Caribbean Paradise." *Environment and Planning A: Economy and Space* 41, no. 6: 1386–1403.

Sidaway, James. 2010. "'One Island, One Team, One Mission': Geopolitics, Sovereignty, 'Race' and Rendition." *Geopolitics* 15, no. 4: 667–83.

Sinnerbrink, Ingrid, Derrick Silove, Annette Field, Zachary Steel, and Vijaya Manicavasagar. 1997. "Compounding of Premigration Trauma and Postmigration Stress in Asylum Seekers." *The Journal of Psychology* 131, no. 5: 463–70.

Smith, Seyda T., Kyle D. Smith, and Abdulgaffar Peang-Meth. 2010. "University-Based Services for Asylum Seekers on Guam: Empowerment, Culture Learning and Community." *International Journal of Intercultural Relations* 34, no. 2: 150–62.

Sobhanian, Farahnaz, Gregory Boyle, Mark Bahr, and Tindaro Fallo. 2006. "Psychological Status of Former Refugee Detainees from the Woomera Detention Centre Now Living in the Australian Community." *Psychiatry, Psychology, and Law* 13, no. 2: 151–59.

Solzhenitsyn, Alexander Isaevich. 1974. *The Gulag Archipelago, 1918–1956: An Experiment in Literary Investigation*. 1st ed. New York: Harper and Row.

Sparke, Matthew. 2006. "The Neoliberal Nexus: Economy, Security and the Biopolitics of Citizenship on the Border." *Political Geography* 25, no. 2: 151–80.

Sperandio, Elisa. 2019. "Setting the Stage: Resident Experiences with Enforcement Rescue and Spectacle on Lampedusa." MA thesis, University of Kentucky. https://pdfs.semanticscholar.org/d352/6407af44deffccec49bdbce 8fbb72ad147a8.pdf.

Spiegel Online. 2011. "European Leaders Struggle with Wave of Tunisian Migrants." February 15. http://www.spiegel.de/international/europe/des tination-lampedusa-european-leaders-struggle-with-wave-of-tunisian -migrants-a-745669.html.

Spijkerboer, Thomas, Tamara Last, Paolo Cuttitta, Theodore Baird, and Orcun Ulusoy. 2015. "Human Costs of Border Control." http://www .borderdeaths.org/.

Squire, Vicki. 2009. *The Exclusionary Politics of Asylum: Migration, Minorities and Citizenship*. Chippenham, U.K.: Palgrave Macmillan.

Squire, Vicki. 2011. *The Contested Politics of Mobility: Border Zones and Irregularity*. Abingdon, U.K.: Palgrave Macmillan.

Steel, Zachary, Derrick Silove, Robert Brooks, Shakeh Momartin, Bushra Alzuhairi, and Ina Suslijik. 2006. "Impact of Immigration Detention and Temporary Protection on the Mental Health of Refugees." *British Journal of Psychiatry* 188, no. 1: 58–64.

Steinberg, Philip. 2005. "Insularity, Sovereignty and Statehood: The Representation of Islands on Portolan Charts and the Construction of the Territorial State." *Geographiska Annaler* 87, no. 4: 253–65.

Stepick, Alex. 1982. "Haitian Boat People: A Study in the Conflicting Forces Shaping U.S. Immigration Policy." *Law and Contemporary Problems* 45, no. 2: 163–96.

Stevenson, Mark. 2019. "Hours after Mass Escape, Migrants Chant for Food, Freedom." Associated Press. https://apnews.com/2529d3d392394f3c87bd246 d75d81213.

Stewart, Catrina. 2012. "Israelis Build the World's Biggest Detention Center." *Independent,* March 10. http://www.independent.co.uk/news/world /middle-east/israelis-build-the-worlds-biggest-detention-centre-7547401 .html.

Stierl, Maurice. 2020. "Of Migrant Slaves and Underground Railroads: Movement, Containment, Freedom." *American Behavioral Scientist* 64, no. 4: 456–79.

Stillman, Sarah. 2013. "Lampedusa's Migrant Tragedy, and Ours." *New Yorker,* October 10. http://www.newyorker.com/online/blogs/comment/2013/10 /lampedusas-migrant-tragedy-and-ours.html.

Stoler, Ann. 2011. "Colony." *Political Concepts: A Critical Lexicon* 1. http:// www.politicalconcepts.org/issue1/colony/.

Stoler, Ann, ed. 2013. *Imperial Debris: On Ruins and Ruination.* Durham, N.C.: Duke University Press.

Stratford, Elaine, Godfrey Baldacchino, Elizabeth McMahon, Carol Farbotko, and Andrew Harwood. 2011. "Envisioning the Archipelago." *Island Studies Journal* 6, no. 2: 113–30.

Sudbury, Julia, ed. 2005. *Global Lockdown: Race, Gender, and the Prison Industrial Complex.* London: Routledge.

Tang, Andrea, and David Hammond. 2014. "The Push Back Situation in Australia: A Case Study on Human Rights Abuses for Indonesian Migrants and Refugees Trying to Seek Refuge in Australia." Human Rights at Sea. http://9bri.com/wp-content/uploads/2014/09/20140910-HRAS_Case _Study_The-Push-Back-Situation-in-Australia.pdf.

Taussig, Michael. 1997. *The Magic of the State.* New York: Routledge.

Taussig, Michael. 2004. *My Cocaine Museum.* Chicago: University of Chicago Press.

Taylor, Diana. 1998. "Border Watching." In *The Ends of Performance,* edited by Peggy Phelan and Jill Lane, 178–85. New York: New York University Press.

Taylor, Jessie. 2009. "Behind Australian Doors: Examining the Conditions of Detention of Asylum Seekers in Australia." https://www.safecom.org.au /pdfs/behind-australian-doors-examining-the-conditions.pdf.

Taylor, Savitri. 2005. "Sovereign Power at the Border." *Public Law Review* 16, no. 1: 55–77.

Tazzioli, Martina. 2011. "Cronologia degli accordi Italia-Tunisia" http://www .storiemigranti.org/spip.php?article1004.

Tazzioli, Martina. 2015. "Which Europe? Migrants' Uneven Geographies and Counter-mapping at the Limits of Representation." *movements: Journal for Critical Migration and Border Regime Studies* 1, no. 2. https://movements -journal.org/issues/02.kaempfe/04.tazzioli--europe-migrants-geographies -counter-mapping-representation.html.

Tazzioli, Martina. 2016. "Border Displacements: Challenging the Politics of Rescue between Mare Nostrum and Triton." *Migration Studies* 4, no. 1: 1–19.

Tazzioli, Martina. 2019. "Governing Migrant Mobility through Mobility: Containment and Dispersal at the Internal Frontiers of Europe." *Environment and Planning C: Politics and Space.* Advance online publication. https:// doi.org/10.1177/2399654419839065.

Tazzioli, Martina, and Glenda Garelli. 2019. "Counter-mapping, Refugees and Asylum Borders." In *Handbook on Critical Geographies of Migration*, ed. Katharyne Mitchell, Reece Jones, and Jennifer L. Fluri (London: Edward Elgar, 2019).

Teaiwa, Katerina. 2015. *Consuming Ocean Island: Stories of People and Phosphate from Banaba*. Bloomington: Indiana University Press.

Thiranagama, S. 2011. *In My Mother's House: Civil War in Sri Lanka*. Philadelphia: University of Pennsylvania Press.

Ticktin, Miriam. 2011. *Casualties of Care: Immigration and the Politics of Humanitarianism in France*. Berkeley: University of California Press.

Tolia-Kelly, Divya P. 2006. "Affect—an Ethnocentric Encounter? Exploring the 'Universalist' Imperative of Emotional/Affectual Geographies." *Area* 38, no. 2: 213–17.

Tsiolkas, Christos. 2013. "Why We Hate Refugees." *Monthly*, September, 22–31.

Turnbull, Sarah. 2015. "'Stuck in the Middle': Waiting and Uncertainty in Immigration Detention." Criminal Justice, Borders, and Citizenship Research Paper 2540549. https://doi.org/10.2139/ssrn.2540549.

Tyler, Imogen. 2013. *Revolting Subjects: Social Abjection and Resistance in Neoliberal Britain*. London: Zed Books.

UNITED for Intercultural Action. 2014. "List of 18759 Documented Refugee Deaths through Fortress Europe." http://www.unitedagainstracism.org/pdfs/listofdeaths_09.pdf.

United Nations High Commissioner for Refugees. 2005. "UNHCR Deeply Concerned over Lampedusa Deportations." Press release, March 18. http://www.unhcr.org/news/press/2005/3/423b00a54/unhcr-deeply-concerned-lampedusa-deportations.html.

United Nations High Commissioner for Refugees. 2007. *2006 Global Trends*. Geneva: UNHCR.

United Nations High Commissioner for Refugees. 2008. *Asylum Levels and Trends in Industrialized Countries, 2007*. Geneva: UNHCR.

United Nations High Commissioner for Refugees. 2012. "More than 1,500 Drown or Go Missing Trying to Cross the Mediterranean in 2011." Press release, January 31. http://www.unhcr.org/news/latest/2012/1/4f2803949/1500-drown-missing-trying-cross-mediterranean-2011.html.

United Nations High Commissioner for Refugees. 2014a. "Statement of Boat Incident off Greece Coast." Press release, January 21. http://www.unhcr.org/news/press/2014/1/52df83d49/unhcr-statement-boat-incident-greece-coast.html.

United Nations High Commissioner for Refugees. 2014b. "World at War:

Global Trends, Forced Displacement in 2014." http://unhcr.org/556725e69 .html.

United Nations High Commissioner for Refugees. 2015a. "Lesvos Island— Greece. Fact Sheet." November 12. http://www.unhcr.org/protection /operations/5645ddbc6/greece-factsheet-lesvos-island.html.

United Nations High Commissioner for Refugees. 2015b. "States Parties to the 1951 Convention Relating to the Status of Refugees and the 1967 Protocol." http://www.unhcr.org/protect/PROTECTION/3b73b0d63.pdf.

United Nations High Commissioner for Refugees. 2016a. "2015 UNHCR Country Operations Profile—Lebanon." http://reporting.unhcr.org/node /2520#_ga=2.250186246.1823715134.1516390225-1117963682.1509333338.

United Nations High Commissioner for Refugees. 2016b. "Syria Regional Refugee Response." http://data.unhcr.org/syrianrefugees/settlement.php?id =176&region=77&country=107.

United Nations High Commissioner for Refugees. 2016c. *UNHCR Global Report 2016.* http://reporting.unhcr.org/publications#tab-global_report& _ga=2.253775496.1823715134.1516390225-1117963682.1509333338.

United Nations High Commissioner for Refugees. 2016d. "UNHCR Population Statistics." http://popstats.unhcr.org/en/time_series.

United Nations High Commissioner for Refugees. 2017. *Global Trends: Forced Displacement in 2016.* June 21. http://www.refworld.org/docid/594aa38e .html.

United Nations High Commissioner for Refugees. 2019. *Global Trends: Forced Displacement in 2018.* http://www.unhcr.org/5d08d7ee7.pdf.

United Nations Special Committee on Decolonization. 2009. "Special Committee on Decolonization Approves Text Reaffirming Principle of Self- Determination as Fundamental Human Right." Press release, June 19. http://www.un.org/press/en/2009/gacol3197.doc.htm.

Urry, John. 2014. *Offshoring.* Cambridge: Polity Press.

U.S. Border Patrol. 2015. "Southwest Border Deaths by Fiscal Year." https:// www.cbp.gov/document/stats/us-border-patrol-fiscal-year-southwest -border-sector-deaths-fy-1998-fy-2018.

U.S. Border Patrol. 2017. "Southwest Border Deaths by Fiscal Year [1998–2017]." https://www.cbp.gov/sites/default/files/assets/documents/2019-Mar/bp -southwest-border-sector-deaths-fy1998-fy2018.pdf.

U.S. Government Accountability Office. 2011. "Commonwealth of the Northern Mariana Islands: Status of Transition to Federal Immigration Law." http://www.gao.gov/products/GAO-11-805T.

U.S. Immigration and Customs Enforcement. 2009a. "Detention Facility

Average Daily Population as of December 12, 2008." https://www.ice .gov/foia/library.

U.S. Immigration and Customs Enforcement. 2009b. "El Paso Processing Centre March 2007–March 2009." https://www.ice.gov/foia/library.

U.S. Immigration and Customs Enforcement. 2015. "ICE Detention Facility Listing 2015." https://www.ice.gov/foia/library.

van Liempt, Ilse, Maybritt Jill Alpes, Saima Hassan, Sevda Tunaboylu, Orcun Ulusoy, and Annelies Zoomers. 2017. *Evidence-Based Assessment of Migration Deals: The Case of the EU–Turkey Statement: Final Report.* December. https://www.borderline-europe.de/sites/default/files/projekte _files/20171221-Final%20Report-WOTRO.pdf.

Van Selm, Joanne, and Betsy Cooper. 2006. *The New "Boat People": Ensuring Safety and Determining Status.* Washington, D.C.: Migration Policy Institute. https://www.migrationpolicy.org/sites/default/files/publications /Boat_People_Report.pdf.

Varsanyi, Monica. 2008. "Immigration Policing through the Back Door: City Ordinances, the 'Right to the City,' and Exclusion of Undocumented Day Laborers." *Urban Geography* 29, no. 1: 1–29.

Vaughan-Williams, Nick. 2015. *Europe's Border Crisis: Biopolitical Security and Beyond.* Oxford: Oxford University Press.

Vine, David. 2009. *Island of Shame: The Secret History of the U.S. Military Base on Diego Garcia.* Princeton, N.J.: Princeton University Press.

Vine, David. 2012. "The Lily-Pad Strategy." *TomDispatch* (blog), July 15. http:// www.tomdispatch.com/archive/175568/.

Vogt, Wendy A. 2013. "Crossing Mexico: Structural Violence and the Commodification of Undocumented Central American Migrants." *American Ethnologist* 40, no. 4: 764–80.

Vosko, Leah, Valerie Preston, and Robert Latham, eds. 2014. *Liberating Temporariness? Migration, Work, and Citizenship in an Age of Insecurity.* Montreal: McGill-Queens University Press.

Vradis, Antonis, Evie Papada, Joe Painter, and Anna Papoutsi. *New Borders, Hotspots, and the European Migration Regime.* London: Pluto Press.

Walters, William. 2004. "Secure Borders, Safe Haven, Domopolitics." *Citizenship Studies* 8, no. 3: 237–60.

Walters, William. 2008. "Bordering the Sea: Shipping Industries and the Policing of Stowaways." *Borderlands E-Journal* 7, no. 3: 1–25.

Walters, William. 2012. *Governmentality.* London: Routledge.

Weber, Leanne, and Sharon Pickering. 2011. *Globalization and Borders: Deaths at the Global Frontier.* London: Palgrave Macmillan.

Weiss, L. 2016. "Central American Refugees Struggle for Protection in Southern Mexico." NACLA, September 19. http://nacla.org/news/2016/09/19/central-american-refugees-struggle-protection-southern-mexico.

Welch, Michael. 2002. *Detained: Immigration Laws and the Expanding INS Jail Complex*. Philadelphia: Temple University Press.

West Australian. 2010. "Gillard's Indian Ocean Solution to Boat People." July 7, 1.

Whyte, Sarah. 2014. "Abbott Offers Asylum Seekers $10k to Go Home." *Sydney Morning Herald*, June 21. http://www.smh.com.au/federal-politics/political-news/abbott-offers-asylum-seekers-10k-to-go-home-20140620-3ajr6.html.

Williams, Jill. 2014. "The Safety/Security Nexus and the Humanitarianisation of Border Enforcement." *Geographical Journal* 182, no. 1: 27–37.

Williams, Jill. 2015. "From Humanitarian Exceptionalism to Contingent Care: Care and Enforcement at the Humanitarian Border." *Political Geography* 47, no. 1: 11–20.

Williams, Kira. 2018. "Arriving Somewhere, Not Here: Exploring and Mapping the Relationship between Border Enforcement and Migration by Boat in the Central Mediterranean Sea, 2006–2015." PhD diss., Wilfrid Laurier University.

Williams, Kira, and Alison Mountz. 2016. "Rising Tide: Analyzing the Relationship between Externalization and Migrant and Boat Losses." In *Externalizing Migration Management: Europe, North America, and the Spread of Remote Control,* edited by Ruben Zaiotti, 31–50. New York: Routledge.

Williams, Kira, and Alison Mountz. 2018. "Between Enforcement and Precarity: Externalization and Migrant Deaths at Sea." *International Migration* 56, no. 5: 74–89.

Wingrove, Josh. 2014. "Refugee Claims Reach 'Historic Low': Ottawa Accused of Brushing Aside Valid Cases by Deterring Applicants from Countries Deemed Safe." *Globe and Mail,* January 23, A17.

Winterson, Jeanette. 2001. *The PowerBook*. Toronto: Vintage Canada.

Wright, Melissa W. 1997. "Crossing the Factory Frontier: Gender, Place, and Power in the Mexican Maquiladora." *Antipode* 29, no. 3: 278–302.

Wright, Melissa W. 2006. *Disposable Women and Other Myths of Global Capitalism*. New York: Taylor and Francis.

Zaiotti, Ruben, ed. 2016. *Remote Control: The Externalization of Migration Management in Europe and North America*. New York: Routledge.

Zolberg, Aristide. 1999. "Matters of State: Theorizing Immigration Policy." In *The Handbook of International Migration: The American Experience,* edited by Charles Hirschan, Philip Kasinitz, and Josh DeWind, 71–93. New York: Russell Sage.

Zolberg, Aristide. 2003. "The Archaeology of 'Remote Control.'" In *Migration Control in the North Atlantic World: The Evolution of State Practices in Europe and the United States from the French Revolution to the Interwar Period,* edited by Andreas Fahrmeir, Oliver Faron, and Patrick Weil, 195–222. New York: Berghahn Books.

Index

activism, xxix–xxx, 14–17; antidetention, 197–98; and body as technology, 201–2, 219. *See also* countertopographies

archipelago: carceral, 19, 73–74; as metaphor, 19–20

asylum: and activist networks, 211–14; in Australia, xxiv, 16–17, 44–45, 104–23, 135, 142; claims data, xiii, xvi, xviii; criminalization of asylum seekers, xvi, 33, 38–39, 166, 176–77, 183; and detention, 131–34, 160; in the European Union, 11–12, 61; evolution and conventions, xi, xv; and geopolitics, 125–26; on Lampedusa, 75, 78–79; and migration crises, xix; and *neo-refoulement,* 247n2; offshoring of, xxi–xxii, 12–13, 59; spaces, xxv–xxx. *See also specific countries*

Australia: activists in, 203–4, 212–14; detention infrastructure and state practice, 104–18

bilateral arrangements, 33–34, 52, 70–71

boats: arrivals, 39–50; Cuban and Haitian arrivals, 39–43; securitization of arrivals, 177. *See also specific boats*

"bogus refugees," xiii, xvi, 49, 168, 177, 189

borderlands, xix, xxv, 6, 13, 68, 228, 232; and islands, xxiv, 22

borders: in Australia, xxiv; in Canada, 168–71; deaths, xxii, 6–7, 23, 204–6, 230, 237

budgets: in European Union, xxiii; externalization, 10, 58; in Italy, 14–15, 75–77, 237; mobilities, 57–58; offshoring, xxi, 5–6; topological, 71; in United States, xiv, xxiii–xxiv; walls, xx–xxi, 54–55, 229, 235–36. *See also* enforcement

"burden," 77; of enforcement, 65; "sharing," 68–69

Butler, Judith, xiv, xxi–xxiii, 4, 201–2

Canada: boat arrivals, 175; conventions and law, 168–73; Designated Countries of Origin List, 183–85; detention in, 189–91

Canada's Immigration and Refugee Protection Act (IRPA), 171, 178–79, 186

history of, 34–35, 50–54; United
States, xviii, 36; United States
and Guam, 49; United States,
Haitians, and Cubans, 39–44

Frontex, xxiii–xxiv, 8, 52, 65, 84,
208

geopolitics, 14, 66–67, 183–86
Global Detention Project, 155–57,
187–88, 210–11
Golden Venture (boat), 43. *See also*
boats
Gregory, Derek, 14–15, 18–22, 37–38
grievability, xvi, xxii
Guam, 20, 49, 101–2, 144–53
Guantánamo Bay, 15, 21, 31, 42, 55,
98–101, 143

haunting, 96–97, 101–3, 225–26
"hot spots," 61, 78; islands as, xxvii,
2–3
humanitarian: discourses, 88;
enforcement, 190, 232, 237;
rescue, xxiii, 3, 8, 43, 47, 67, 189
human rights: abuses, xxx, 15, 177;
access, xxvii, 79–80. *See also*
conventions

Immigration, Refugees, and
Citizenship Canada (IRCC). *See*
Citizenship and Immigration
Canada
Indonesia: "alternatives to
detention," 116; detention,
100–101, 114–15, 120–21, 248n2;
Lombok, 114–15; smuggling, 109.
See also transit
interception, xvi, 229–30; and

Australia, 45, 48, 112–16, 122; and
Canada, 166, 178, 183; Cuban
and Haitian, xvi, 4; and Italy, 47,
66–67, 80; and Spain, 46; and the
United States, 35, 148. *See also*
externalization
interdiction, 11, 169–70, 183;
enforcement, 40, 59, 64
International Organization for
Migration (IOM), 10–11, 60, 102,
109, 187–89; and Canada and
AVRR program, 187–90; and
migrant deaths, 7, 143, 208, 237
islands: as camp, 93; and colonial
histories, 98, 109, 243; detention
on, xv, 93–94; as interstitial
places, 74, 102, 125; as militarized
locations, 21, 98; as mirror, xxi,
225; as sites of experimentation,
20; sovereignty on, 94–95, 102–3,
124, 126; as stage, 83, 104–5, 231;
"strategic island concept," 95, 145.
See also borderlands; military
bases; *specific islands*

Komagata Maru (boat), xiii, 175. *See
also* boats

Lampedusa, 8, 13, 15–17, 66–67;
in Berlin, 240–42; and boat
arrivals, 46–47; and death, 208–9;
and memorials, 207; offshore
processing, 74–87
law: legal ambiguity, xxviii, 99,
130–31, 143; legal geographies,
10, 18–19, 105, 175–76; legal
limbo, 22, 58, 131, 240; legal
microgeographies, 31, 126, 141;
legislation, 38, 44, 165–66, 171,

Alison Mountz is professor of geography and Canada Research Chair in Global Migration at Wilfrid Laurier University. She is author of *Seeking Asylum: Human Smuggling and Bureaucracy at the Border* (Minnesota, 2010) and of *Boats, Borders, and Bases: Race, the Cold War, and the Rise of Migration Detention in the United States.*